RubyMusic

Caitlin Press Inc.
3375 Ponderosa Way
Qualicum Beach, BC V9K 2J8
www.caitlinpress.com

Text and cover design by Vici Johnstone
Edited by Mary Schendlinger
All of the photos in this book were taken by Connie Kuhns, unless otherwise noted.
Printed in Canada

Caitlin Press Inc. acknowledges financial support from the Government of Canada and the Canada Council for the Arts, and the Province of British Columbia through the British Columbia Arts Council and the Book Publisher's Tax Credit.

Library and Archives Canada Cataloguing in Publication
Rubymusic : a popular history of women's music and culture / Connie Kuhns
Names: Kuhns, Connie
Identifiers: Canadiana 20220453373 | ISBN 9781773861012 (softcover)
Subjects: LCSH: Women musicians—Canada. | LCSH: Women composers—Interviews. | LCSH: Women punk rock
  musicians—British Columbia—Vancouver.
Classification: LCC ML82 K96 2023 | DDC 780.82/0971—dc23

RUBYMUSIC

A Popular History of Women's
Music and Culture

DEBRA ROONEY

CONNIE KUHNS

Caitlin Press 2023

RUBYMUSIC

102.7FM

10 YEARS

VANCOUVER, CANADA

To my mother
Wilma D. Kuhns

And to my mentor
Karlene Faith

CONTENTS

FACE THE MUSIC   —139

TESTIMONY —165

BONUS TRACKS —223

INTRODUCTION

I'M A RADIO

RUBYMUSIC

with **CONNIE KUHNS**

Friday night

7:30 - 9:30
CFRO 102.7 FM
VANCOUVER
CO-OPERATIVE
RADIO

(Rubymusic is rebroadcast in part   on Friday mornings beginning at 10:30)

It's not all here.

In my room are boxes of cassette tapes and large Ampex reels. I have perhaps a thousand pages of transcribed interviews, done on a typewriter, and notebooks full of actual notes that have lost all context. There are four file drawers of newspaper clippings and at least another six or seven boxes full of promo kits, posters, scrapbooks and other mementoes given to me by women who wanted me to tell their story. What you're holding is a selection of what has been published.

I got hooked early. I knew all the weekly top ten hits (and the flip sides) from looking through the record display at the dime store. On Saturdays I would ride my bike out to the radio station and buy demo records for ten cents apiece. I had *American Bandstand* in the afternoons, and at night, in shared bunk beds with my brother, I listened to far-off beats on my turquoise transistor, a Christmas gift from my parents when I was ten. In my teens, I discovered KOMA in Oklahoma City. Rock and roll, rhythm and blues, Brill Building pop, Philly and Motown—the great music of the era—found its way into my bedroom. The best reception was on our car radios, at night, after all the local stations had gone off the air. We drove around as late as we were allowed, listening as the music blasted its way over the Great Plains to the Canadian prairies.

Some of the bands I heard about on the radio played at our teen centre. But my world was amplified in the summer when I stood against the cool, tiled walls of the National Guard Armory, listening to the magnificent R&B bands swinging in step with their horn sections, looking smooth and sleek in matching baby-blue suits. Our little town was on the circuit. When I could, I deejayed my junior high school dances or formed separate lines of boys and girls to dance the Continental Walk. For a shy kid, this was surprising, even to me.

An older boy in the neighbourhood became the nighttime deejay at our local station. He gave me my first Rolling Stones album. One night, when my parents thought I was somewhere else, I went down and watched him work. The studio had its own magic. Turntables. Dials. Lights. I already knew I wanted to be a writer, but this was something else.

I went to college and quietly got my third-class radio licence from the Federal Communications Commission—a requirement to work at the college radio station—before flunking out first year. In 1968, no one paid attention to the lone eighteen-year-old female at the back of the class. In those days, becoming a journalist or having a career in radio was wholly imaginary for a woman. There were limits. One morning I got up and left.

In my first months on the road I used panhandling money to buy MC5's album *Kick Out the Jams* and Spirit's "I Got a Line on You," which I still have. (It didn't matter that I had no place to play them.) When I got to California, the money I earned working at an amusement park got me tickets to Led Zeppelin and Three Dog Night. Legitimate employment paid for rent and more concerts: Sly and the Family Stone; Crosby, Stills & Nash; Iron Butterfly; the Rolling Stones. But underneath it all was Janis Joplin with her tortured call to be true to oneself. Eventually, over the endless drum solos, I started to hear the voices of Joni Mitchell, Carly Simon, Bonnie Raitt and Carole King. Music finds a way.

I wrote my first concert review in 1976. I was crashing at a youth hostel in Vancouver, waiting out the rain. Each day on the bus I would pass by the Status of Women office on Fourth Avenue. One day I went in and asked if they needed any help. When they found out I was from California, they sent me out to review a Meg Christian concert for their in-house feminist monthly, *Kinesis*. Meg Christian was the first artist to record on the newly formed feminist label (out of California) Olivia Records. The women's movement had taken hold, and there was growing opportunity in its parallel universe. I was no longer invisible. A few years later I ended up writing a monthly women's music column in *Kinesis*, the companion to my new adventure: *Rubymusic*, a radio program featuring music by women, exclusively.

Rubymusic went on the air on May 15, 1981. When I climbed the stairs to the studio for the first time in late 1979, I knew this was where I needed to be. Vancouver Co-operative Radio was a revolutionary start-up, not just in ideology but in practice. At any time, a handful of different languages could be heard in the editing room, each representing a country or community in turmoil or construction. The music programming was the best in the city. There were women everywhere: writing, producing, operating the board, even running the place. They were open and ready for me, but as I wrote in my essay "A Woman's Place Is on the Radio," the station only gave me a thirty-minute time slot because they were unsure if there was enough music by women to fill the hour I had requested. In the guide copy for opening night, I wrote: "On this special occasion, take your radio in your arms and dance." When I retired the program fifteen years later, I had been on air for two hours every Friday night, rebroadcast on Friday mornings, and had produced hundreds of hours of special programming. *Rubymusic* was among the first of its kind in Canada, but it had become so much more.

The opening essay in this collection, "Women's Music and the Mothers of Invention," was made possible by an Explorations Grant in 1986 from the Canada Council for the Arts. With that money, I was able to interview at least a hundred women musicians, songwriters, composers, singers, technicians, concert producers and coffee house collectives, as well as the maker of the Picasso guitar. I crossed Canada meeting women in

1985: You're listening to Vancouver Cooperative Radio, CFRO, 102.7 FM, and on a variety of cable frequencies throughout British Columbia and northwestern Washington. Good evening. I'm Connie Kuhns, and this is *Rubymusic*. Photo: Sharon Knapp

airports, hotel rooms, kitchens and city parks, backstage at concert halls and folk festivals, and at the Toronto Women's Club. Four years later I received a Canada Council travel grant to speak on the history of women's music in Canada at the annual convention of the Association of Women's Music and Culture in San Francisco. The talk was part of a larger presentation on the hidden history of women's contributions that I had given in Vancouver at Simon Fraser University, the University of British Columbia, Langara College and the World Conference of Community Radio Broadcasters. *Rubymusic* was my platform and became part of the zeitgeist. When Joan Turner offered me a place in her anthology *Living the Changes* to make my research permanent, it was a major opportunity. Also, during this time, on the recommendation of Ruth Dworin, the woman behind Womynly Way Productions in Toronto, and with the assistance of editor Mark Miller, I was asked to write the very first entry on "feminist music" for the second edition of *Encyclopedia of Music in Canada*. It was published in 1992.

For a couple of decades, I carried around a Marantz tape recorder, an EV 635 microphone, a few feet of cord and a small mic stand. I kept it all in a Samsonite carryall with my name on the strap. I was almost eight months pregnant when I hauled my equipment around Vancouver's

Stanley Park at a concert protesting the evictions carried out by the city for the upcoming Expo 86. The concert featured, among others, Pete Seeger, Arlo Guthrie, Four the Moment and D.O.A. It was my first story for the *Georgia Straight*, and one of the hottest summers on record. An old friend, Brent Gibson, had recommended me to Charles Campbell, the *Straight*'s editor (who, if I remember correctly, really wanted more women on staff). He put my first story on the cover and later allowed my Amy Grant interview to appear in Q&A form, which was usually the purview of the publisher. (Full disclosure: I had just left town and he couldn't reach me to do a rewrite.)

My relationship with the Canadian literary journal *Geist* was my cosmic reward. Mary Schendlinger, co-founder and, at that time, senior editor of *Geist*, had been a long-time listener of *Rubymusic*. When we finally met in 2011, she asked to read whatever I was writing. I handed her some papers across the table. When that essay (not included in this collection) was published in *Geist*, it was reviewed in the *Globe and Mail*, nominated for a magazine award and named a "notable essay" in the *Best American Essays* series. I had found my place. Assistant Publisher AnnMarie MacKinnon asked me to write about punk music in Vancouver. We changed the focus. The result was "Strange Women," a history of the women involved in Vancouver's punk scene. AnnMarie had remarkable instincts. "Strange Women" and my extended essay on Yoko Ono—after AnnMarie had become publisher and editor-in-chief—would not have happened without her skill and trust.

I wish I could tell you everything—all those moments behind the scenes that are the foundation of this collection. Sawagi Taiko surprised us big time from the *Rubymusic* stage at the Vancouver Folk Music Festival by playing "Wipe Out" on Japanese taiko drums. Linda Tillery and the Cultural Heritage Choir made their first Canadian appearance on the *Rubymusic* stage and returned the next year. (Thank you, Dugg Simpson.) I spent a weekend in the recording studio with jazz musician and composer Mary Watkins and pianist Marcia Meyer during the recording of Marcia's atmospheric instrumental album *Oregon Summer*, and I got to be a fan girl backstage with Gloria Steinem when I showed her a photograph of me from the 1970s, with my hair parted down the middle, wearing a copy of her signature aviator glasses. There was also the night my friend Bill Grant called me from a pay phone and told me to get down to the Savoy immediately; a young wild woman in a bridal gown from Alberta had taken over the club. I interviewed k.d. lang the next day, and a few months later I introduced her from the stage of the Commodore Ballroom when she came back to Vancouver to headline a benefit for Co-op Radio.

Etta James was the full package. After our interview, I emceed her concert at the Town Pump, took photographs of her during her performance and danced in front of the stage while she smiled down at us. The late singer and musician Elizabeth Fischer and I found ourselves awake and online one morning before dawn while I was writing "Strange Women." She was the only person besides my editor to read that essay before it was published. We didn't know Elizabeth would not be with us much longer. In 2021, we lost the extraordinary slide guitarist and singer Ellen McIlwaine. I wish I had more of her to offer you and more of her for myself.

In addition to my mother, who passed away just as I was finishing "Strange Women," this book is dedicated to Karlene Faith. We met in the summer of 1982 at the Vancouver Folk Music Festival. I had just been rightly brushed off by Holly Near, whom I interrupted while she was listening to music, but her friend, who was sitting next to her, got up and followed me. Karlene had just moved to Vancouver from California to head the Simon Fraser University School of Criminology's distance education program. She had heard about my show and wanted to help. Karlene became my mentor.

Karlene Faith was a revolutionary feminist. She had worked in Eritrea with the Peace Corps and in Jamaica with the Rastafarians and had led writing workshops with prisoners at Soledad in California. But as co-founder in the early 1970s of the Santa Cruz Women's Prison Project, she brought feminist consciousness and self-esteem to the women incarcerated at the California Institution for Women (CIW). With volunteers that included artists, teachers, students, poets, professors and other community activists, women's studies became the curriculum, college credits included. (At the warden's invitation, Karlene was asked to introduce the three women we knew as the "Manson girls" to feminism in hopes that these women could be "deprogrammed" and reclaim their humanity. Karlene became their teacher.)

Through Karlene's program Music Inside/Out, Meg Christian, Holly Near, June Millington, Linda Tillery and other musicians from the emerging women's music scene performed behind those walls. Hundreds of musical instruments were donated. A concert tour called Women on Wheels travelled around California bringing attention to the issue. Karlene also taught the very first class on the history of women in American music at the University of California, Santa Cruz. (She had been denied the previous year because the subject matter was considered "too narrow.") As this was an undiscovered field, with little to no research available, when word got out, many women in the business came as special guests. The class produced a 172-page book on a typewriter titled *Women's Music*, itself a historical document.

I had been at the 1975 California National Organization for Women convention, where a handful of women from CIW were allowed to spend the day. They were returned to prison that evening while Cris Williamson and Margie Adam were performing. They stopped the concert. I was also in the audience at Women on Wheels. I knew Karlene without knowing her.

Always humble, Karlene referred to herself as simply "a witness." She believed in me and what I was doing. Karlene was a guest on *Rubymusic* multiple times, and she introduced me to *everybody*. Eventually Holly Near did come on *Rubymusic* (she was campaigning for Jesse Jackson at the time), and I got to know her accompanist when we were trapped for a couple of hours in a crowded elevator in New York City, missing the after-party—Holly and Ferron had just performed at Carnegie Hall. Things have a way of coming full circle.

Karlene died May 15, 2017.

In 1988, June Millington, co-founder of the rock and roll band Fanny, and later of the Institute for the Musical Arts (which trains young women and girls in musicianship and business), said to me: "One of the things that concerns me is that we find a lot of women coming into women's music as part of our audience who have no idea of the history of even those of us who are still alive, not to mention women who have done music and have passed on."

I cannot stress strongly enough how the contributions of female musicians and the women who support their networks have been overlooked and dismissed, even into our modern times. In a story that may be familiar to some, my mother was the nighttime cleaning lady at her hometown radio station. In the dark and damp basement, she found hundreds of demo 45s that had been thrown away. She saved them for me. Most of those records were by women. This is where we find our history: in those dark and damp places, in used record stores, old magazines and photographs and in the memories of others.

There is a spirit that connects the women in this book. There is accomplishment, as in the work of Rosetta Reitz, who single-handedly gave us back our blues; there is sadness as Etta James recalls her encounter with Janis Joplin; and there is courage in the words of Holocaust survivor Esther Bejarano, who was selected to play in the "women's orchestra" at Auschwitz-Birkenau as the trains arrived. I have been so fortunate to know these women, if only for a moment.

In their honour, I submit to you this history, before our words are lost again.

Founded in 1973, the Vancouver Women's Bookstore at 804 Richards Street became part of an international feminist network. In addition to books, posters and pamphlets, it was the only place where one could buy "women's music." Arson was suspected when it burned down in 1980.

WOMEN'S MUSIC AND
THE MOTHERS OF INVENTION

Living the Changes, edited by Joan Turner, University of Manitoba Press, 1990

In the summer of 1974 I performed an original song at the local bar where I worked. Up until that night, my repertoire had included "Four Strong Winds," "Take It Easy" and "The Night They Drove Old Dixie Down." On this night I wanted to give my audience something more personal. In my naïveté, I thought a tongue-in-cheek talking blues about my recent abortion would be appropriate. I called it "Abortion Baby Blues." I will never forget the silence that followed my last chord. Likewise, I will never forget the applause that erupted once everyone caught their breath. Those cheering the loudest would later go out and hold up half the sky. My life changed that night, too; it was only a matter of time before I was writing and singing to the all-women audiences that thrived during the '70s.

What I had written was "women's music," inspired by the euphoria of the women's movement. It was in reaction to that nameless emptiness many of us felt while listening to the radio, to our records or to the music in clubs. Although there were notable exceptions, most of the music in the 1970s did not encourage independence in women. It was rare to hear music that accurately described our lives.

In 1974 a woman did not have to belong to the women's movement to feel its power. Women's liberation was the coffee-break topic of the year, whether that coffee was being poured in the kitchens of Saskatchewan and Nebraska or in the office lunchrooms in Toronto and Denver. No woman was left untouched. It was an incredible feeling to stand poised, ready to make history.

Women's music was born during these urgent times. It was music that valued honesty. It encouraged women to take control of their lives. Its subject matter was rich and varied. Some women wrote hard-edged, overtly political lyrics. Others chose to celebrate the accomplishments of women they knew: mothers, grandmothers, sisters, friends. Still others documented the intricate subtleties of relationships between women, including between lesbians, and some composers dared to demonstrate female sensibilities in purely instrumental music. Bravely, songwriters revealed the painful secret of abuse. Women's music was easily recognizable. It was to the women's movement what civil rights music was to the '60s, and it paved the way for the freedom of expression that newer female artists now enjoy. Historically, it was an unforgettable force.

With the growing acceptance of socially conscious songwriting in popular music today, and with the acknowledgement by women of the hard-fought gains made by our musical foremothers, the term *women's music* is not easily defined. In fact, many Canadian performers with feminist sensibilities now find the term vague, or inappropriate and limiting. But it was not so in the early years.

Although women's music could certainly be considered a spontaneous outburst, one of the first written definitions of women's music is traceable to California and the all-women recording company Olivia Records. In 1974 it described women's music as music that "speaks honestly and realistically to women about our lives—our needs, our strengths, our relationships with each, our anger, our love." And the creators of this new music committed themselves to confronting oppressive behaviour and bigotry.

As time passed, however, and a sophisticated women's music network developed in the United States, the term *women's music* was often used to mean "lesbian music." Lively debate still continues in the United States among concert and festival producers, musicians and supporters

1987, Toronto: Guitarist Elaine Stef makes a rare solo performance at a Mayworks event, aided by her "assistant," her 1970 Fender Jazzmaster.

as to whether this is true. Also, confronting discrimination and prejudice in the world at large is often a difficult process until we have confronted it in the world within.

But in the mid-1970s, many Canadian feminists involved in the growing women's independent music scene acknowledged and accepted the definition of women's music as envisioned by the American pioneers; this was particularly so in Vancouver, where there were more cultural exchanges with Washington, Oregon and California than with the western provinces, and in Toronto and Montreal, where the Michigan Womyn's Music Festival provided an annual cultural fix.

Through the work of Anne Michaud, the organizers of the Michigan festival became aware of the existence and needs of the French-speaking women of Quebec and made it possible for there to be French translations of all relevant material as well as space for francophones to meet. Later, those services grew into a multicultural and international support service with Anne as the coordinator. Anne explained:

"At the same time, it was important for me that the road be open for francophone performers and musicians. It took a couple of years of lobbying to get them to have Lucie Blue Tremblay. I really wanted Lucie to be the first one because she was speaking and performing in both languages. I was sure it was a great way to have a francophone woman start

1987, Montreal: Organized by Concordia University student leader Kamari Clarke (*left*), speaker Angela Davis returns to the stage to join musician and activist Faith Nolan (*Africville*), Clarke, and Andrea Currie (*right*) from Four the Moment.

in the States. It's still a part of my work that is close to my heart.

"Having access to Michigan has been very important in terms of having a strong sense of community. Because there are so many lesbians in the States and money to have, there are more possibilities in terms of what you can do. For me, it was a place to get the nourishment that I needed to come back to my own community and go on with the work I had to do. Michigan is the only place in the world where for two weeks your choices as a lesbian are validated.

"[At the Michigan festival] there is also the part of listening to all that music that is part of your day-to-day. That music is very connected to what we live when we are among each other. But there are few places out there where we can be with each other. So, to be outdoors, to be with so many women and to see live onstage those women you listen to when you do your dishes, or when you are with your lover, is another reason won.en go."

Michigan was also the place where Canadian women learning sound engineering got a chance to work. Engineer Nancy Poole and Womynly Way Productions producer Ruth Dworin are still an important part of the women's festival scene in the United States, and Edmonton sound engineer Cathy Welch made her debut at Michigan in 1988. As for performers, what started as a trickle sixteen years ago with classical musicians Carol Rowe and April Kassirer (known in Toronto as C.T. and April) taking the stage at the National Women's Music Festival in Illinois has turned into a stream. Most feminist performers in Canada have found their way to the major festivals in the United States. Quebec's Lucie Blue Tremblay has signed with Olivia Records; Connie Kaldor, Sherry Shute, Ferron, Lillian Allen, Faith Nolan, Lorraine Segato and Heather Bishop have all made names for themselves south of the border.

Heather Bishop's manager and business partner, Joan Miller, and Ruth Dworin sit on the board of directors of the Association of Women's Music and Culture, which meets yearly in the United States. For two years I wrote a regular column called Live! From Canada in *Hot Wire*, the Chicago-based journal of women's music and culture. But, however connected many of us were, and still are, to this American movement, here at home a transformation was taking place that was uniquely our own.

In Canada, in the mid-1970s, there were coffee houses and clubs that offered women-only space on a full- or part-time basis. These places became centres for the development of women's communities. Among them were the Full Circle Coffee House in Vancouver, Clementine's (later renamed the Three of Cups) and the Fly by Night in Toronto, and the Powerhouse Gallery and Co-op Femme, also known as Co-op Lesbienne, in Montreal. Almost every Canadian city had one women's coffee house

1984, Vancouver: Famed recording engineer Leslie Ann Jones is photographed backstage at the Vancouver Folk Music Festival. "As I recall, I was there because I had engineered Ferron's *Shadows on a Dime*. A classic and one of my faves."

during this period, whether it was in temporary quarters in the YWCA in Halifax, down an alleyway in some guy's dance studio in Dalhousie, at Women's Night at the Guild in Regina or an evening of live music at the Women's Building in Winnipeg. Some coffee houses offered an evening for women and their men friends, and on occasion some concert producers designated lesbian-only space. But this usually occurred only when American performers Linda Shear or Alix Dobkin came to town.

Most cities had an all-women production group, although for the most part the women were novices, with only their energy and desire to guide them. Often these women were associated with a women's group or political organization that produced concerts for a particular benefit. However, there were some exceptional companies that produced the first women's music concerts in the country, for example, Womankind Productions in Vancouver and Sappho Sound in Toronto (which later gave birth to Womynly Way Productions).

These women took on an incredible task as they imported talent, often at their own expense, and introduced us to our own kind. They also weathered a lot of criticism as they tried to respond to the needs of a growing political community trying to define itself.

In conjunction, there emerged a small garden of women's music festivals, beginning on the West Coast and eventually spreading to Nova

1987, Montreal: At CentreVille radio, Charlene Boudreau co-produced female pow-ered current affairs. But her passion was music: Wonder Brass, Les Poules, Mat'chum, Danielle Dax, and the Slits. "I got to play the Au Pairs at 7 in the morning."

Scotia. The talent was often local, and trappings were few, but for those women, and in some cases men, who openly celebrated the contributions of women, while being videotaped by local police (as was the case in the Kootenays of British Columbia), and who hiked into the backwoods to sit on the ground and get eaten by bugs, there were great rewards: the a cappella and acoustic music of women on the edge of time, including Ferron and Rita MacNeil.

It is appropriate that the first Canadian women's festivals took place in the Kootenays. The area has a mixture of Doukhobor people, the rural working class, urban exiles, American expatriates and an active women's community. Even a provincial tourism brochure states that the area has a reputation for seclusion and several generations of settlers have found a safe haven here from the anxieties of religious persecution or social unrest.

The first festival, held in 1974 in Castlegar, BC, was organized by Marcia Braundy for the Kootenay Women's Council, an ad hoc group of Status of Women organizations in several small towns. The two-day fes-tival featured local and regional musicians, workshops on witchery and crafts, a film festival, square dancing and an arts and crafts fair. It was open to both women and men.

The second year, the festival was held in nearby Kaslo and lasted for four days. The first two days were for women and their invited guests

1987, Toronto: Working in her studio, Linda Manzer, creator of the archtop flat-tip acoustic and multi stringed harp guitars, smooths and shapes each instrument with her hands. From watching her father in his workshop to building her first dulcimer fifty years ago, Manzer guitars are considered works of art.

and the final days were for women only. These were historic events. It was revolutionary for women to put themselves first and to celebrate and promote each other. To designate women-only space, especially in a public place, was entirely new. Equally groundbreaking was a workshop on lesbianism led by the Lesbian Caucus of the British Columbia Federation of Women. But as one woman told me, "lesbianism was not an issue" for rural women at these festivals. The primary purpose was to bring all rural women together for the first time. As Rita MacNeil sang "Angry People in the Streets," so did the Doukhobor Women's Choir sing the music of their culture.

Although the idea of women-only space was controversial in the '70s and often misunderstood in the '80s and '90s, within that environment something wonderful happened. Women spoke honestly to each other. They sang together. They loved one another. They rejoiced in the telling of their stories and secrets. With music as the salve, women were healed. For a brief time, the slumber party had come of age.

However, Canada has yet to support a national women's music festival on an ongoing basis. The West Kootenay Women's Festival in British Columbia, now in its fourteenth year (at the time of publication), is the oldest. For the 150 women who attend, this festival is primarily a com-

1987, Toronto: Marva Jackson, under headphones at a local benefit, was a rock and alternative deejay, as well as a music and spoken word programmer at CKLN. Although she injected music by women into the reggae scene, she was highly influenced by the riot girrrls movement. She became station manager of CKLN in 1992, leading the charge for continued funding.

munity celebration complete with potluck supper, talent show, auction and dance. The Kingston, Ontario, Womyn's Music Festival has been in business since 1985 but operates on private land that accommodates only about 300 women. Both festivals are for women only with some restrictions placed on boy children.

In 1988 avant-garde musicians Diane Labrosse, Danielle Roger and Joane Hétu produced the ambitious five-day Festival international de musiciennes innovatrices in Montreal. Nadine Davenport, Carol Street and a dozen other dedicated souls produced Vancouver's First Women's Music Festival. In 1989 and 1990, Vancouver offered Women in View: A Festival of Performing Arts, which featured mostly theatre. Ruth Dworin of Womynly Way Productions remains one of our most prolific producers, as she continues to organize two- and three-day events for the Toronto area, including Spectrum: A Festival of Music, Theatre, Dance, Skillbuilding and Strategizing (1985), Joining Hands: A Deaf and Hearing Theatre and Music Festival (1987) and Colourburst: Multicultural Women in the Arts Festival (1987). She has also worked on several co-productions, including Spirit of Turtle Island: Native Women's Festival, co-produced with Dakota-Ojibway Productions (1985), and the Rainbow Women's Festival, co-produced with Multicultural Womyn in Concert (1984). But, overall, women's music festivals in Canada are sporadic. And, with the Kootenay and Kingston festivals being the exceptions, women-only festivals are rare.

When Ruth Dworin founded Womynly Way Productions in 1980, she decided on an open-door policy for her concerts and festivals. She says: "At the time, I wanted to do something politically that would nurture and support women, feminists, who were out doing frontline organizing work. I also wanted a situation that would educate people who were just coming for the entertainment value, and I figured a concert was the ideal way to do both. Art is a really strong tool for consciousness-raising because it goes for people's emotions and in a lot of senses bypasses their intellect.

"It may be a little bit annoying for some women to sit at a concert and be singing along and hear male voices singing along, but the trade-off is the fact that those women aren't having to make themselves personally vulnerable and the men are learning more about our issues. As far as I'm concerned, it's probably the most painless way to educate people."

It is on this point of exclusivity that the Canadian experience differs radically from that of American women. It became obvious in 1984 when Our Time Is Now! Canadian Women's Music and Cultural Festival was held in Winnipeg. Although it was intended to be a once-in-a-lifetime experience, the festival continued for three years. And it came to symbolize what Canadian women's music had become. Quite accidentally, it was the first national festival that defined women's music in a Canadian context—but not without controversy.

Produced by Joan Miller and a core group of five women, at the request of a Winnipeg organization called the Same Damn Bunch, Our Time Is Now! was the largest gathering of Canadian women musicians ever assembled in this country. The first festival introduced dub poet Lillian Allen, Inuit throat singers Lucy Kownak and Emily Alerk and Indigenous singers Suzanne Bird and Alanis Obomsawin, as well as Connie Kaldor, Arlene Mantle, Nancy White, Ferron, Marie-Lynn Hammond, Four the Moment, Heather Bishop and Suzanne Campagne, in a program composed of almost fifty women performers. The second festival, produced by a newly formed Canadian Women's Music and Cultural Festival Inc., presented seventy individual women, including comedian Sheila Gostick, jazz musicians Wondeur Brass and the Swing Sisters, gospel and blues performer Louise Rose and the punk band Ruggedy Annes. Canadian women's music was not limited to one musical genre. Nor was it the sole expression of one race or sexual orientation. Breaking from an early tradition, women's music was not for women only.

The organizers knew what many of us did not: that the established women's community could not support a women-only festival of this magnitude. Musicians born out of the movement would not make a living if they sang only to women. This was devastating news to women who were accustomed to the American women's festivals—which, with the exception of Sisterfire, are closed to men and to boy children—and to women who needed the lesbian-positive atmosphere that women-only festivals provide.

The issue was further complicated when the festival organizers did not designate a lesbian stage. It was their belief that the musicians had the right to choose how they would identify themselves. It was an acknowledgement, as well, that many performers in Canada who are lesbian choose not to declare their sexual preference publicly or to make it the focal point of their careers, regardless of their public stands on issues. And this right to privacy had to be respected.

Despite this painful controversy, the majority of the feminist press applauded the festival, as did the *Winnipeg Free Press*. Ironically a few letters to the editor appeared in that paper complaining of "women hugging and kissing each other in this family-based park," and that "taxpayers' money is being spent on hate propaganda," but the responses from other readers were swift and encouraging. Heather Bishop told me: "What it did for all of us women musicians was just short of a miracle. It put us all together in the same place. It changed people's lives. That's a victory."

Although the attendance at the second festival in 1985 was over two thousand people, the organizers were left with a deficit. They chose to hold a much smaller festival in 1986 and then to discontinue producing the festival for the time being. But they had already made a bold statement about women's music in Canada. Women's music could benefit everyone. This was not news to the performers.

For over a decade the Vancouver and Winnipeg folk music festivals have been promoting music by women at their annual gatherings. For at least three years Winnipeg had a women's theme tent, and Vancouver has consistently brought new songwriters and regional legends from around the world, including the first wave of feminist and lesbian performers. It was on these stages that women's music met the music of the world. In an atmosphere of tolerance, the ideals and issues so sacred to women's music received an international hearing as politically aware performers—women and men, gay and straight, white and of colour—stood together, worked together and learned each other's songs. Likewise, the audience was integrated, giving women an opportunity to gather and yet be part of the whole. To stress this point, Rosalie Goldstein, artistic director of the Winnipeg festival since 1987, told me: "I think there are some important principles around which the festival operates. I mean, in addition to its concern about women. Its concern in general is about people who live in a society that's alienating. And the concern is to bring them together, the artists, the audience, the volunteers, and give them a quality-of-life experience which is something hopefully they take away with them and use as a model for their lives on a daily basis. Because I really think that is how the world changes."

Certainly, the Vancouver Folk Music Festival is an example of this as well. At its peak, twenty thousand people gather for two days and three nights at an oceanside park in a beautiful area of the city. The counterculture attends, as well as seniors, politicians, teenagers, students, children, professionals and a large contingent from the feminist and lesbian community.

When women's music began to rise to prominence in the United States, Canadian artistic directors took note and, urged on by women working in the ranks (in particular in Vancouver by Susan Knutson and Wendy Solloway), began to book the first wave of feminist and lesbian performers. In his first year as artistic director for the Vancouver festival, Gary Cristall sent talent scouts to Michigan. He called "someone who knew someone" who eventually got him in touch with Holly Near. And in 1980 the floodgates opened. Onstage in Vancouver, in front of ten thousand people, were Sweet Honey in the Rock, Cathy Winter and Betsy Rose, Ferron, Robin Flower, Nancy Vogl, Laurie Lewis, Barbara Higbie, and Holly Near and Adrienne Torf.

"Feminist" appeared as a music category alongside "Gospel" and "Celtic" in the festival publicity. The festival program printed articles about women's music and songs by Rosalie Sorrels, Ferron, Holly Near and Betsy Rose. There was a workshop with women performers called A Good Woman's Love. All of this happened in an environment that included traditional folk and blues music, and performers from other parts of the world. In varied proportions, it has remained this way ever since. (It should be noted that in 1978, the festival's inaugural year, there was no programming devoted to women or their issues. Although Gary Cristall was not booking the festival—he was festival coordinator—in 1979 he managed to get a graphic with a woman's symbol, an equal sign, musical notes and a clenched fist as the title of a workshop. When he was given the chance to choose one act by artistic director and founder Mitch Podolak, who also created the Winnipeg Folk Festival, Gary chose Ferron. Gary would not become artistic director until the following year, but he was already looking and listening for what was starting to emerge from "women's music.")

The big breakthrough at the Winnipeg Folk Festival came in 1982, when Heather Bishop, Holly Near, Betsy Rose and Cathy Winter, Meg Christian and Diane Lindsay, Ginni Clemmens, Frankie Armstrong and Mimi Fariña were invited by Mitch Podolak to appear in the Big Tent.

Winnipeg also introduced a women's theme tent, which operated for three years between 1984 and 1986. In 1984 nearly thirty women appeared on this stage, including Toshi Reagon, Judy Small, Anne Lederman, Teresa Trull and Barbara Higbie, Heather Bishop, Holly Near, Ronnie Gilbert, Patsy Montana and the Reel World String Band. In 1985 newcomers included k.d. lang, Margret RoadKnight, Four the Moment and Rory Block. The final year was a blowout with Ellen McIlwaine, Christine Lavin, Tracy Riley, Heather Bishop, Connie Kaldor and Sweet Honey in the Rock, among others.

Despite its popularity, when Rosalie Goldstein became artistic director after the festival in 1986, she disbanded the women's stage. "I did so with the most loving care," she told me, "because I believe it's important for women to be dispersed throughout the entire body of the festival. I would not put up a tent at the festival and say, 'Here are all the blacks,' or 'Here are all the Jews.' And that's exactly what was happening with women. I don't think that's fair. I don't think it shows women to their best advantage. I don't think that it invites people who might, under other circumstance, come and see that programming. It doesn't make it easy for women, whatever their sexual orientation, to put their music across. And I want that to happen in a serious way. It's what I believe in."

The feminization of the Winnipeg and Vancouver folk festivals came about in part because of the large number of women who volunteer each year to work on the events. Currently half of the eight hundred volunteers at the Winnipeg festival are women, and in Vancouver, women are in the majority. The inclusion of women was also aided by musicians such as Connie Kaldor and Heather Bishop, who carried around lists of Canadian women performers to show any and all who would blame the lack of participation by women performers on the fact that there were not any, and by Marie-Lynn Hammond, one of the first Canadian feminists to grace the main stages of festivals. Connie Kaldor called her "the shining light in that scene."

Although the Vancouver and Winnipeg festivals are now the biggest producers of women's music in the country (with Womynly Way Productions an impressive contender), it should be noted that not every folk festival has been open to the idea. The Regina Women's Production Group operated a women's stage for three years at the Regina Folk Festival against all odds.

But the feminization of the Canadian music business in general has been aided by our feminist musicians who, while supporting our independence movement with their music, did not separate themselves from the rest of Canada. They fought for equal access, for their right to perform in the best venues in the country, for their right to control their own careers and their creativity, for their right to speak out on behalf of women. Now a collective consciousness is at work spreading the word.

Our job is not over yet. There are wounds to heal and bridges to mend from those early years. There is living history that must be analyzed and documented. And there are issues that are as urgent today as they were in the beginning.

The advent of women's music brought new standards to concert production; it brought sign language interpretation, wheelchair accessibility, provision of child care and the lowering of the barrier between performer and audience. The network that supported women's music gave women the opportunity to develop skills that had previously eluded them: concert production, photography, sound engineering, music journalism, management, graphic arts, record production and distribution. It also ushered in a wave of unprecedented criticism.

Because the performers of women's music became the voices for a newly forming and still largely silent women's community, their accountability was demanded by the women they represented. In the early years a performer could just as easily be chastised for wearing makeup or shaving her legs as she could for making a racist remark. There was no qualitative difference. The length of a performer's hair and the style

1987, Toronto: A cappella group Four the Moment performs at an event in support of their first album *We're Still Standing*. Natives of Nova Scotia, their music called out injustice through original songs and historic covers. *Left to right:* Debbie Jones, Kim Bernard, Delvina Bernard, Andrea Currie.

of her clothing could be used as indicators of the depth of her political commitment. Appearance was a serious business as women attempted to reject images that were perceived to be contrived, traditionally "feminine" or "man-made."

Although women's audiences were notably enthusiastic, a musician was often judged more by the content of her material than for her skill. It was the message, not the means, that won over an audience. And since the primary battle at that time was designated to be between women and men, performers who chose to sing about being mothers, or the wives and lovers of men, were not always welcome. Children were not always welcome either, as women asserted their right to be with women only.

There is no gentle way to say that these times were not always the best of times. Often, as one group of women claimed its territory, it did so at the expense of another. Any history of oppressed people includes the difficulties encountered as those people define their issues and themselves.

Many of our musicians were victims of our desire to design a perfect woman's world. Heterosexual performers were made to feel like traitors, lesbian performers who made their sexual preference public were taken for granted, and women whose careers began before or outside the women's movement were seen as having no validity. (This was particularly the case if they played anything other than acoustic music.)

We also failed to recognize cultural, racial and class differences between women. Assimilation was required by all, with one language spoken here.

The Alliance for the Production of Women's Performing Arts / l'Alliance Femmes et Arts de la Scene is attempting to address these problems, as well as to unite women in communities across the country. Although hundreds of women worked tirelessly to create and support women's music in Canada, they have often done so in isolation. Their stories are just beginning to be told. There are also voices to be reckoned with: the black women of Nova Scotia, the immigrant women from the Caribbean, the Indigenous women from across the country and the women of Quebec.

Today the mothers of invention are hard at work. Many of the early performers are now keeping pace in the music business. Other women are at home, choosing instead to nourish their communities with their very personal music. Women's music is still changing lives. It is also changing the way Canadian society feels about women. And each time a woman decides to tell her story, a revolution takes place.

We must always remember how these changes happened. We must honour our predecessors and the women who work daily to enrich our cultural lives. History is a precious gift. It is how we learn. Only with hindsight will we shape our vision. Only with vision can we carry on.

FEMINIST MUSIC

Encyclopedia of Music in Canada, second edition,
University of Toronto Press, 1992

Feminist music (or Women's music). Pop music with lyrics written from a feminist perspective and usually, but not exclusively, sung for feminist audiences. The description has also been applied generally to pop music performed by groups whose membership—i.e., all, or in the majority, women—implies a statement of self-determination. Employing folk, rock, punk, reggae and rap styles, women's music has given voice to the issues raised by the feminist movement of the 1970s, 1980s and 1990s. Subject matter includes childbirth, parenthood, sexual orientation, violence against women and children, and discrimination and equality in the workplace.

Feminism first found expression in Canadian music in 1975 in the songs of Rita MacNeil's first LP, *Born a Woman,* and in Jacqueline Lemay's "La Moitié du monde est une femme." Other early feminist singers, songwriters and instrumentalists included Eileen Brown, Ferron, Jeanette Gritanni, Jane Perks, Connie Smith (Kuhns), Carol Street and the band Contagious on the West Coast; Heather Bishop, Connie Kaldor, Noelle Hall, Kris Purdy and the band Walpurgis Night on the prairies; C.T. and April, Sara Ellen Dunlop, Marianne, Beverly Glenn-Copeland, Marie-Lynn Hammond, Arlene Mantle, Lorraine Segato, Sherry Shute and the band Mama Quilla II in Ontario; and Angèle Arsenault, Édith Butler and the bands Marianna Bazooka and Wondeur Brass (Justine) in Quebec.

In Canada, the feminist and folk music scenes overlapped in the 1980s—i.e., feminist singers appeared at folk festivals as well as at events sponsored by women's cultural or political organizations (in marked contrast to the USA, where women's music is generally independent of mainstream contemporary folk). The earliest Canadian performers, however, worked exclusively within the women's community—at coffee houses (e.g., Full Circle in Vancouver, Clementine's, or the Three of Cups, and Fly by Night in Toronto, and the Powerhouse Gallery and Co-op Femme, or Co-op Lesbienne, in Montreal), art galleries and social and health centres—and have continued to flourish through an independent network of production groups (e.g., Womankind Productions in Vancouver, Sappho Sound in Toronto), community and college radio programs, etc. For the most part, recordings have been produced for independent labels owned by the musicians themselves—e.g., SPPS-Disques (Arsenault, Butler,

Lemay), Mother of Pearl (Bishop) and Lucy (Ferron).

Feminist music has been a major component of the small West Kootenay Women's Festival, first held in 1974 at Castlegar, BC (later relocated to near Nelson). Many concerts and larger events have been organized in Toronto by Womynly Way Productions (established in 1980), while the Canadian Women's Music and Cultural Festival was held annually in 1984–86 in Winnipeg, and the Festival international de musiciennes innovatrices was organized

by Productions Super Meme in 1988 in Montreal. Women's music was first introduced into the contemporary folk mainstream at the 1980 Vancouver Folk Music Festival and the 1982 Winnipeg Folk Festival and has subsequently been heard at many similar events across the country.

Among other Canadian women aligned in the 1980s and early 1990s with feminist music were Lillian Allen, Suzanne Bird, Micheline Goulet, Faith Nolan, Alanis Obomsawin, Louise Rose, Itah Sadu, Djanet Sears, Gwen Swick and Lucie Blue Tremblay. Ensembles, in a variety of styles, have included Assar Santana and Chanel #6, Demi-Monde, Four the Moment, the Heretics, , No Frills, Parachute Club, the Pillow Sisters, Ruggedy Annes and Tête de vache. Several Canadians have been popular on the US women's music scene, including Allen, Bishop, Ferron, Kaldor, Nolan, Tremblay and the guitarist Shute. Ferron's "Testimony" became an international anthem of women's music in the early 1980s. Other significant songs in Canadian feminist music include MacNeil's "Born a Woman," Kaldor's "Strength Love and Laughter" and Parachute Club's "Rise Up."

SELECTED DISCOGRAPHY

(As originallly published in *Encyclopedia of Music in Canada*)

Suzanne Bird, *Heart Full of Soul* (1988), Rayne Productions, unnumbered (cass.)

Marianne Girard, *When It Hurts* (1982), Sailor, SAIL-2002

Beverly Glenn-Copeland, *At Last!* (1983), Atlast Records, ALR-010

Heretics, *Mass Hysteria* (1991), Fringe, FDP-3105 (CD)

Mama Quilla II, *Mama Quilla II* (1982), Tupperwaros, TR-001 (EP)

Arlene Mantle, *Class Act* (1986), On the Line, OTL-003; *In Solidarity* (1988), On the Line, OTL-006

Moral Lepers, *Turn to Stone* (1982), Mo-Da-Mu, 006

Faith Nolan, *Africville* (1986), MWIC, 11161; *Sistership* (1987), MWIC, 11162; *Freedom to Love* (1989), Aural Tradition, ATR-302

Kris Purdy, *Kris Purdy*, Bang Clunk, BC-1 (cass.)

Ruggedy Annes, *Jagged Thoughts* (1985), Tabb Records, unnumbered

Sherry Shute, *Sherry Shute* (1986), Lois Carroll Music, unnumbered (EP)

Lucy Blue Tremblay, *Lucie Blue Tremblay* (1986), Olivia, LC-947; *Tendresse* (1989), Olivia, LC-955

Label text:

TURN TO STONE
DEAD OF NIGHT
SUICIDE
CHINA RAG

SIDE 1   MOM-6
45rpm

MORAL LEPERS

Made in Canada 1982

WHAT'S THAT SOUND?

THERE IS A WIND THAT NEVER DIES

THE LIFE OF YOKO ONO

Geist, no. 114 (Fall 2019)

I follow Yoko Ono on Twitter. She is my daily devotion, my addiction. She reassures me that *Good things will come later* and she urges me to *Remember love*. Her words would go nicely on a refrigerator magnet. I was not quite a woman when she arrived uninvited, a grey mist over a blond sea. But as I aged, she became my mystery to solve, my road less travelled.

Her early instructional writings tell me to imagine the clouds dripping, to send the smell of the moon (to someone), to see the sky between a woman's thighs. She once labelled polished beach stones and shards of glass as past and future mornings, to be sold at dawn from her rooftop. She took a childhood game called Telephone and turned it into performance art. (When she introduced *Whisper Piece* at the Destruction in Art Symposium in London, in 1966, asking the audience to whisper the same word from ear to ear, many of the male artists asked that she be removed.)

Yoko is a woman with machismo, who was relentless in creating her own way through the exploratory art movements of the 1960s, straight into the heart of popular culture, celebrity, politics and feminism. She is a question mark and a contradiction. At almost eighty-seven years old, she still vibrates.

It has been fifty years since her marriage to the late John Lennon, a relationship that brought her into the public consciousness. It was a union that broke up two marriages, leaving two small children behind, and, truthfully, helped bring about the end of the revolutionary Beatles. The couple's public behaviour and the legal battles that followed destroyed friendships and families. It's a saga of infidelity, drug busts and addiction; but also of transformation, collaboration and creation. Together they gave the world "Imagine," and this year, on the anniversary of their honeymoon performances, known as the Bed-Ins for Peace, their life together is celebrated.

When John and Yoko met in London in 1966, she was already an experienced entrepreneur and performance artist, and an early interpreter of what was known as Concept Art. Born in 1933, in Japan, a descendant of Samurai warriors, Yoko was an older woman.

From her loft in New York City, in 1960, she had organized a series of performances with her friend, the composer La Monte Young. In this environment artists were encouraged to move outside the boundaries of historical and conventional creation. Her first husband, the classical pianist and composer Toshi Ichiyanagi, whom she married in 1956, had introduced her to the composer John Cage, the dancer Merce Cunningham and others, which placed her directly in the evolving art scene. From her associations, especially with the enterprising George Maciunas, the Fluxus art movement was identified and named. Simply put, art was no longer in the eye of the beholder to be passively viewed. It was art that would be created in the mind of the artist and completed only by participation. Art was anything. Art could be nothing. Her self-published book *Grapefruit: A Book of Instruction and Drawings*, in 1964, was Yoko's contribution to this mind game.

Her instruction poems, including the earlier reference to dripping clouds, ask the reader to *imagine*, to "draw a map to get lost" ("Map Piece"), to "put your shadows together until they become one" ("Shadow Piece") or to "stir inside of your brains with a penis. Mix well. Take a walk" ("Walk Piece"). She made five hundred copies. With *Grapefruit* reissued in 1970 with an introduction by John Lennon, and again in subsequent years (most recently in 2000 and still very much in print), it is easy to see how her work at the time may have been misunderstood for its intangible nature. Not so now.

The sky never ceased to be there for us. (Twitter: April 22, 2019)

In 2013, the Schirn Kunsthalle Frankfurt presented the exhibition *Yoko Ono: Half-a-Wind Show*. She was eighty years old. This was the first major retrospective of her work in Europe, although at any given time, her art is being shown somewhere in the world. There are no fewer than thirty solo and group shows either in galleries now or scheduled to be presented by 2020. The Schirn retrospective featured more than two hundred objects, installations, photographs, drawings and films, as well as a special room dedicated to her music. The exhibition travelled to Denmark and Austria before moving to the Guggenheim Museum in Bilbao, Spain, in 2014.

The collected volume of her work, amassed in one place, as well as the documentation of her growth, her innovations and her contributions to the avant-garde art movements, as illustrated in the gallery's publication, is (to use appropriate terminology) mind-blowing. Her brilliance is everywhere, wrapped in her humour, her boldness, her sexuality and perhaps even her disrespect. It is often repeated that John Lennon referred to her as "the world's most famous unknown artist: everyone knows her name but no one actually knows what she does." In the two-hundred-page catalogue for the *Half-a-Wind Show*, she is referred to as pioneering and "mythic."

Yoko was one of just a handful of women in the early 1960s who were expressing themselves outside acceptable boundaries. (Her sisters included the late Carolee Schneemann, who famously filmed herself and her husband having sex, partly from the point of view of their cat, and the late Shigeko Kubota, who was among the first artists to use video in her work. Kubota strapped a paintbrush to her underwear and, squatting down, painted a picture resembling Japanese lettering, henceforth known as the *Vagina Painting*.)

Yoko's early films, most co-produced with John Lennon, used nudity both to shock and to un-shock. *Bottoms* and *Up Your Legs Forever* were easy enough, as friends and strangers lined up to be filmed. But her film *Fly* was more difficult to orchestrate as it involved following a fly as it crawled over the body of a naked woman. Collecting flies from piles of garbage and restaurant kitchens around the Bowery and then gassing them with carbon dioxide eventually produced the desired results.

Freedom, a one-minute short of a woman trying to unhook the front clasp of her bra, can send multiple messages. The film *Self-Portrait*, a forty-two-minute single shot, of Lennon's penis getting an erection, is its own statement between lovers, as is a film of his smile. More controversial was her film *Rape*, meant as a condemnation of the paparazzi but interpreted years later as an exposé on "male visual lust." Yoko sent a two-person camera crew to follow a random woman around the streets of London for three days, filming her without her permission, and finally chasing her right into her home. The woman had been set up by her sister without her knowledge.

"Feminist" is a label that has been mostly applied by others. How else to explain her behaviour and her impact? Her performance of *Cut Piece*, first staged in Kyoto and Tokyo in 1964, and later at the Carnegie Recital Hall in 1965, featured Yoko sitting motionless on the stage, fully clothed, "wearing the best suit I had," she said, with a pair of shears nearby. Audience members were invited to cut off a piece of her clothing until there was nothing left, or until Yoko decided she was finished. She restaged this piece in Paris in 2003, sitting on a chair, as she was at that point seventy years old and sitting on the floor was difficult. Her vulnerability and the potential for harm or humiliation make *Cut Piece* radical in any era.

During Cut Piece, I felt whole when I was sitting. (Twitter: February 14, 2019)

Yoko's essay "The Feminization of Society," included in the liner notes of her album *Approximately Infinite Universe* in 1973 (but previously published in an abridged form in the *New York Times* in 1972 and unedited in the San Francisco countercultural magazine *SunDance*), certainly contributed to her status as a feminist seer. Yet for angry and dogmatic times, Yoko's analysis is very unstructured and free-flowing. She touches on the subject of child care—"We definitely need more positive participation by men in the care of our children"—and lesbianism "as a means of expressing rebellion toward the existing society through sexual freedom," but asks, "How about liberating ourselves from our various mind trips such as ignorance, greed, masochism, fear of God and social conventions?" and she suggests the reader harness "the patience and natural wisdom of a pregnant woman."

As if she were looking ahead, Yoko writes: "We can, of course, aim to play the same game that men have played for centuries, and inch by inch, take over all the best jobs and eventually conquer the whole world, leaving an extremely bitter male stud-cum-slave class moaning and groaning underneath us. This is alright for an afternoon dream, but in reality, it would obviously be a drag."

Another version of this essay was published in 2018 on the Drop, the online music component of Refinery29, a young women's lifestyle website. It was in conjunction with an interview by Courtney E. Smith and a music video of Yoko's reworking of some of her earlier songs in the newly released collection *Warzone*. In the interview, Ms. Smith asks Yoko: "What influence has watching the Women's March and seeing women get more involved in American politics, running in record numbers in 2018, had on your work or your hopefulness for a female revolution?"

Yoko answers: "I don't think that revolution is necessary, I prefer the world 'evolution.'" This response is consistent with her approach in interviews for decades. No matter how pointed the question, whether about politics or difficult and private events in her life, she always takes the less direct road, a pacifist's trip to understanding. Imagine no ideology.

Remember many feminists have followed the ways of men and hurt their health by drinking, smoking and pursuing more money and power by intense competition. Think of your health and think of being you, instead of having an intense competition. (Twitter: July 23, 2018)

When John Lennon was murdered on December 8, 1980, Yoko released the album *Season of Glass* within six months of his death. The cover photograph was of John's bloodied glasses on a window ledge beside a glass of water, half empty and half full. Their son, Sean, who was five years old at the time and whose voice can be heard telling a story on the recording, said decades later this act of his mother's showed him how to turn struggle into art. Yoko had never been a silent partner, nor was she a silent widow.

Yoko and John collaborated on ten albums during their twelve-year relationship. (Two more were released posthumously.) But their work can be bookmarked by two albums: *Unfinished Music No. 1: Two Virgins*, where they appeared naked on the cover, front and back, and *Double Fantasy*, released right before John's death. *Two Virgins* (recorded while on acid during their first night together, in the house John shared with his wife Cynthia and their son, Julian, while Cynthia was away) was immediately censored for its graphic photos and highly criticized for its content. There was nothing on the twenty-eight-minute album, condensed from over fourteen hours of tape recordings, that actually resembled music. But more than their nudity and their nerve, *Two Virgins* was a shocking redefinition of who John Lennon was becoming under her influence.

Their final album together, *Double Fantasy*, released on November 17, 1980, three weeks before his death, was their love song, or their swan song, depending on which account one wants to believe; they were each, allegedly, reconsidering their future together. In an interview with Chrissy Iley writing for the *Telegraph* in 2012, Yoko said: "I was very aware that we were ruining each other's careers and I was hated and John was hated because of me."

Double Fantasy is a conversation between long-time partners, alternating songs. It is highly autobiographical and details problems they've had during their years together. John sings "I'm Losing You." Yoko sings "I'm Moving On." They both sing about their love for their son. But Yoko's contributions were still jarring in contrast to John's traditional song structure. Their son, Sean, has remastered his mother's music as a gift to her. He has said that "the albums need to be understood within the context of the avant-garde world."

"*Double Fantasy* was a great joy for John and me," Yoko wrote in *Rolling Stone* in 2010. "John knew what I was up against and protected me to the end. ... But there was a strong feeling that this record should have been just John, and I was an extra thing that they had to put up with." *Double Fantasy* received the Grammy for Album of the Year in 1981.

It's significant that during these tumultuous years, John Lennon, in a very public way, acknowledged his jealousy and his violent temper. (Both his first wife, Cynthia Lennon, and his lover May Pang wrote of violent episodes in their respective memoirs.) According to a named source in a Lennon biography written by Albert Goldman in 1988, a beating may have contributed to the loss of John and Yoko's son, John Ono Lennon II, who died in 1968, in utero, at five months. Other sources attribute this loss to the stress of a recent drug bust. The couple immortalized his unrealized life on their album *Unfinished Music No. 2: Life with the Lions* by recording five minutes and thirty seconds of the baby's heartbeat, followed by two minutes of silence. John continued to speak openly in interviews and on talk shows about his treatment of women until the end of his life.

> *Don't fight against the monster, fight yourself, your ignorance.*
> (Twitter: September 27, 2018)

It was during Yoko's hospital stay that she sent her cameraman Nicholas Knowland to film *Rape*. Of this, Yoko wrote (in part): "Violence is a sad wind that, if channeled carefully, could bring seeds, chairs and all things pleasant to us. ... Nick is a gentle-man who prefers eating clouds and floating pies to shooting *Rape*. Nevertheless, it was shot."

In 1972, John and Yoko wrote and recorded "Woman Is ...," released on their album *Some Time in New York City*. The full title (redacted here) was taken from a comment Yoko had made in an interview with *Nova* magazine in 1969. The song received very limited airplay as most radio stations refused to play it because of the use of the racial epithet. The couple were allowed to sing it on *The Dick Cavett Show* only after Cavett was forced by the network (ABC) to make a pre-taped apology. However, the National Organization for Women presented Yoko and John with a Positive Image of Women award in 1972 for the song and its flip side, Yoko's "Sisters, O Sisters."

Their most triumphant song was "Imagine," honoured in 2017 by the National Music Publishers' Association as song of the century. After decades of trying to get the songwriting credit that John Lennon said she deserved, Yoko was acknowledged as co-writer. John had been inspired by her 1964 book *Grapefruit* and had used her words and sentiments to write his lyrics. He blamed his chauvinism for not crediting her at the time. Their son, Sean, accepted with Yoko. Patti Smith stood at the podium and sang "Imagine," breaking down once, accompanied by her daughter on piano.

> *I love all words, even so-called bad ones, since they have been created by us, human beings for some emotional necessity. You can use the word YES negatively, too. Our word games are very complex.* (Twitter: April 5, 2019)

In the fall of 2018 Yoko curated a major tome, *Imagine John Yoko*, documenting in detail the making of the album *Imagine* at their home in 1971.

Included are photographs, postcards, video stills, handwritten notes and first-person accounts by everyone involved in this album who is still alive. Co-producer Phil Spector presumably wrote from prison. However, Yoko speaks for May Pang, who was their assistant on many films and recordings, and later, at Yoko's invitation, according to Pang, John's lover and protector during one of their separations. The release of this book coincides with the documentary *John & Yoko: Above Us Only Sky*, where Yoko is clearly regarded by all participants as muse, mentor and now crone.

Yoko received the Venice Biennale's Golden Lion for Lifetime Achievement in 2009, just *one* of several important and deserved acknowledgements of her oeuvre. But in the spring of 2019, Yoko Ono was honoured for something very specific. As part of the Los Angeles Philharmonic's Fluxus Festival, over seventy-five women, including a fourteen-piece music ensemble, a twenty-five-person choir, nine dancers and twelve guest artists, paid tribute to Yoko Ono and her *music*, at a sold-out event. With few exceptions, all stage crew, musicians and performers were women.

Breathewatchlistentouch: The Work and Music of Yoko Ono was produced by Girlschool, a group of women-identified artists founded by violinist Anna Bulbrook, from the LA band Airborne Toxic Event. It was an emotional night as performers as diverse as the lead singer of the band Garbage, Shirley Manson, Marisol Hernandez from the band La Santa Cecilia, the songwriter Miya Folick and violinist Sudan Archives reimagined Yoko's music. Electronic music artist and activist Madame Gandhi read from Yoko's written works, and then, under the musical direction of Shruti Kumar, she invited the audience to scream, as part of Yoko's "Voice Piece for Soprano." The choreographer Nina McNeely prepared two dance pieces.

Yoko had been trained in her youth in opera—German Lieder and French chanson—but her recordings and performances more often included screaming, wailing, high-pitched fluttering and deep guttural sounds, more in keeping with female throat singing or a vocal interpretation of gagaku, a Japanese instrumental music known for its minimalism, both unfamiliar to most fans of rock music. It could be unlistenable and her message was often lost. When she released *Warzone* in 2018, at age eighty-five, she rerecorded many of her earlier works, but with stripped-down, cleaner production. It was now apparent, especially sung with her older woman's voice, weary and childlike, how mindful and passionate her songs actually were. Yoko had remained committed to her music, recording dozens of songs and continuing to perform decades after John's death, but it was a younger generation of musicians, influenced by club music, punk and noise, that finally understood her. Experimental musicians remixed her songs. She performed in a band with her son,

Sean. At the age of eighty, she collaborated with Kim Gordon and Thurston Moore, of Sonic Youth. Yoko's current catalogue lists at least forty singles and almost two dozen albums.

As part of the LA tribute, musicians were given permission to reinterpret Yoko's music, and they did so to much acclaim. Although it was not known if Yoko would be able to attend, she was brought in as the lights went down, in a wheelchair. The final performer of the night, singer St. Vincent, led the house in singing "Imagine" to her.

"Who influenced John Lennon to be focused on peace?" the event programmer Anna Bulbrook asked journalist Jessica Gelt in an interview with the *Los Angeles Times*. "Yoko Ono has literally changed the world, and she's had to do it from a position of being publicly overlooked and spurned." In the film *Above Us Only Sky*, assistant Dan Richter says: "I love John, but [Yoko] was speaking through him. I don't think the world's got that quite yet. The language that you see from the time they got together forward is Yoko's language. She taught him this language."

> *You must work on what you love to work on. In my case it was music and art. Work is sacred. It saves you from sad thoughts. I have been wronged by the whole world. But I'm still here. Lies, ultimately, cannot destroy you, unless you join the liars.* (Twitter: June 26, 2018)

As the city of Montreal marked the fiftieth anniversary of the Bed-In for Peace, which took place at the Queen Elizabeth Hotel on May 26, 1969, the Fondation PHI pour l'art contemporain in old Montreal opened *Liberté Conquérante/ Growing Freedom: The Instructions of Yoko Ono and the Art of John and Yoko*. The exhibition filled two buildings, one focusing on Yoko's individual participation works, for example *Mend Piece*, where attendees glue broken pottery back together in any shape (mending the world), while the other building highlighted her work with John, in particular the Montreal bed-in.

The eight days they spent at the Queen Elizabeth Hotel launched a new public approach for the couple. Their message was so simple as to be naive. *Imagine peace*. Celebrities and politicians visited, including the prime minister of Canada. John and Yoko made endless telephone calls to world leaders and gave dozens of press interviews from their bed. They spoke to the leaders and participants of the People's Park protests in Berkeley, pleading for non-violent action, and it was from this room that they made their recording of "Give Peace a Chance." It was a spectacle. (There had been a previous bed-in in Amsterdam right after their wedding, but they ended up at the Queen Elizabeth Hotel in Montreal because John was denied entry to the US because of his drug arrests.)

"Some people took us seriously and were attacking us," Yoko told Peter Watts in the April 2019 edition of *Uncut* magazine, "but actually, it was a big clown thing. And through clowning we communicated the idea of world peace as being very important." The Fondation PHI recorded the personal stories of many of the individuals who made it in to room 1742.

Significantly, *Growing Freedom* featured Yoko's exhibit *Arising*, which records a different kind of story. "Women of all ages, from all countries of the world: you are invited to send a testament of harm done to you for being a woman." Yoko asks that each woman write in her own language, sign only her first name and include a photograph of her eyes. It is particularly sad that *Arising* was mounted in Montreal, as on December 6, 1989, at École Polytechnique, fourteen female engineering students were separated from their male classmates and killed. Fourteen other students—ten women and four men—were also shot but survived.

In any gallery where *Arising* is staged, the walls are covered with the printouts of women's testimonies, eyes and words. As the walls fill up, the older stories are archived. *Arising* premiered as part of the Venice Biennale in 2013 and has been shown around the world, including in Germany, England, Norway, Japan and Peru. Women continue to contribute. I submitted mine.

The year before *Arising* was seen for the first time, Yoko opened *Remember Us* as part of the exhibit *Our Beautiful Daughters* at the Vadehra Art Gallery in New Delhi, India. In coffin-like boxes filled with charcoal, she displayed headless, dismembered, naked female body parts, made of silicone. At the far end of the room were bowls of ashes, a final nod to the horror of sati (an outlawed Hindu practice that requires a widowed woman be burned to death on her husband's funeral pyre). Each evening Rajasthani women covered the bodies with shrouds, woven with their own hands in their tradition. On the walls, "I am uncursed" and "Uncurse yourself" were written in dozens of languages.

Use your skills to heal what was destroyed in the past. (Twitter: March 6, 2019)

Concurrent with this remarkable life, Yoko's detractors still had much to work with. Even her biggest supporters had difficulty with how Julian Lennon, John's son with his first wife, was denied any inheritance and had to buy back at auction sites any personal items of his father's that were meant for him. And as Yoko is the first and last word regarding how John Lennon is to be memorialized, Cynthia Lennon was prevented from organizing her own tributes, including one at the Brandenburg Gate. Bad publicity also followed Yoko into the pages of the *New York Times* in 2006, when her chauffeur and bodyguard of ten years was charged with grand larceny. On the twenty-sixth anniversary of John's death, the chauffeur confronted Yoko with a letter detailing his demands, including $2 million to keep quiet about her personal affairs. He claimed to have photographs taken with hidden cameras and "thousands of hours of recordings." In his letter, he accused her of "sexual harassment," at the same time writing that he had been her lover. His plans included writing a tell-all book for release in his native Turkey, and on the internet in Iran. Even more disturbing, in conversations with Yoko's lawyers, he said he had people "on standby" to kill her and her son, Sean, if he didn't get the money. The matter was ended quickly when, after sixty days in jail, he reached a plea agreement and was handed over to Immigration. The *New York Times* printed paragraphs from his salacious and demented letter, the publication of which served only to humiliate Yoko and compromise her privacy, even though she was the victim. In one story, the *Times* referred to the case as a "melodrama." Yoko was seventy-three at the time. In 2017, dozens of items were recovered in Berlin that had been stolen by the chauffeur and an accomplice, including three of John's diaries.

Yoko will always remain Mrs. Lennon, even after taking a lover within months of John's death. (She and Sam Havadtoy lived together for twenty years.) The writer and performance artist Lisa Carver said it best when she wrote in 2012 in her book *Reaching Out with No Hands: Reconsidering Yoko Ono*, "Yoko does not believe in arbitrary walls, or gates, or time frames for locking and unlocking, or any rules at all. Yoko's no hypocrite. ... Yoko's beliefs are in her body, and her body is in her beliefs." John's death brought about a reconciliation between Yoko and her long-lost daughter, now grown. Kyoko had been raised by her father, Yoko's second husband, Anthony Cox; their whereabouts were unknown for decades. That loss had been another price Yoko paid.

If you are still alive, you must have had the experience of surrendering. (Twitter: April 17, 2019)

Yoko's belief in peace and unification between people has been her primary message for decades. She has supported initiatives to end hunger and spoken about autism. Her tweets often ask that women and men listen compassionately to each other. She stays away from labels, insisting that she is a "citizen of the world."

She established the LennonOno Grant for Peace, and Yoko encourages others to participate by "imagining peace," her mantra, and by contributing artistically to her projects through her website imaginepeace.com. (She also sells merchandise.) Recipients of the Grant for Peace, who are given a substantial amount of money for their causes, are as diverse as the Russian punk band Pussy Riot, Doctors Without Borders, the Chinese artist Ai Weiwei, *Rolling Stone* co-founder Jann Wenner and the Wounded Warrior Fund at Walter Reed National Military Center.

On what would have been John's birthday, October 9, 2007, she unveiled the Imagine Peace Tower on Viðey Island, outside Reykjavik Harbour in Iceland. The tower is lit between sunset and midnight on days of special significance to the couple and during winter solstice. Anyone can send their "wishes" to be stored in capsules and buried surrounding the tower. More recently, she published two more volumes of instructions, and in October 2018, she designed *Sky*, the mural at the newly reopened Seventy-Second Street subway stop outside her home in New York City near Strawberry Fields in Central Park. It's theme: *Imagine peace.*

In a tweet from May 2019, just months after her eighty-sixth birthday, she wrote: "It's okay to have a rest from being creative," but her force remains strong. Among her latest works is *Add Color (Refugee Boat)*. In a room, with just an empty boat, participants are asked to colour everything.

I'm always listening to the voice of my soul. Are you? (Twitter: October 7, 2018)

A few years ago, I saw Yoko Ono in New York City. We were heading up Central Park East when she appeared. She was walking quickly while having an animated conversation with a friend. As she passed, I held my breath. I imagined a refraction of light bouncing off each one of us, shimmering and beautiful. The street life halted. As instructed, we began a game of Telephone, our own *Whisper Piece*, as her name, "Yoko Ono," was whispered from ear to ear.

"There is a wind that never dies" is a line taken from Yoko Ono's essay "To the Wesleyan People," January 23, 1966.

JONI MITCHELL

FIFTY YEARS IN REVIEW

Geist, no. 108 (Spring 2018)

Just months before she was found unconscious in her home in California, in the spring of 2015, Joni Mitchell was the new face of an Yves Saint Laurent clothing campaign called the Music Project. In photographs taken by creative director Hedi Slimane, Joni is wearing an embroidered tunic and wide-brimmed hat from Saint Laurent's Folk Collection and holding her guitar. At seventy-one years of age, she is regal.

It was an image to hold on to, as confusing reports circulated regarding her condition. Eventually it was revealed that she had suffered a brain aneurysm. Almost two years passed before there was some public evidence of a slow recovery when she attended a Chick Corea concert in Los Angeles.

For those of us who came of age, grew up and grew old listening to her music, Joni Mitchell gave women a more serious understanding of themselves. She made women visible to the outside world. She was a romantic and a lover, and a woman who was constantly moving forward. She rebelled against categorization and often suffered the consequences. For Joni, who started out as a painter and took to heart the creative sacrifices her grandmothers were forced to make, there was no question that her art came first.

After dropping out of art school in Alberta and drifting east in the mid-1960s toward a heightened folk scene in Toronto, Detroit and New York, Joni rose to fame quickly. She got immediate attention for her beauty, but soon enough for her songwriting and unconventional phrasing. Her tunings were unusual, too, an accommodation she made for a left hand weakened by polio when she was nine. Decades passed before her "chords of inquiry," as she called them, could be broken down and translated into songbooks for novices.

From the beginning of her recording career in 1968, Joni Mitchell expected and received full artistic control, a right rarely given to a new artist and never to a woman. She refused to work with producers (her friend David Crosby, who produced her first album, *Song to a Seagull*, was more of a gatekeeper), and she selected, directed and replaced musicians on her records until she got the sound she wanted. In a very short time, she went from accompanying herself on piano and guitar to working with jazz musicians, as she found they were the only players who could follow her inside her head. She recorded and produced nineteen studio albums, thirteen of them and the live album *Miles of Aisles* with her faithful engineer Henry Lewy, a legendary sound engineer who became a close friend. "She's the only true genius I've ever met," he once said. Joni also released another live album, nine compilations and four video albums. She was prolific, profound and articulate. She was feted and maligned.

Since her near-fatal brain injury, her contribution to modern music has undergone re-evaluation. She is in the top ten of *Rolling Stone*'s 100 Greatest Songwriters of All Time, and on NPR's list of the top 150 albums by women with her 1971 release *Blue* in the number one spot. Essays have appeared in the *Atlantic*, the *New Yorker*, the *Ringer* and other publications. In the UK, an international symposium called Court and Spark was held at the University of Lincoln, with dozens of international speakers exploring "the images of freedom, travel and liberation within Joni's work." A book of scholarly essays from this conference will be published in 2019.

Meanwhile, in the realm of music journalism, Barney Hoskyns, co-founder of the online music library Rock's Backpages and author of the books *Hotel California* and *Small Town Talk* as well as other significant works, compiled a comprehensive selection of album and concert reviews, interviews and commentary covering almost fifty years of Joni Mitchell's career. Released in the UK in 2016 (by Constable) with the title *Reckless Daughter: A Joni Mitchell Anthology* (I found my copy last spring at Blackwell's Music Shop in Oxford), the book was published in North America in the fall of 2017 (by Picador), under the title *Joni: The Anthology* so as not to be confused with another fall book, a biography of Joni Mitchell by David Yaffe titled *Reckless Daughter*.

The forty-eight career contributors to Hoskyns's anthology represent more than a hundred magazines, newspapers, radio broadcasts and other media in the US, the UK and Europe. Most are influential writers in their field, and the "Contributors" page is its own historical document.

With the exception of an introduction by Hoskyns and an informed essay by music journalist Nicholas Jennings on Joni's early years, individual pieces in the anthology are presented without commentary or explanation. For the most part they are chronological, which makes the book even more illuminating, as the writings naturally reflect the attitudes of the times in which Joni worked. The late Paul Williams, founder of *Crawdaddy!*, one of the first magazines of rock criticism, shows his hand when reviewing *Song to a Seagull*—which he *liked*—when he writes: "A great many ladies have their heads so full of all they've read and heard and seen about why a man loves a woman that they can think of little save how lovable they are. But Joni even knows that a woman can have a will without being unfeminine or unyielding herself."

In the transcribed interviews, Joni is candid and intelligent. She stands out for being reflective and uncensored. *Rolling Stone*'s Larry LeBlanc talks with Joni backstage at the 1971 Mariposa Folk Festival, where she tells him about her time in the caves of Matala. Kristine McKenna ("I was pleasantly surprised to find a warm and open woman of impressive intelligence") questions her in 1982 in *NME* about fame and Joni's sometimes combative relationship with the press. Writing for *MOJO* in 1998, Dave DiMartino has an expansive conversation with Joni about her life as a painter and about an industry slow to recognize her immense contributions. Robin Eggar, reporting for the German edition of *Rolling Stone*, is with her in 2007 at the premiere of her ballet *The Fiddle and the Drum* with the Alberta Ballet.

In the reviews of her early albums and concerts, much is made of Joni's tunings, her "confessional" style of songwriting and the way women are drawn to her. But there is wonderment in some of the writing as the critics, most of them male, sense there is something here that is not like the other.

Geoffrey Cannon, in reviewing a concert in London for the *Guardian* in 1970, writes: "I believe that Joni Mitchell is better able to describe, and celebrate, what it means, and should mean, to be alive today, than any other singer. She tells us what we already know, but have felt obliged through life's circumstances, to forget: that we are free. That we have love. And she does this by scrupulous observation and thought only of what she herself has heard and seen and felt."

That same year, Jacoba Atlas writes in *Melody Maker*: "Her ability to understand and transform has made her almost a legend in the United States. Critics and listeners alike rhapsodize over her songs and her psyche. She is fulfilling something of a 'goddess' need in American rock, a woman who is more than a woman; a poet who expresses a full range of emotions without embarrassment. ... She is virtually without competition. ... She is without comparison. Her work, for now, goes almost totally without question, without debate."

However, the negative criticism of her work and of her, personally, is dismissive, brittle and ugly.

Richard Williams, in 1972, in a review for *Melody Maker* of Joni's fifth album, *For the Roses*, writes: "More songs of transient euphoria and stabbing loss, played out against an ambiguous background of relentless fatalism and constant hope, mingled in approximately equal proportions from the poorest little rich girl in Laurel Canyon."

In fact, those very first albums were filled with grief.

In 1990, Joni was blindsided by Trevor Dunn on GLR (Greater London Radio), in the middle of an interview about her exhibition of paintings in London, with a question about a child she had given up for adoption when she was twenty-one years old. It was a thoughtless and cruel act and she struggled to answer, stumbling between shock and defensiveness.

She had shared this heartbreak privately with husbands and lovers, and she even looked for her daughter in the crowds. But it was still a shameful secret. In a time when young, unmarried women and girls were forced to give up their children, Joni had given birth in the charity ward of a Toronto hospital. Not even her family knew. This experience shaped the rest of her life.

Completely alone and devastated, she began to write songs and sing as a way to support herself and find her way through. She had written more than twenty songs before she stepped into a recording studio for the first time. "Little Green," a song to her daughter, was among them.

While reviewing a concert in Long Island, New York, in 1976, Michael Gross writes in *Swank*: "Where are all the world's beautiful, ripe fourteen-year-old girls? Where are all those Lolitas we've heard so much about, with their pert tits, hard bums, yadda yadda yadda? The answer? They're home listening to Joni Mitchell albums, of course." He concludes: "By the time of her third album, Joni had grown, if not to complete womanhood, to at least an inkling of her own self-sufficiency, couched as it was in the counter-cultural garbage of making cookies in the canyon."

In the late '70s, in what was considered in all camps a very controversial move at the time, Joni accepted an invitation to collaborate with the legendary jazz composer and bassist Charles Mingus. He had been impressed with her album *Don Juan's Reckless Daughter* (on the cover of which she had appeared dressed and made up as a black man). Mingus was said to have been "intrigued by the audacity of that act." He was dying and he wanted his last project to be with her.

Joni had been working with Tom Scott's jazz group L.A. Express since *Court and Spark*, and she had experimented with world music—before it had a name—on *The Hissing of Summer Lawns*. She was already moving away from what was seen as her "traditional" place. *Don Juan's Reckless Daughter* was truly reckless, particularly as it included "The Tenth World," a dynamic conga jam with Don Alias, Manolo Badrena, Alejandro (Alex) Acuña, Airto Moreira and Jaco Pastorius. Among the background vocalists was Chaka Khan.

In a conversation with Ben Sidran, the *Rolling Stone* writer whose essay in *Joni: The Anthology* explains how these two artists' lives converged, Joni recalls the moment when Mingus asked her to write some lyrics that would suggest "the things I'm going to miss."

"We all have some things in common experientially," she said. "And there are things in common musically. We both have a broad range of feeling. And there's literariness to his writing. And within his idiom he's an eccentric; some of his eccentricities are parallel to mine." Mingus wrote six melodies for her, named and numbered "Joni I–VI." He died before the album was completed.

In a review of the album *Mingus*, released in 1979, Sandy Robertson writes in *Sounds*: "The liner notes reveal how much Joni held Mingus to be some kind of mystical black saint figure, the typical dizzy white people's view of black people, the stupid idea that they're privy to some inner secrets that us poor honkies will never understand."

Quite a contrast with the remarks offered by actor Laurence Fishburne two decades later, in 2000, during the Joni Mitchell All-Star Tribute in New York, as he introduced a visual tribute to her work with Mingus, followed by Cassandra Wilson's interpretation of one of the songs from the album. Joni Mitchell had responded to Mingus with an enthusiastic, open heart, honouring him but also being true to herself. It's all context. ("The reviews were mixed," she told Kristine McKenna.)

Joni received a Grammy Award in 1969, and another in 1974, but more than twenty years passed before the industry acknowledged her again. When the awards started coming in 1996, she won two Grammys, including Best Pop Album (for *Turbulent Indigo*), followed by the US National Academy of Songwriters Lifetime Achievement Award, the inaugural Billboard Century Award, Sweden's Polar Music Prize and a Grammy for Lifetime Achievement. (In 2016, she received a Grammy for Best Album Notes, bringing her total to nine.)

In Canada, she was inducted into the Canadian Music Hall of Fame in 1981, but she did not receive a Juno Award until 2001, and it was for Best Vocal Jazz Album. In time, she received the Governor General's Performing Arts Award for Lifetime Achievement and a star on Canada's Walk of Fame. She was also appointed a Companion of the Order of Canada, Canada's highest civilian honour. In 2007, she was inducted into the Canadian Songwriters Hall of Fame and she was featured on a postage stamp.

In 1997, Joni was finally included in the Rock and Roll Hall of Fame, after the *New York Times* writer Stephen Holden accused the organization of anti-women bias. Joni agreed and didn't show up to accept. In the interview with Dave DiMartino in the anthology, she explains her position: "Unfortunately, I don't have a good attitude about the Rock and Roll Hall of Fame and you can say this. It was a dubious honour in that they held me out conspicuously for three years. To go, Oh, thank you, thank you, I mean having conspicuously ostracized me for a few projects, how can I be gracious, really. And the other complaint I had is that it was gonna cost about twenty grand to take my family."

That year, she had begun a very public search for her daughter. "Little Green" had started looking five years earlier. Her name was Kilauren Gibb. She was living in Toronto and pregnant with her first child when she learned she was adopted, and she wanted to find her birth mother.

It is a dramatic story of closed files and waiting lists, unanswered emails and someone remembering someone they once knew. Finally, Kilauren had a lead. She received a registered letter from the Children's Aid Society with this piece of non-identifying information: "Your mother was from a small town in Saskatchewan and left for the US to pursue her career as a folksinger." By the time they met, Kilauren had given birth and Joni was a grandmother.

Perhaps reflecting on that time decades ago, when she had left art school, pregnant and without possibilities, and her life had come full circle, Joni told Dave DiMartino in the *MOJO* interview—after a production where her paintings hung in a circle around the stage—"I'm really a painter at heart, and I can say this now, since, you know, Kilauren has come along. Music was a hobby for me at art school, and art was serious. Art was always what I was going to do; I was going to be an artist."

She had taken intermittent breaks over the years, but in 2002, Joni Mitchell walked away from the music business. "I'm quitting because the business made itself so repugnant to me," she told Dave Simpson, writing for the *Guardian*. "Record companies are not looking for talent. They're looking for a look and a willingness to cooperate." Simpson writes that Joni's sales have never matched her influence and critical standing. Despite her landmark deals for artistic control, she still fought a thirty-year battle with record companies.

In her interview with Dave DiMartino, she says: "You only get about five or six years before they're sick of you in the business generally and they let you ride. They don't put any money or effort or interest into you, really. They just let you sit there like manure in the pasture, as a procurer of young artists at the label. For the last twenty years, I've had no record company support, no radio support.

"My predicament wasn't one in which effort worked anyway. I was just *shut out*, period, after the Mingus album."

She tells Robin Eggar, writing for the German *Rolling Stone*: "You are supposed to stay neatly in your decade and then die. From my sixth album on [critics] were dismissive while I knew I was still growing. It was an extraordinary rejection of good work. Everything was compared unfavorably to *Court and Spark*."

This could also be said of her fans, many of whom were unable to make the trip from her powerful early writing through her experimental years. In recalling a tour she did with Van Morrison and Bob Dylan in 1998, she says of the Vancouver concert: "It was a difficult show for me because I'm not used to playing big sports arenas and there was a lot of milling, a lot of going for beer and a lot of talking really loud through all the shows. It seemed to me that that crowd had come for beer and the event itself, not to listen. And I thought that was a shame." I was in the audience that night and I confirm that the auditorium was on the move, particularly during Joni's set. They really had come for *Court and Spark*.

"I came to hate music and only listened to talk shows," she told Paul Sexton when he visited her home in 2007, on assignment for the *Guardian*.

True to her word, Joni stayed away for ten years.

In the 2003 American Masters documentary *Joni Mitchell: Woman of Heart and Mind* (produced by Susan Lacey), Bill Flanagan, author and editorial director of MTV Networks, sums up Joni's power when he describes "the really potent popular image of the California girl, the Beach Boys' girl, the beautiful golden girl with the long blond hair parted in the middle. And Joni not only *was* that girl, but she was also the Bob Dylan, the Paul Simon, the Lennon and McCartney. *Writing it.* She was the whole package. She was the subject and she was the painter."

In *Joni: The Anthology*, Barney Hoskyns adds the names Brian Wilson and Stevie Wonder to Joni's list of peers when he refers to her "masterful albums" and describes her songs as "great art." He writes: "She's struggled to bear the weight of her talent and intelligence in an arena better disposed to the crass and the facile." Referring to his own interview included in this book, he writes: "I've always felt privileged to have met this genius of North American music."

Joni Mitchell's last CD of original music was released in 2007 by Starbucks' Hear Music (Hoskyns reviews it in the anthology). *Shine* was her first attempt at writing since 1998, and she describes the CD to Robin Eggar as "a late birth." The songs were written at her home on the Sunshine Coast of British Columbia, the same place where she wrote *For the Roses* in 1972.

"All around the house the wild roses were blooming," she writes in the liner notes. "The air smelled sweet and salty and loud with crows and bees. My house was clean. I had food in the fridge for a week. I sat outside 'til the sun went down.

"That night the piano beckoned for the first time in ten years. My fingers found these patterns which express what words could not. This sound poured out while a brown bear rummaged through my garbage cans."

The CD is dedicated to her grandchildren, Marlin and Daisy.

Having come fully out of retirement, she had two other major creations that year: the ballet *The Fiddle and the Drum*, a collaboration with choreographer Jean Grande-Maître of the Alberta Ballet; and a major art show (LA, New York, Toronto, Dublin) featuring sixty-four of her paintings, which had also been used as set directions. Up until her injury, she had been promoting *Love Has Many Faces: A Quartet, A Ballet, Waiting to be Danced*, a four-CD boxed set released in 2014.

Joni: The Anthology reveals the work of the real star-making machinery—the critic, whose opinions can encourage exploration or cause chaos. It also has a valuable story to tell, especially as it rests on a larger truth.

Joni would have been a successful musician and songwriter under any circumstances. But it was the pain of bearing and then giving up her child—a uniquely female experience—that took her work into unknown territory and unlocked a talent so infinite and raw, she was propelled beyond the expectations and limitations of her womanhood, into a pure, undefined form of musicianship. No one else could have done this. Joni Mitchell is brilliant and brave. She lives.

STRANGE WOMEN

Geist, no. 95 (Winter 2014)

The Dishrags, the Zellots, the Persisters, the Moral Lepers and the Animal Slaves are just some of the revolutionary women's groups that came out of the culture of the 1970s—at a time when it was a radical concept to claim a musical space for women, when coming out as a feminist was a daring admission, and came with conswequences.

Punk was not unique, and I say that with great respect. It *sounded* different; it was louder and faster. For an audience not used to dancing to their politics, who preferred the black sounds in the gay discos, or harmonies and endless free-form drumming, it was unlistenable. Punk was *difficult*. But it was also similar to what had gone before. The scene could be violent; it could be angry. It most certainly included drugs. The desire to "stick it to the man" was not that different from the discrimination felt by hippies, and beats, and any other outsider group who rejected the lifestyle and political choices of their time. And no one trusted the police. Punk was also a boy's club. Its sexism grew out of the same misinformation and blurred vision as every other institution. It shared the same historical prejudices. Women had been making music since the beginning, but it was within punk that women stood up and screamed.

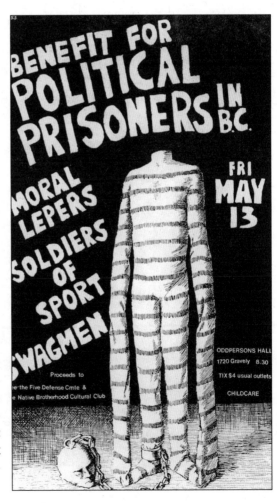

The "do it yourself" dictum was already in motion in the women's movement. In 1972, anti-war activist Holly Near started Redwood Records in California as an outlet for her political beliefs. A year later, an East Coast lesbian collective, Lavender Jane, began work on *Lavender Jane Loves Women*, an album written and produced exclusively "by and for lesbians." That same year, 1973, while being interviewed on an early feminist radio program, songwriter Cris Williamson, who had released an album on Ampex Records (a label shared with Creedence Clearwater Revival, Todd Rundgren and Gil Evans), suggested a "women's music" label be formed.

That label was Olivia Records, a launching pad that soon became a landing strip as many musicians who were already in the business, working in isolation, arrived at the door in California to offer their services. They produced and engineered albums, played backup, arranged music, raised money and packed boxes. Women taught each other. This was the big idea.

By the mid-1970s a renegade network of women's coffee houses and bookstores, women's centres and festivals supported by other women-run recording labels and women's production and distribution companies, publicized by a growing number of female music journalists and historians (the late Rosetta Reitz of Rosetta Records and others), began spreading throughout the Western world. It was mail order and word of mouth and long-distance calls on Sunday when the rates were down.

The first women's music festival in Canada took place in 1974 in the Kootenay region of British Columbia, an area described by a provincial tourist bureau as having "a reputation for seclusion. ... Several generations of settlers have found a safe haven here from the anxieties of religious persecution or social unrest." The two-day festival featured local and regional musicians, workshops on witchery and crafts, a film festival, square dancing and an arts and crafts fair. It was open to both women and men.

Almost every city in Canada had a women's coffee house or an area set aside for women only: Clementine's and the Fly by Night in Toronto, the Powerhouse Gallery and Co-op Femme in Montreal, the Women's Building in Winnipeg, the Guild in Regina and a place down an alleyway in some guy's dance studio in Dalhousie. In 1972, after returning from her first women's liberation meeting, Rita MacNeil wrote her first song.

Vancouver's early women's community caught fire during this time. Coffee houses rotated between the basement of the New School (the Gay Alliance Toward Equality did child care), the Vancouver Women's Bookstore on Richards, Ariel Books in Kitsilano and finally the Full Circle at Eighth and Main. Laurine Harrison and Gisele Perreault, from their communal house off Oak Street, along with Kim Albertson and Christine Morissette, started Womankind Productions, hosting women-only dances at Simon Fraser University and producing concerts for many high-profile musicians coming out of the feminist movement in the US. Womankind also took a turn at hosting a women's music festival. Local musicians Susan Knutson and Wendy Solloway worked with artistic director Gary Cristall to integrate the stages of the Vancouver Folk Music Festival with feminist-themed music (they went as talent scouts to the newly happening Michigan Womyn's Music Festival), and in 1977, Ferron, one of the most prominent singer-songwriters to emerge from this era, released her first album on her own label, Lucy Records. (More than ten years later, she performed with Holly Near at Carnegie Hall.)

It cannot be overstated how radical a concept it was in the 1970s to actually claim a space just for women. With the exception of outdoor festivals and concerts, it was still unacceptable in many clubs and bars for women to dance alone or with a female friend. It took a lot of courage to walk into a lesbian drop-in or decide to attend a consciousness-raising group at the Vancouver Status of Women on West Fourth Avenue. To come out as a *feminist* was a daring admission. There could be repercussions.

The music during this time was exclusively about the story. The personal was political. It was the lyrics that mattered most. In the tradition of the troubadour, abuses, struggles and triumphs were documented and shared. An enemy was identified. Although many of the songs could be joyful and healing—Elaine Stef, a guitarist with the Moral Lepers, once described the genre as music for women to hold hands and sway—the words were also raw and bleeding. The delivery was crucial. Even the angriest protest song was sung a cappella or with an acoustic guitar. It was the only form of music that was acceptable.

In this way, the women's movement mirrored the biases of society. Girl groups of the '60s, blues and country singers of decades past and "straight" folkies were wrongly dismissed and discredited as being mix-and-match, or drug-addicted victims of their men, or skinny perfect blondes pining for Jackson Browne. No one clued in that Karen Carpenter played drums, or that Bo Diddley had Peggy Jones behind him on rhythm, or that guitarist Ellen McIlwaine had jammed with Hendrix or that she *even existed*. But it may not have mattered. All would have been seen as pawns of the male-controlled music industry. Generally, the women's movement did not respect women who played any kind of rock and roll. It was particularly problematic if you came from a jazz or rhythm and blues background and wanted to express yourself in that way. Plugging in was seen as male-identified. It was a curse like no other.

It must be said that no history of women's contributions to music was being taught. There were no special university courses. There were no books or magazines in the library. Obviously, there was no internet. Any piece of information about a woman playing music was most likely found in a bin in a used record store. The radio "rule" was no more than two female singers in a row. This held true even for the earth-shattering FM format, which blasted great music to hungry minds barely weaned off transistor radios. (When my mother was a cleaning lady for a small radio station in the American Midwest, she used to save all of the demo 45s for me that had been thrown away. Most of these records were by women:

the band Fanny, country singer Skeeter Davis and Aretha Franklin's sister Erma singing "Piece of My Heart.") But even among the leftists, there was an assumption that women weren't making music. In 1981, when I went on the air with *Rubymusic*, a radio show specializing in this very subject, even my radical (and very supportive) radio station, Vancouver Co-operative Radio, was concerned that I might not be able to find enough music by women to fill half an hour every week.

The emergence of women players in Vancouver came in fits and starts and was largely invisible. Although it coincided with the early punk scene in Vancouver, the two political communities did not mix and they had no real awareness of each other's existence or importance.

Ad Hoc was a familiar band in the left-wing and feminist communities. They played at least a hundred benefits, rallies and dances beginning with their first gig on International Women's Day in 1978. They were a very politically conscious mixed band with an equal number of men and women. They struggled publicly to overcome sex roles, which at that time included the difficult fact that most women did not have the technical knowledge needed for set-up or sound production. Even the act of carrying one's equipment or getting a beer for a male band member could be viewed through a political lens. American recording engineers Karen Kane and Leslie Ann Jones notwithstanding, the shortage of trained female sound personnel was a problem everywhere throughout the early women's movement, brought home when it was "discovered" that the female tech on some of Olivia's feminist and lesbian-focused albums had previously been a man.

Sapphire, an all-women band produced by Womankind, came together in 1976 in Vancouver for a few dances but has disappeared from memory. Contagious was another matter. So rare was it to see a band made up of all women that Contagious was constantly referred to as "that women's band," the assumption being that there was only one. The women first got together in 1977 at drummer Jorie Cedroff's old house on Alberta Street, "to see what would happen," and the band stayed together for three years. As was typical of the era's politics, they functioned as a collective. They worked hard to create a sound and image that they saw as different from the music they considered produced and created by men. At one point they debated whether to let a good male friend be their manager and first sound engineer. (They did, although it was uncomfortable at women-only dances. Jin Hong later trained for the job.) So sensitive was the issue of technical ability that when one of the musicians commented from the stage that they (the band) didn't know how to use microphones, she was reprimanded by other band members who didn't want to reinforce that image of women not knowing anything about sound equipment (an issue

the band
from Vancouver

New Playing
At...

that also surfaced in punk music). Everything was new.

Janet Lumb, a founding member of Contagious, recalls: "It was through this band that we learned to call ourselves musicians. The realities of a collective band: touring and performing hungry, cold, sick, exhausted, vulnerable, pissed off at someone, and the show is on. On the road, we were seven women including the sound person, one van, one Volkswagen bug, three children and two dogs." On one tour, "we arrived at a gas station that had a phone booth, filled up on gas and parked. Wendy [Solloway] pulled out our box of food supplies, bulbs of garlic, veggies, crackers, bread, water and fruit. We fed the kids and ate. Everyone at the gas station stopped in awe and disbelief to see Jin, our car mechanic and sound person, under the hood fixing the radiator amidst a troop of women, kids and dogs in two vehicles packed to the brim. We phoned the venue organizers to say that we were on our way. They'd already heard."

The emotional attachment felt by the women's community for this band was so deep that more than four hundred people (mostly female) showed up for a farewell concert on March 17, 1980, at the Vancouver East Cultural Centre. A music critic for the *Province* newspaper wrote at the time:

"There was once an all-woman band from Vancouver that had the germ of an idea. They called themselves Contagious. ... These ladies didn't want to be confined to the traditional female role of vocalists; they had to play instruments, too.

"If there is one lesson these women might take with them as they go their separate ways, it is: This kind of music (swing, be-bop, or whatever you want to call it) requires much discipline. It looks easy and easy-going when people like Dan Hicks and His Hot Licks are doing it, but don't be fooled. To get to that point, you need to sweat and swear and wear your fingers to the bone. Anyway, Contagious has made its point. Let's see more brave women spreading germs on the musical front."

The same week that Contagious ended their run, the Dishrags went into the recording studio. Contagious had not been the only band of women in town.

⊙

When Contagious first began defining itself within the women's movement, other women in Vancouver were also forming bands or joining with men they knew. But this time, the women were not openly connected or supported by feminism or even aware of an established feminist community. They were young musicians answering a different call, and their escape from their bedrooms was into the basement practice spaces of the very harsh and very male world of punk rock. It was emotional anarchy combined with a desire to play—loud and hard.

In a flash it had begun. The Dishrags, the Devices and the Zellots became bands. Mary, renamed Mary-Jo Kopechne (after the young woman left to drown in a submerged car by US senator Ted Kennedy), took up guitar with Wasted Lives and then the Modernettes. Ebra Ziron and Nathan Holiday, calling themselves Tunnel Canary, stood downtown at the corner of Georgia and Granville, and with Nathan playing his electric guitar, Ebra wailed like a banshee. "It was like plugging into a very creative stream of energy that we thought was quite beautiful, not frightening," Ebra said years later, in a 2011 interview with Allan MacInnis in the *Big Takeover*. "Like a thunderstorm would be beautiful."

In an article in *Kinesis*, the Vancouver women's newspaper, in 1982, journalist Janie Newton-Moss wrote: "For the majority of us growing up in the '60s and early '70s, fantasies about performing in a rock band were quickly obliterated when it became apparent that our role was to be consumers not producers of rock music. Like it or not, we had to content ourselves watching brothers and boyfriends experiment in garages or basements and listening endlessly to the radio."

It has been noted occasionally that some of these young women had connections to male relatives, boyfriends, or husbands or ex-husbands who were musicians in the scene, as if this explains and justifies their presence. It could also be said that when the door was open, they walked right in.

"We felt very strongly about what we were doing," says Scout Upex, the drummer with the Dishrags and later Blanche Whitman. "I was thrilled to be able to express how I felt. It was like all the oddballs joining the same club—artists, writers, musicians, all feeling encouragement from one another, often trying out each other's mediums. In the beginning, it was a love fest." She was just sixteen when she gave it up for rock and roll.

Barbara Bernath also hit the Vancouver streets as an underage drummer a few years before the birth of Bolero Lava (in 1983) and played with a "wild 'n' wonderful cross-section of other creative people, ranging from hardcore speed punks and exotic east-side strippers to scholarly experimentalists and downtown art boys." She remembers: "The time was all about brave manifestation. You had to be fully committed to the moment in every way. You had to show your stuff, walk your walk, talk your talk. And you had to do it *live*."

In addition to her band 50% Off, Barbara played (again, underage) in the Braids & Arthur, a.k.a. the Sweet Shadows, "a self-assembled group of exotic female dancers I met downtown who worked the big strip clubs like No. 5 Orange and the Marr during the day and then played as musicians at night in various warehouse parties and off-the-grid events. This was way before the current burlesque revival, and another example of women in the scene who were bold and unapologetic toward mainstream life."

Heather Haley, a founding member of the Zellots (with Conny Nowe, Jane Colligan and Christine deVeber), having returned to Vancouver from working and studying music in Edmonton, also entered the punk scene searching and ready: "Just as young people were becoming fed up with staid, institutionalized, inaccessible and *barely* rock music, I was floundering, confused, aimless. Punk brought rock back to its roots, its essence, with a vengeance and provided me with a catalyst, direction and drive."

"We asked the Subhumans and D.O.A. if we could use their practice place if we swept up after their rehearsals," says Susan MacGillivray of her days with the Devices. "Kim [Henriksen] and I would move our gear using a skateboard and onto the city bus." The girls were seventeen and fourteen years old. "The scene moved very quickly back then. I was given a guitar from a youth centre and started saving for my first Gibson, purchased later that year. The Devices were born out of a group effort in naming our new band. 'IUDs' was suggested."

Me (to Kim): "Were you aware that it was unusual for young women to be playing in a band?"

Kim: "Not at all. It was normal to us."

For bass player Mary-Jo Kopechne—who, one music critic wrote, provided some "much needed glamour" to the scene—punk provided something more: "I was a runaway from age thirteen. I had nothing and no one. I went to an east-end party. Victorian Pork was playing and I danced the dance of the devil to them. Party's over and I went back to the house that was keeping a roof on my head. I heard voices; the guy hosting the party told the Pork where my head lay. They found me, took me away and were my father son brother sister mother guiding light. I was saved from a life of desperate prostitution. I was fucked without them and they took me in like I was their little sister. I went from a go-go girl dancer to a 'Hey, wait a minute, if they can play so can I' girl."

There is a scene in Susanne Tabata's 2010 documentary *Bloodied but Unbowed* in which the Dishrags are onstage and a voice is heard in the audience shouting an obscene demand. Tale as old as time—those same words could have been said to Janis Joplin. (They were most certainly repeated years later to riot grrrl band Bikini Kill.) It is a brief but potent moment, a reminder that these young women, while immersed in a raging joy, must be put back in their place. They need to be *reminded*. It's an irony that was not lost on the Dishrags when they were denied an opportunity to compete in a 1978 Battle of the Bands yet were asked to play backup for the other bands competing.

"We dressed differently from other girls," says Jade Blade, guitarist and singer. "We wore leather jackets and T-shirts and torn jeans—in other words, we dressed like boys, and people found that shocking. We were the novelty group. People would come and see us, but not take us seriously, and would often berate us or hurl other kinds of verbal abuse (and the occasional beer bottle). The punk scene in Vancouver was pretty good to us, given the usual attitudes of the time. It was when we played to non-punk crowds that things often went off the rails—that was when people, mostly guys, but sometimes women, too, would yell horrible things at us, often of a sexual nature; we really made ourselves vulnerable, simply by the act of strapping on instruments and getting onstage. I'd like to think that doesn't happen anymore."

Nancy Smith (a.k.a. Rita Ragan), one of the few certified women sound engineers in Vancouver during this time and a valuable member of the Dishrags team ("I had something a lot of the other local musicians didn't have: a car"), remembers a night in Seattle when the Dishrags were opening for the Ramones. "The girls had already played a couple of songs and the audience was enjoying the music, pogoing, waving their hands. All of a sudden, the manager of the club came out onstage, stopped the Dishrags mid-song and announced that Joey Ramone was sick and the band wouldn't be playing. The angry audience started hurling their bottles at the stage, beer and glass shards flying everywhere. The backstage crew worked fast, hustling the girls offstage. Shortly after that, the City of Seattle made it illegal to sell beer in bottles in clubs; it had to be served in plastic or paper cups."

"One afternoon at the Smilin' Buddha," recalls Jane Colligan, the guitarist with the Zellots, "the RCMP and a bunch of plainclothes police rushed in and busted a bunch of innocent punk bands, sound men and friends, in the middle of the afternoon. It was our first taste of police brutality and totally unprovoked. John McAdams rushed me out of the back door to any alleyway and hid me on the floor of a car, but I saw an undercover cop dragging Chrissy [the Zellots' bass player] out by her hair. She was handcuffed behind her back and slammed face down on the hood of a cop car. Her crime? She couldn't produce enough ID. If I wasn't particularly anarchistic before that day, I sure as hell was after."

"Like many of my peers," Heather Haley says, "it was a struggle to survive, find work, pay the rent. Sexism, being condescended to, left out, left off, despite a lot of forward-thinking punk rockers. The status quo largely remained in place. Many record companies and radio stations were reluctant to promote female artists. Violence. At various times I was harassed, stalked, raped, nearly strangled to death. It was a dangerous time, often. One had to be aware. I adapted."

But they were not out there alone. Uncontrollable, appalling sounds were coming out of the UK. The Sex Pistols, the Buzzcocks and the Clash rolled over the landscape like a tank, but when the Slits walked out onstage in 1977, they didn't break ground; they broke rock. At the time, their unconventional looks and deliberate rejection of traditional roles were shocking. Not only did they claim the same rights as men in the punk movement—such as the right to learn while doing—they called themselves by *that name*! The Slits were too disturbing to be dismissed, and they were often the target of violence at clubs and on the street. (Ari Up, the lead singer, was stabbed twice.) Others enlisted: the Raincoats, Eve Libertine, Poly Styrene, the Bodysnatchers, Delta 5, Siouxsie and the Banshees, Vi Subversa, the Au Pairs, Mo-Dettes and Pauline Black. They shouted out their abuses, struggles and triumphs. In Vancouver, the Visitors were soon to follow.

⊙

Marian Lydbrooke met Jill Bend outside the Paddington Street police station in London, UK, in 1978. They were both protesting the arrest of a group of so-called anarchists (dubbed "Persons Unknown") on conspiracy charges. Jill was in London as an "associate" for the Vancouver-based anarchist newspaper *Open Road*. She was also very active in the anti-prison movement. Marian was getting ready to travel to North America.

"I'd come from the squats in London, where Nazi gangs roamed the streets outside at night," she says. "There was the anti-Nazi movement and Rock Against Racism and bands like the Clash, X-Ray Spex, Steel Pulse, Gang of Four and women's bands like the Raincoats and other agitprop women musicians playing at feminist conferences. I'd seen Holly Near play at a women's conference in London and loved the lyrics (at the time). When I arrived in Vancouver, I was exhausted, exhilarated and angry."

Although Marian had seen "large, colourful *Open Road* posters in every anarchist squat in London" by David Lester, a graphic designer and one-half of the future Mecca Normal, they didn't meet until she got to Vancouver. She rented drums, moved in with David and his brother Ken (later the manager of D.O.A.) and started jamming. She was joined by Rachel Melas, a bass player from an all-women bar band, the Distractions, and by guitarist Bonnie Williams. "And then Annie [Moss] came around with some songs she'd written, I added some of mine and voila!" They called themselves the Visitors. Their coming-out party was at the Windmill on Granville Street. "The gig at the Windmill was a watershed moment," says Marian. "It was the first feminist punk gig to hit Vancouver. I sang 'Suicide' [co-written with David Lester] and 'Witches in the Wood,' which was a big hit with the more adventurous radical dykes who'd heard we'd be playing and packed the place."

The Visitors played a few other gigs, including the men's prison at Matsqui ("I told them we are musicians; we are not 'pretty girls'") and benefits for Betsy Wood and Gay Hoon, activists who had been charged with attempted murder and complicity during a bungled escape attempt at the BC Pen while they were visiting inmates. (They were acquitted.)

At one of these prison benefits, Contagious and the Visitors shared the bill. It was an all-too-common culture clash. A member of Contagious let it be known that they considered the Visitors too aggressive and male-identified. Janet Lumb, of Contagious, remembers: "The conversation flew back and forth with the Visitors responding to what Contagious understood as punk, versus the history, movement and principles of punk which the Visitors believed in, stood for and was fighting for. In the end, an understanding was laid out and initiated. In the end, I became a punk and still consider myself to be a punk." As the Visitors sang in "I Can See Right Up Your Nose," "Don't give me all that feminist crap / if all that it leads to is another trap." Janet later joined the reformed Visitors when they became the Moral Lepers.

"It was a time in Vancouver when there was an incredible political community," Marian says. "The *Open Road* anarchist paper was incredibly well organized and had an amazing office and a mailing list of thousands from all over the world. So much was going on. But the people working in social justice, food co-ops, rock and folk bands, bookstores, radical presses, rape crisis centre–type places weren't too enamoured with the punk scene, which up to that time had been mostly male.

"There was a certain hostility from feminists around sexism in the punk community, understandably. Some of the feminists who came out to see the Visitors were still suspicious of rock music. They were reeling from the real sexist part of rock music that had happened in the '60s. Seeing women up onstage being able to do it and being angry and strong changed their minds to some extent.

"Also, some of the male music community in Vancouver hadn't really rubbed shoulders with lesbians and feminists. The Visitors (and particularly the Moral Lepers) started bringing more of those people together."

When Jill Bend returned to Vancouver and to her work with the organization Women Against Prisons, she had been pushed further into battle by her meetings with the Clash in London and by "the militancy of political activism" she had encountered in the UK. She called an open meeting for all women musicians in the scene. The idea was to come together to raise money for a bail fund for women in prison. ("A First Nations woman in Vancouver, Geri Ferguson, had been working with Women Against Prisons on her case, which involved charging a male guard from the Oakalla women's prison with assaulting her while locked in one of their isolation cells. She'd been picked up on a minor charge and needed bail. We had to get her out!")

By all accounts, between fifteen and twenty musicians showed up. Jill says: "Ideas were flowing and combinations of instruments, personalities and genres tossed back and forth. Some rejected, some embraced, and out of that confusion and madness came a kind of natural selection. It had seemed like an unlikely project, that what normally needs months of time and space to create even one band could coalesce in one meeting. But that spark can ignite something greater and I guess it was one of those nights when more happens than you had expected."

From that night came a short-lived reggae band called Lionchild, a funk band with women from Ad Hoc and Contagious called the Persisters, and the rebirth of the Visitors as the Moral Lepers. Bail was raised.

"Moral Lepers were a huge influence on me," says Jean Smith of the duo Mecca Normal (with David Lester). "Even though I didn't see them live, hearing their record brought an entirely new vantage point to my awareness. Being in a band had potential. For me. There was always something of a comprehension barrier watching guys in bands. I didn't imagine myself in D.O.A., for instance, but it was different somehow with women. The configurations they played and sang—their intensity— seemed accessible to emulate, in a way. Likely, it's because of the Moral Lepers that I ever dared to take a chance on singing feminist themes with an electric guitar."

"We *were* Moral Lepers," says Marian, "which was attractive to a lot of different people for a lot of different reasons. We were very conscious of the lyrics we were writing, really working hard on our instrumentals. Working together collectively. In a sense we were like a political and cultural statement in ourselves."

Elaine Stef says: "We were a hardcore feminist, political band. We were strange women who were fairly unpredictable."

⊙

By now, the spectacularly developed early feminist music network, which had heralded a new musical revolution, began to fray, particularly in the US. The debate as to what constituted "women's music" was in full force. It was a black hole. Although there were extremely significant songwriters and musicians in the movement, the genre remained artistically narrow. It had also evolved into a politically separatist scene, with its own subsets, divisions and concerns.

For a growing number of musicians, regardless of their sexual identification, "women's space" was fast becoming a ghetto. Goodwill gestures at mainstream music festivals to have a "women's stage" served in the long run only to isolate women musicians from the rest of the festival lineup, even though in the beginning it seemed like a solution to a problem.

In 1986 the artistic director of the Winnipeg Folk Festival, Rosalie Goldstein, disbanded the women's stage. "I did so with the most loving care," she told me at the time, "because I believe it's important for women to be dispersed throughout the entire body of the festival. I would not put up a tent at the festival and say, 'Here are all the blacks,' or 'Here are all the Jews.' And that's exactly what was happening with women. I don't think it shows women to their best advantage."

Elizabeth Fischer, for ten years the force behind the artistic punk trio Animal Slaves, says: "I considered myself a feminist, of course, although probably of a different variety than most, at that time. I considered myself perfectly equal and I always had, in brains, in talent, in ability, in potential. I refused female 'roles' as much from women as men. Men and women [as] equals, which also manifested itself in Animal Slaves, and in any other band I have played with since ... I never felt that artists should be ghettoized. I felt that artists were a necessary brick in the village."

⊙

By the early '80s, there were dozens of women musicians in Vancouver inspired by punk and its offshoots. In addition to the Dishrags, Devices, Zellots, Persisters, Moral Lepers and Animal Slaves, the bands Junco Run, Perfect Stranger, Twin Twist, Work Party, Bolero Lava, Playdoh Republic, Industrial Waste Banned, Quantum Leap and Liquid Wrench were sharing bills and musicians. Kitty Byrne and Danice Macleod were part of U-J3RK5. Emily Faryna was out there solo with her Casio keyboard. Mec-

ca Normal was on the cusp. Even Katari Taiko, Vancouver's first Japanese taiko drumming group, formed with women at the core.

In December 1983, the anarchist newsletter *BC Blackout* featured a cover story, "Play It, Don't Spray It!" on the "emerging women's new music scene." They noted that "along with such familiar staples as war, eco-devastation and mindless consumerism, women musicians are insisting that a range of topics from sexual stereotyping to porn and child abuse get serious attention." The newsletter questioned whether these women were indicative of a "full-blown movement" but noted: "They have played alongside men in a variety of mixed bands, they have written their own songs and arranged their own gigs (no boyfriends or brothers to haul the speakers), they have swapped expertise and equipment and they have put together a number of bands that have already started to make a dent across Canada." The newsletter gave the Moral Lepers and Industrial Waste Banned as examples. There was also a notice that the "all-women" Persisters would be playing for their final time that month. There was no mention of whether the Persisters would be carrying their own equipment.

In 1984, when Bolero Lava won the Hot Air Show, a Battle of the Bands at the University of British Columbia sponsored by the radio station CiTR, not much had changed in the way women musicians were regarded. Like Contagious, they were "that women's band."

"Being an all-female band like Bolero Lava was a blessing and a curse," says drummer Barbara Bernath. "We were overly adored in some ways, and then fully disrespected in other ways. Either way, being female always seemed to be our primary tag and identity. I remember one gig in Victoria at the New Era Social Club, we dressed in reverse drag as an "all-male band" to show the irony of our situation. I mean, what male band of *any* genre is *ever* referred to as an 'all-male band'?

"It shows intrinsically what we were dealing with every day as women publicly expressing our musicality. I also remember constantly having to prove ourselves as musicians in ways that men would never have to—especially in a scene that was supposed to be nonconformist. (I always loved sitting down for the drum check and knocking the socks off an unsuspecting soundman who was expecting me to not be able to play.) Sexism was definitely all around us, but we blasted onward, enjoying each other and the thrill of doing something as a team of stunning underdogs."

Christine deVeber, bass player for the Zellots, says: "We knew that the 'all-girl' initial draw was only good for the first few minutes. We had to back it up with strong original material, and in the back of our minds, wanting to be taken seriously as artists, we embraced hard-to-play or sometimes challenging musicianship because of this. We could have played it very simple with three-chord rock and that would have been fine, but at the time, we liked challenging ourselves and came up with a little more sophisticated songwriting, while keeping the basic energy of punk as the mainstay."

Echoing these experiences, Nancy Gillespie, bass player in her band SHE, a group that played regularly at the Town Pump and shared the stage with D.O.A., the Sons of Freedom and the Scramblers (and also played at the Matsqui prison), says: "We worked really hard to be good musicians and to have a strong, clear sound, which was sometimes held against us as that was seen as being too professional. But as women musicians we wanted to be fierce and to be taken seriously. Thus, we were not as raw as the riot grrrls, but we had a solid, driving edge. And we were a little ahead of them historically. Being a woman musician was a little bit more difficult then, I think. We were a band on our own, in between the waves, so to speak, in between significant historical moments, and not part of a 'scene,' so we often get forgotten about, fall through the cracks of history."

By the end of the decade, the Moral Lepers had become a perfect seed band spreading out across the country. Marian Lydbrooke and Elaine Stef were part of Demi/Monde in Toronto and Janet Lumb joined Mat'Chum in Montreal. Rachel Melas teamed with Animal Slaves in Vancouver and later was reunited with Elaine Stef and Conny Nowe to play the Michigan Womyn's Music Festival with the Lillian Allen Band and multiple individual projects. Two Devices became Dishrags ("Sue's songs were epic," Scout Upex remembers). Heather Haley went to LA with the Avengers, and the remaining Zellots reformed back east. Bolero Lava changed musicians, Danice Macleod became BAMFF, Elizabeth Fischer regrouped, and Mecca Normal kept on playing, becoming an early inspiration (along with Toronto's Fifth Column) for the incoming riot grrrls. In 1988, in Vancouver, newcomer Nadine Davenport produced a women's music festival. The bands Cub and Maow, and Bif Naked, were still to come.

Unfortunately, the riot grrrls of the '90s fought the very same battles for visibility, credibility and access as their mentors in the punk scene and their sisters in the early women's movement. The debate over women's stages and the general lack of representation of women musicians on the Warped Tours and other heavy metal punk-like festivals is still loudly contested. Musician Shira crashed the 2004 Warped Tour with her pink box truck (named the Shiragirl Stage) and hosted more than two hundred female-fronted bands. She continued to do this for several years. "There is always the argument of 'Why is it separate?' But it's either that or nothing," she said. "No one else is coming in and fighting for the women"—a sentiment lived first-hand by Canadian musician Sarah McLachlan during her three years, 1997–99, producing the all-women Lilith Fair concert tours.

CBC music blogger Holly Gordon recently wrote: "Dear Canadian Music Festivals. Show Us the Women," as she tabulated the percentages of women performing at festivals across Canada, finding that the numbers came up short. Even in the UK, the punk music mother ship, artists and writers point out with regularity that punk still has a problem with women.

As for the Michigan Womyn's Music Festival, now in its fortieth year, its booking policies have opened up to include performances by the "queer punk" bands, and former Bikini Kill Kathleen Hanna's band Le Tigre. (After this essay was published in 2014, the "Michfest" team, led by founder and spokesperson Lisa Vogel, chose to retire the week-long event at the close of its August 2015 festival, owing in part to ongoing protests and boycotts over the festival's "womyn-born womyn" attendance policy.)

⊙

For those first musicians in the late '70s and early '80s, punk had been the new world. For a woman (or a girl) whose soul was wrapped up in the chaotic, physical thrill of punk music and the political issues it championed, there was no better place to create, to be in control and to be fully oneself. *It was natural.* Not since the all-female jazz bands of the '40s did so many women musicians storm the barricades en masse. To the *BC Blackout*, yes, it had been a "full-blown movement," full of contradictions and turmoil and opportunity. Without exception, every woman interviewed for this article who was on the scene during those years is still involved in music, the

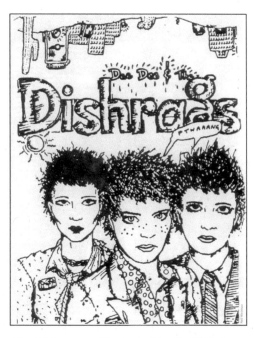

The Dishrags as illustrated by Neil Wedman for an album insert.

creative arts or community activism almost forty years later. Not bad for a girl.

"When I got involved in music, punk meant more than just testosterone-fuelled guitar-drum bashings," Elizabeth Fischer says. "It was a social movement, both political and creative, and it was inclusive of many different voices, people experimenting, redefining and creating new musical expressions. And importantly, there were the women: women playing instruments, angry women, intelligent women, thoughtful women, who presented themselves as equals in every way to the hitherto mostly male-dominated musical community. That community was politicized, redefined. That was truly revolutionary."

MORE STORIES FROM "STRANGE WOMEN"

Mary Armstrong, bass, vocals, Wasted Lives, Modernettes:
It never ends though. Playing music fed me, put a roof over my head, and no matter how smug you get in life, it's always there for you. You can give the finger to big banks, your case managers, your backstabbing co-workers who lie to get you fired and nab your job. You can step up out of the gutter of those that try to take your soul and die the death when they realize they can't pull it off without you. And you sit back and take a conscious breath and say, "Tomorrow I will walk forward with my head held high knowing that I am the One and I am still here and I am still a better man than that."

Jill Bend, activist, band support, Moral Lepers:
We were always organizing benefits for righteous radical causes. Rock Against Prisons, Rock Against Sexism, Rock Against Nukes, Rock Against Reagan, Rock Against Racism … the list is long! We provided the political face of the Vancouver punk scene and the bands had a venue and a cause to be allied with.

> Our local and early punk scene had lots of women around and never felt uncomfortable or unwelcoming to me. It was very real and working-class. The dynamics were no-bullshit and nonconformist but never felt like people were falling into nihilism. There was an authenticity to the scene of early Vancouver punk that was inclusive of all of us weirdos, and that is what made it so beautiful. The original roots here are akin to the British punk roots … working-class rebellion.
>
> Of course, the scene evolved, which it should, and "new wave" and "art punk" and all variations on a theme came along. The only arrival that ever caused universal animosity was THE POSEUR! To quote the Moral Lepers, "fashion loves to take what's real and crush it dry!"

Barbara Bernath, drummer, various bands, Bolero Lava:
The late '70s and early '80s were a wild, raw and exciting time, with all kinds of creative people coming together to share themselves through original music, new politics, visual art, live performance, self-publishing, contemporary dance, warehouse living, satellite galleries, extreme fashion and flexible sexuality. It was especially interesting and edgy at the beginning when the scene was still very underground. What tends to be overlooked is the sheer bravery, variety and raw beauty of what was going on in Vancouver then—it was every outsider's dream.

> All of this alerted me as a teenager to a bigger cultural shift happening everywhere, with protests and angry public demonstrations demanding nuclear-free zones, the end to prisons, women's rights, racial equality and individual freedoms of all kinds. Collective consciousness and creative expression were all being forced to the next level.

Jade Blade, guitar, vocals, the Dishrags:
Being teenagers in a small, conservative, rural community was pretty stifling; music was what fed us, and motivated us. And the punk aesthetic absolutely inspired us! That was also so liberating. I remember hearing the first Ramones album for the first time; it was like, whoa, where did these guys come from? That first Ramones album was so pure, so unlike most of what was on the radio in those days. We'd get home from school and pogo around our parents' basements to all of the great new bands coming out of the US and UK, and this would take us a million miles from Central Saanich. As for politics and feminism, I think that came later—music and punk in particular was what inspired us to play music ourselves, and through that we became more engaged in the political aspects of the scene.

The Dishrags. Dale, Jade and Scout. Photo: Eric Foto

Being in an all-female band, it was kind of impossible not to be political. Gender cut both ways for us, but it was always rather painfully apparent that we were the novelty act, always the backup band, that we usually had to play on crummy equipment when we opened for bands we didn't know as they seemed to think we'd wreck their gear because we were girls. So, just being taken seriously was probably our biggest issue, because not only were we female, but we were also, like, fifteen years old! Okay, well, not the whole time, but [the Dishrags] was disbanded by the time I was eighteen, so I was pretty much retired from punk by that age.

> My favourite moment was when we opened for the Clash in 1979. It was really a great privilege to be able to meet and play with some of our musical heroes, like the Ramones and the Clash; but at that first Clash appearance we played "London's Burning" as our encore, and I looked over and saw the Clash dancing to us playing their song by the side of the stage.

Jane Colligan, bass, Zellots:

I doubt I would have ever played an instrument if it wasn't for punk. You didn't have to play arpeggios or do runs faster than light speed to play punk. Punk was raw. I'll never forget the first time I heard the Sex Pistols album and that wall of sound, that buzzed-out guitar sound. Rock and pop music in 1975 were the product of the big machine, "the music industry" that had a stranglehold on dictating what bands would ever be signed to a label, and what music would ever be recorded and get airplay.

Playing punk meant that I could buy a fifty-dollar Kent bass and learn to play. There were no rules and no musical snobbery. Chrissy [deVeber] played guitar and she had a complete repertoire of Led Zep songs, which proved that she could play guitar very well. She rented me a bass for my eighteenth birthday and we commenced. We were inspired by Heart and the Pretty Things in our early days. Heart was soon replaced by Patti Smith, Bowie by the Velvet Underground. The Stones made us puke now.

Christine deVeber, guitar, Zellots:

This time in history makes me believe all the more that suppressing expression of any kind, even if you personally find it "vile" or "repulsive" (like some powers that be described punk as), would be a crime against humanity and art as a whole. Total freedom of expression is really important, as is challenging authority in order to keep a balance against the faceless grinding bureaucratic regime. Plus, it's *waay* more fun!

Meeting Heather Haley brought us immediately into the centre of the scene. She seemed to know everyone and all about everything going on in the underground scene at that time. At first we felt a little like outsiders, but we quickly realized we were in a most exciting scene. There was so much going on and such a wild energy, the most imaginative and shocking artistic expression and high-energy tireless performances.

As far as how we were received, in the big picture we were received really well. There may have been some "purists" who perhaps thought we were too female or not butch or tough enough, but I think our musicianship and our music stood its ground.

My very first influence was when I was thirteen and heard the screeching cascading guitar leads on Janis Joplin's records. I was mesmerized and I think that is when the desire to play electric guitar first got hold of me.

Emily Faryna, Casio keyboard, solo:
I didn't really like high school at all. I had long feathered hair. Got my mom to buy me jeans. It still didn't work. Nobody wanted to be my friend. So one day I came to class with a safety pin in my ear.

When the hardcore scene first popped up in Vancouver, I really fit right in. It was the first time I had a feeling that I belonged. I was totally an outsider in high school because I wasn't cute. I was kind of a hairy, gawky girl. I was just not cool.

Elizabeth Fischer, vocals, keyboards, Animal Slaves:
What exists as punk in my brain was not the boys playing three chords really fast, but that it also included people like me. *Soi-disant* brain-racked artist howling at humanity accompanied and inspired by excellent, creative musical partners who believed in the same things I did. Being inspiring in turn. An artistic exchange. Men and women alike.

Heather Haley, vocals, Zellots:
My first punk rock concert was D.O.A. at the Windmill, and that definitely constituted a turning point, an awakening. The volume and raw power blew my mind. I admired the Dishrags, listened to a lot of female artists like Lene Lovich, Poly Styrene of X-Ray Spex, Chrissie Hynde and the Slits.

Kim Henriksen, bass, Devices:
It was a very special time that could never be relived now due to internet, iPhones, etc. We had freedom from all of that to do what we wanted. It was fun, fast-paced and had a family feel to it. Everybody cared about everybody. Even when the Clash came to town, they came to the Windmill to watch the bands and we all partied together. They stayed in our homes as well. It was a very close-knit community.

David Lester, guitar, Mecca Normal:
At the time, I was more inspired by the existence of certain bands rather than directly by the sounds they were making. While squatting in England I saw the Raincoats at a Rock Against Sexism concert, and the Gang of Four at an anti-nuclear rally in Trafalgar Square. It was incredibly exciting because these bands were challenging the stereotypes of what a band is and what music is, politically and socially. Locally there was the Moral Lepers, whose guitarist Elaine Stef continues making dynamic music in LOUD. The music evolved but the punk inspiration remains. I was inspired by D.O.A. and the Subhumans because of their energy and political bravado. Even now I admire Joe Shithead's stamina to continue to speak out on issues with his music.

Of course, Jean [Smith] is my biggest influence. I'm lucky to be in a band with a singer who writes such amazingly literate lyrics.

The first-ever Mecca Normal show took place on July 27, 1984. We opened for D.O.A. at the Smilin' Buddha. I feel the same intensity playing live today as I did on that night thirty years ago and the same passion of political expression that fuelled us on that night. The issues of feminism, poverty and inequality have not gone away with the passage of time. "I Walk Alone" remains as relevant to feminism as it was thirty years ago. Perhaps even more so now. For a song's relevance to travel that many decades is both sad and inspirational.

Danice Macleod, violin, U-J3RK5, BAMFF:
On U-J3RK5:
Kitty [Byrne] and I showed up at every rehearsal and were considered equals with the guys, even when carrying gear. The only problem I remember was when we temporarily practised in a top floor of the Ace Building with no elevator or washroom.

On BAMFF:
I was repeatedly asked my age by interested big-time A&R [artists and repertoire] who considered me an "older woman." Plus, the industry couldn't categorize the music. Getting signed was not the initial motivation but became more important to keep a band together. Replacing musicians continued to be a stalling factor. I became less the artist and more a small label: designing graphics, recording product, booking gigs and promoting.

Conny Nowe, drummer, Zellots, Moral Lepers, Twin Twist, Work Party, others:
Music is universal and its language should not be wasted with insignificant words lacking thought and depth. (*Kinesis* interview with Tory Tanner, March 1985)

Vanessa Richards, lead vocals, Bolero Lava:
It was powerful to be part of a movement and making one's own culture. There was a great deal of camaraderie between bands and other artmakers. The politics, the do-for-self approach, the regional and international youth movement that could reach back to the history of leftist culture while demanding change now and for the future, was inspiring.

I first learned about apartheid when I was in high school from a pamphlet I was handed at a D.O.A. Rock Against Prisons show. That made me question what I was learning in school. The rebirth of ska music gave me a black culture distinct from my parents' and the African American experience. It was like a rebirth for me as well.

Jean Smith, vocals, lyrics, Mecca Normal:
Punk was the very loud abhorrence of injustice, and that, for me, was articulated by the audience—dancing, colliding, sweating and engaging without relying on our own voices; we were out there bashing around in response to a very pure form of music that demonstrated our dissatisfaction and dissent.

For whatever reason, when I decided to participate in the punk scene as the singer in a band of two (Mecca Normal), I realized I wasn't part of whatever I thought I was part of as an audience member. That is to say, people didn't like us. They ignored us, basically. We were what you call room clearers, which turned out to be okay, because we ended up going on tour pretty quickly and found scenes in other cities where we were welcomed and included. Our first out-of-town shows were in Montreal, where we played two sold-out nights at an anarchist café and got standing ovations. It was totally weird.

Part of the idea for creating Mecca Normal was a reaction to the lack of women in bands in Vancouver. It definitely seemed like the guys were in bands and the girls watched the guys. It was annoying. To me, starting a band demonstrated a solution to the issue.

After we released our first album (on our record label) someone "in the scene" said we shouldn't have released it because there were bands more deserving than us. I recall someone saying that we hadn't paid our dues. That phrase really stuck with me. From time to time, thirty years and sixteen albums later (thirteen Mecca Normal, one solo, two as 2 Foot Flame), I still wonder if I've paid my dues.

Jean Smith, about the cover of Mecca Normal's 1988 album *Calico Kills the Cat***:**

> The cover of *Calico Kills the Cat* is a drawing I did of what
> a woman sees when she's looking at her legs when she's

sitting on the toilet. It's one of the few times we see our own bodies in front of us without mirrors, without society projecting standards of beauty and acceptability.

The title of the album, while quite obscure, speaks to the same thing. Calico cats are typically female and it's the idea of naming the cat *calico*—of naming things at all—that tends to limit what that thing can be seen as. It's no longer just a cat; it's a calico cat that fits into a box of stereotypes about calico cats in the same way as blonde, redhead, slut, bitch, etc. tend to limit the myriad of complexities that describe a whole person.

Nancy Smith (Rita Ragan), sound engineer, the Dishrags; drums, Playdoh Republic, Nash Metropolitan:
The Japanese Hall. D.O.A. It was the first time I saw the music live and I still remember almost every minute of the evening. I was wearing a dress. I think it was the last time I ever wore "normal" clothes. I sat cross-legged on top of a table off to the side, away from the crowd down front.

I swear to this day (even though he denies doing it) that I saw Joey [Shithead, D.O.A. lead vocalist] pee off the stage. I remember a golden liquid stream arching out and the crowd backing up as fast as it could.

(Memorable night): It was a hall gig. The Dishrags and I were in the audience watching the Subhumans, who were the headliners that night. Iggy Pop was going to be playing Vancouver for the first time a couple of nights later, and everybody was hugely excited about that. There was a wave of whispers through the crowd; Iggy was in the audience. Everybody was surprised at how short he was and how very drunk he was. Iggy was notorious for his pursuit of women. He immediately made a beeline for the Dishrags, started to chat Jade [Blade] up, leaned close to her and threw up massively on her shoes. His minders hustled him out.

Elaine Stef, guitar, Moral Lepers:
The Vancouver punk scene wasn't only punk bands and people who like punk music. There were reggae bands and art bands, experimental bands and noise bands as well as punk bands, and they were all making relevant music. There were people who organized benefits almost every weekend. In fact, the punk scene was single-handedly funding a lot of grassroots political causes. People were involved, they were organizing, they were in the streets protesting, and they were educating themselves and each other. It was a healthy community that way. I was involved in organizing gigs and rallies. We silkscreened T-shirts and ran a printing press to get information out to people. We hauled *a lot* of gear.

I was surrounded by musicians who had an influence on me. I owe a lot to Bonnie Williams, who was one of the original members of the Moral Lepers. She got me hooked on working with delay, which, aside from the guitar, is the best tool I've ever found. I'm still not sick of it.

Music is my thing. Back then I was playing the guitar around eight hours a day, writing music and taping things on a plastic cassette recorder that I found in the garbage.

Lorraine Tetrault, keyboards, Bolero Lava:

We were all very dedicated to one another. We set up a strict schedule, four or five nights a week, and not one of us ever missed a practice unless very sick. We would rehearse from early evening till late, often taking a break to have coffee

1987, Toronto: As a member of Moral Lepers, Demi-Monde, the Lillian Allen Band and others, guitarist Elaine Stef performs solo at a Mayworks event. It's a moment representative of every woman who ever picked up a guitar.

and pie or cake at the Montgomery Café. I remember our first gigs, we had about six songs and at one show we had to repeat all six songs because the audience kept yelling for more. We were all a bundle of nerves!

Scout Upex, drummer, vocals, the Dishrags:

Unlike the drummers in the punk scene who shared instruments and would roadie for each other, often drummers from the "mainstream" bands wouldn't let me play their drums. I think they were afraid I was going to break them, or they just didn't like the idea of a female drummer. So, I would drag my kit to a gig where we had a twenty-minute backup slot. Even as late in the game as 1988, I was drumming for the Unknown and called the drummer for the main act to see if I could use his drums. Nope, wouldn't let me, so there I was dragging my drums in the back of a pickup on Valentine's Day to the 86th Street Music Hall, in the snow.

One of my favourite bands I played in was Blanche Whitman with Kitty Byrne and myself playing drums, Phil Smith and Rodney Graham on keyboards and guitar. Kitty was a great drummer and it was a lot of fun drumming with her. I love how she was really solid and her fills were always just right. She opened up a new way of drumming to me. I had the opportunity to buy her Ludwig wood drums, which I play to this day.

Ebra Ziron, vocals, Tunnel Canary:

A lot of [our lyrics] was commentary about the status quo in society and basically for people to look at what they were doing with their lives— where they were spending their money, how they were thinking—just trying to make them think. And also the gender roles, just trying to open things up in a little bit that way. That there are rooms for different kinds of expression, that maybe things don't have to be a certain way. Just to be open to human beings, and not having to act a certain way because you're male or female. (Quoted in Allen MacInnis, "Tunnel Canary: Musical Terrorists of Olde Vancouver," *The Big Takeover*, no. 74, July 28, 2011)

Song Lyrics

"Suicide"
(M. Lydbrooke, D. Lester: the Visitors, 1979)

> Don't think, don't do a thing
> Hate yourselves and everything
> Never fight, just play it cool
> "Peace and love man," I'm no fool
> That's just suicide
> Suicide Suicide
> Might as well take some cyanide
> You don't have to be dead to commit suicide
> Cop out, run away
> Sell yourselves, till you've got your pay
> Hide yourselves, behind the lies
> Don't come out from your disguise
> That's just suicide
> Fill yourselves with mindless junk
> Dress up just to please
> Spread the war paint on your face
> Till you look like you're diseased
> Shape yourselves to a magazine
> Glue yourselves to a TV screen
> That's just suicide
> Never criticize yourself
> Never change your line
> When your life is miserable
> Pretend everything is fine
> Be unaware, disintegrate
> Only act when it's too late
> That's just suicide

"When Women Were King"
(D. Lester, J. Smith: Mecca Normal, 1985)

> Long ago there was a world
> That you don't know.
> Women were king
> Long ago—
> History don't show
> So you don't know.
> They told you

It's simply not so.
And now you look around.
You think it's always been
this way.
You say,
No, it's not so.
Well, yes it's so.
Women were king.

"Bullshit"

(J. Bain, D. Powers, C. Michaud: the Dishrags, 1978)

It's all we ever hear today
It's what we're taught in school
So, what are we supposed to think about
Or know what's really true?
When it's all bullshit
We see it on the television
Hear it on the radio
Is it a lie or is it true
How're we supposed to know?
When you're all bullshit
It's what we're always telling them
About the things we do
It's what they want to hear from us
They wouldn't believe the truth
So we're all bullshit
Government's another joke
And the crap that they debate
Everything's a front, a lie
Another Watergate
And they're all bullshit

"I Walk Alone"
(D. Lester, J. Smith: Mecca Normal, 1985)

I go downtown
I walk alone.
This city is my home.
I'm not alone in my home.

"Perfect Plastic People"
(The Devices, 1978)

perfect plastic people
churned out of the big machine
perfect plastic people
just like everyone I've seen
clones alone
plasticized
perfect plastic replicas
each girl must be 5'4"
men must be 3 inches more
it's such a laugh hahaha
perfect plastic people
not like all the human ones
perfect plastic people
mass-produced by the ton
clones alone

THE FAMILY TREE
VANCOUVER, CANADA
1977–88

The Dishrags (1976/77–80)
Jade "Blade" Bain, guitar, vocals
Kim Henriksen, bass, vocals (1980)
Susan MacGillivray, guitar, vocals (1980)
Carmen "Scout" Michaud (a.k.a. Scout Upex), drums, vocals
Dale Powers, bass, vocals (1976–80)
Kat Hammond, manager

Contagious (1977–80)
Jorie Cedroff, congas
Bo Conlin, lead vocals, acoustic guitar
Lynda Girard, keyboards
Jin Hong, sound
Ann Knight, violin
Janet Lumb, acoustic guitar, soprano sax, vocals
Wendy Solloway, electric bass, acoustic guitar, flute
Chris Creighton-Kelly, manager, sound

Ad Hoc (1978–82)
The women band members:
Doreen Allen, bass, lead vocals
Sheila Allen, violin, lead vocals
Mona (Jessie) Arens, keyboards
Jorie Cedroff, congas
Madelaine Kierans, vocals
Claire Kujundzic, lead vocals
Jane Leroux, lead vocals
Janet Lumb, soprano sax, tenor sax, lead vocals
Wendy Solloway, bass
Carol Street, backup vocals, harmonica
Kathy Willander, sound

The Devices (1978)
Robert Bruce, drums
Kim Henriksen, bass
Susan MacGillivray, guitar
Eve Posener, vocals

The Distractions (1978–80)
Rachel Melas, bass
Wendy Perry, keyboards
Linda "Sticks" Walker, drums

Tunnel Canary (1978/79–82)
Core lineup:
Nathan (Aleh) Holiday, guitar, electronics
David Sheftel, bass, electronics
Ebra Ziron, vocals

UJ3RK5 (1978–81)
Kitty Byrne, drums, vocals
Rodney Graham, guitar
Colin Griffiths, guitar
Danice Macleod, violin
Frankie Ramirez, lead vocals
Jeff Wall, organ, vocals
Ian Wallace, bass
David Wisdom, keyboards, vocals

Wasted Lives (1978–79)
Colin Griffiths, guitar
Brad Kent, guitar (1978)
Mary-Jo Kopechne (Mary Armstrong), bass, vocals
Taylor Little / Andy Graffiti (1979), drums
Phil Smith, keyboards, vocals

Animal Slaves (1979–90)
Elizabeth Fischer, vocals, keyboards
Rosco Hales, drums (1980–87)
Rachel Melas, bass (1980–87)
Additional players: Paul Brennan, drums (1987–90); Ryan Moore, bass
(1987–90); Steven Nikleva and Pat Sproule, guitar (1987–90); Michael
North, drums (1979)

Junco Run (1979–83)
Alvin Collis, guitar, vocals
Annie Moss, bass
Conny Nowe, drums
Pax Robertson, guitar
Elaine Stef, guitar (1983)

Katari Taiko (1979)
Original lineup:
Joyce Chong
Linda Hilts
Linda Uyehara Hoffman
Connie Kadota
Marilyn Kaga
Lucy Komori
Diane Nishii
Naomi Shikaze
Mayu Takasaki

The Modernettes (1979–83)
Core lineup:
John Armstrong, guitar, vocals
Mary-Jo Kopechne (Mary Armstrong), bass, vocals
John McAdams, drums

The Visitors (1979)
Rachel Melas, bass
Annie Moss, guitar, lyrics, vocals
Marian X (Lydbrooke), drums, lyrics, vocals
Additional player: Taylor Little, drums

The Zellots (1979)
Jane Colligan, bass
Christine deVeber, guitar
Heather Haley, vocals
Conny Nowe, drums
Additional player: John McAdams, drums

Perfect Stranger (1980)
Rachel Melas, bass
Alex Philippides, drums
Bonnie Williams, guitar

Twin Twist (1980–81)
Alvin Collis, guitar, vocals
Judy Kemeny, keyboards, vocals
Annie Moss, bass
Conny Nowe, drums

Magic Dragon / Courage of Lassie (1981–82)
Rachel Melas, bass, cello
Ron Nelson, guitar
Maddy Schenkel, guitar
Additional players: Rod Booth, violin, accordion, keyboards;
Jeff Burke, bassoon; Dermit Foley, synthesizer

Moral Lepers (1981–84)
Jill Bend, band support
Janet Lumb, sax (1983)
Rachel Melas, bass, vocals, lyrics
Naomi Moriyama, vocals (1981)
Conny Nowe, drums
Elaine Stef, guitar
Bonnie Williams, guitar
Marian X (Lydbrooke), percussion, synthesizer, vocals, lyrics
Additional player: Wendy Solloway, bass

The Persisters (1981–83)
Doreen Allen, lead vocals, guitar
Mona (Jessie) Arens, keyboards, vocals
Jorie Cedroff, drums
Jin Hong, sound
Janet Lumb, sax, guitar, vocals
Wendy Solloway, bass

Angel Band (1982)
Susan Knutson, guitar
Kira van Deusen, bass
Kalen Wilde, mandolin
Carol Wright, banjo

Blanche Whitman (1982)
Kitty Byrne, drums, vocals
Rodney Graham, guitar, keyboards
Bob Peterson, bass
Phil Smith, keyboards, vocals
Scout Upex, drums, vocals

Bolero Lava (1982)
Original lineup:
Barbara Bernath, traps, percussion, vocals
Phaedra (Struss), guitar, vocals

Vanessa Richards, lead vocals
Lorraine Tetrault, keyboards
Laurel Thackray, bass, vocals

The Evictims (1982–86; formed to play at evictions)
Original lineup:
Doreen Allen, bass, vocals
Jorie Cedroff, drums
Chris Creighton-Kelly, guitar
Janet Lumb, sax
Wendy Solloway, bass
Additional players: Paul Cruikshank, drums; Rachel Melas, bass
(1983–85); Amy Newman, sax; Alex Philippides, drums

Playdoh Republic (1982–83)
Harley (McCharley) McCanley, guitar
Mina Shum, vocals
Nancy Smith (Rita Ragan), drums

Quantum Leap (1982)
Pam Braithwaite, guitar
Yvonne Daley, drums
Judy Ferrano, bass
Diane Keenlyside, keyboards (Minimoog synthesizer)
Additional player: Michelle Basonby, sax

Work Party (1982–86)
Alvin Collis, vocals, guitar
Brian James, bass
Annie Moss, bass, vocals
Conny Nowe, drums
Pax Robertson, guitar

BAMFF (1983)
Danice Macleod, violin, vocals, electronics
Various collaborators: Karen Anderson, Jeff Corness, Rodney Graham,
Scott Harding, Ron Obvious, Paul Rudolf

Industrial Waste Banned (1) (1983)
Sheila Annis, drums
Jan Berman, vocals, occasional bass
Connie Iverson, synthesizer, vocals
Phyllis Iverson, bass, vocals

Liquid Wrench (1983–84)
Joanne Maynard, bass
M. McPherson, vocals
Rachel Melas, drums
Isis van Loon, guitar, vocals

Nash Metropolitan (1983–85)
Nancy Gillespie, bass
Joe McDonald, guitar, vocals
Nancy Smith (Rita Ragan), drums

Cracked Maria (1984)
Grace Scott, bass
Harris Taylor, sax
Isis van Loon, guitar, vocals
Linda "Sticks" Walker, drums, vocals

Industrial Waste Banned (2) (1984)
Mitch Hill, guitar
Connie Iverson, synthesizer, vocals
Phyllis Iverson, bass, vocals
Alex Philippides, drums
Anne Quigley, guitar

Mecca Normal (1984–present)
David Lester, guitar
Jean Smith, vocals, lyrics

Rockin' Harry & the Hack Jobs (1984–87)
Rachel Melas, bass, occasional percussion
Conny Nowe, drums
Grace Scott, bass (when Rachel played percussion)
Harris Taylor, sax, vocals
Isis van Loon, guitar, vocals

Bob's Your Uncle (1985)
Jamie Junger, guitar
Sook-Yin Lee, guitar, vocals
Peter Lizotte, harmonica
Bernie Radelfinger, bass
John Rule / Karl Cardosa, drums

Key Change (1985–90)
Heidi Archibald, vocals
Brenda Baird, keyboards, flute, sax (1987–90)
Sharon Costello, violin, guitar
Jane Leroux, vocals
Conny Nowe, drums (1986–87)
Jacqui Parker-Snedker, bass (1985–87)
Wendy Solloway, bass (1987–90)
Carol Weaver / Lauri Lyster, drums (1988–90)

A Merry Cow (1985–88)
Lane Bradbury, bass
Sue MacGillivray, lead vocals, lyrics, rhythm guitar
Nancy Smith (Rita Ragan), drums
Additional player: Eric Damianos, lead guitar

Twang Hounds (1985–86)
Nancy Gillespie, bass
Fred Hamilton, keyboards
Joe McDonald, guitar

Crimpolines (1986)
Karen Anderson, accordion, vocals
Sandy Scofield, guitar, vocals

The Brewnettes (1986–87)
Sheila Badanic, keyboards, vocals
Nancy Gillespie, bass, vocals
Daphne Osoba, guitar, vocals
Nina Singh, drums, vocals

Ginger Group with Ginger Snaps (1986)
Brenda Baird, keyboards
Jane Leroux, lead vocals
Wendy Solloway, bass
Ginger Snaps (backup singers): Arlene Adolf, Dolores Cejalvo, Bonnie McCoy
Additional player: Karen Graves, sax, flute

Heebie Jeebies (1986)
Randy Bowman, drums
Nancy Gillespie, bass
Darryl Pettigrew, guitar
Ingrid (last name unavailable), lead vocals

SHE (1987–92)
Suezi Boyer, lead vocals (1990–92)
Sherri Chisolm, drums (1989)
Nancy Gillespie, bass
Trasa Hordiyuk, lead vocals (1989)
Eileen Ryan, guitar
Smokin' Val, lead vocals (1987–89)
Julie Turtle, drums (1990–92)
Lisa (last name unavailable), drums (1987–89)

The Society for the Preservation of Live Music (1988–early '90s)
Heidi Archibald, vocals
Brenda Baird, keyboards
Jane Leroux, vocals
Wendy Solloway, bass
Backup singers: Julie Armitage, Bonnie McCoy, Antonio Roberts
Additional player: Karen Graves, sax, flute

RADIO WAVES

THE NEWSMAGAZINE OF VANCOUVER CO-OPERATIVE RADIO   CFRO 102.7 FM   JANUARY 1985

k.d. lang

"Hey pardner! Come on over to the Commodore, January 12 at 8 o'clock and hear k.d. lang play at Co-op Radio's Benefit Dance!"

On the Road

STEINEM ON STEINEM

SOMETHING HAPPENED ON THE WAY TO
BECOMING A ROCKETTE

The Georgia Straight, February 3–10, 1989

Legend has it that Gloria Steinem charged all the expenses for Cesar Chavez's Poor People's March to her American Express card. It is a matter of record that she raised funds for activist Angela Davis, supported Black Power and aided the former Linda Lovelace in exposing the abuse behind the porn film *Deep Throat*.

Responding to a news story linking her with Kissinger, Steinem once declared, "I am not now and never have been a girlfriend of Henry Kissinger." She remains an anomaly to a confused press, which considers her "too beautiful" to need liberating.

Liberated she is, though, and for the past nine years *The World Almanac* has chosen Gloria Steinem as one of the twenty-five most influential women in America. She has received a number of honorary degrees, journalism awards and the Ceres Medal from the United Nations for her women's rights work. Her writing has appeared in magazines, newspapers and anthologies around the world.

But Ms. Steinem, who will be speaking in Vancouver at the Orpheum on February 8, 1989, as part of an event organized by the Women's Legal Education and Action Fund (LEAF), is most widely recognized and lauded for her actions almost twenty years ago, which had a profound effect on American life.

By the end of the '60s, America was at war with itself. As many as 280 American farm boys and inner-city youths were dying each week in Vietnam, as were untold numbers of Vietnamese. John, Robert and Martin were dead, along with four students in Ohio and two in Mississippi. Across America, 488 college campuses either shut down or went on strike. In the few short years to come, Angela Davis would go on trial for murder, Nixon would go to China, and five men would be arrested for breaking into Democratic headquarters at the Watergate Hotel. Andy Warhol and George Wallace would be shot, and the United States Supreme Court, in the landmark decision *Roe v. Wade*, would guarantee women their constitutional right to abortion. On the sidelines, the nascent women's liberation movement was moving closer to the limelight.

Gloria Steinem entered the debate as a political columnist for *New*

York magazine. Between 1968 and 1972, she wrote about the assassination of Martin Luther King Jr., the Democratic convention in Chicago, the campaign for Richard Nixon and the child-care movement in the inner city. *New York* magazine, a weekly she helped found, was "the only place I've ever been allowed to write about politics," she told the *Georgia Straight* during a recent telephone conversation from New York. "I've always been working in politics, but I was writing about Paul Newman and Barbra Streisand."

However, it was *Ms.* magazine, the groundbreaking women's liberation monthly that began publishing in 1972, that placed Gloria Steinem on the front lines. Images of girdles, high heels and bras thrown into a trash can at a demonstration at the Miss America pageant in 1968 were replaced with cohesive, challenging journalism. Now feminism could be a personal and private transformation, available to women who could muster up the courage to purchase *Ms.* The preview issue sold out across the country in eight days, inspired twenty thousand letters to the editor and garnered thirty-five thousand unsolicited subscriptions. As editor and co-founder of this radical new forum, Gloria Steinem became a major spokesperson for women's rights.

However, for the young Steinem, the daughter of working-class parents in east Toledo, Ohio, who dreamed of becoming a Rockette, there was no sign that she would become one of the most visible symbols of women's liberation in America.

"First of all," Steinem says, "in the '40s and '50s when I was growing up, there was little hint of women's liberation. In fact, if I wanted to do anything it was to be in show business because, I suspect, show business is for many little girls what sports is for little boys in poor or minority neighbourhoods. It's the only place you see someone who looks like you doing something non-traditional.

"I was able to go to college, thanks to the scrimping and saving of my mother. So I gave up show business. But I'm sorry to say that college in the '50s was mostly directed to making you a companion for a better class of male.

"The picture of married life that was presented to us was so drastic that it was very difficult to accept. We really believed that we would totally take the identity of our husbands. Whatever his life would be, our life would be. His name would be our name. His future was our future. So if you really believed, as one of my sociology texts said, that marriage is your only life-changing mechanism, then marriage seemed like a small death because it was the end of choice."

Steinem credits the courage of women in the peace and civil rights movements with proving to her that there were other alternatives.

Although reasonably well known as a journalist, Steinem points out that in the early '70s many women writers and editors, including her, could not do what interested them in existing magazines. This reality, combined with her experience on the lecture circuit ("There was no other way of expressing the great new understanding and changes that came from dawning feminism"), made her realize that there was an eager audience for a different kind of women's magazine, and *Ms.* was born out of that realization.

Steinem remained editor of *Ms.* until last year, when the magazine was sold to "two very nice Australian feminists." Although Steinem says *Ms.* "always had more readers than we knew what to do with," escalating postage and production costs along with advertiser resistance forced some tough financial decisions. "The makers of shaving cream understand that men read ads for shaving cream without having an article every month on how to shave. Unfortunately, the makers of beauty products and food don't understand that women will look at ads without needing recipes or diagrams on where to put your rouge."

However, Steinem says, "I feel proud that we got it started at all with almost no money; that we served as a national forum for issues that hadn't even had names before, like battered women or displaced homemakers or sexual harassment. I'm proudest that we became a portable friend for women who were trying to change their lives, and that we didn't do anything we were supposed to do to survive."

An editorial consultant for the current *Ms.* magazine, Steinem is also a frequent media guest and lecturer on women's issues and a correspondent for various television programs, including NBC's *Today* show.

Regarding *Roe v. Wade* and the US Supreme Court's decision to consider the validity of a Missouri law that prohibits abortion, Steinem says that since the Reagan administration has lost the battle electorally, it has stacked the courts. "The net result, if the Supreme Court gives abortion back to the states to decide (which means many state legislators will make abortion illegal), is that they will breed disrespect for the law, as in the time of Prohibition. It will endanger the lives of many women."

Steinem's third book, tentatively titled *The Bedside Book of Self-Esteem*, will be published this year (*Revolution from Within: A Book of Self-Esteem* was published in 1992), and she asserts that self-esteem is at the root of liberation. It's that quality that parents should be imparting to the next generation of women. Steinem says, "I think the deepest way we are made to conform is to feel that we won't be loved or approved of unless we obey an outside source of authority. The more you read and the more you talk to people, the more it's clear. You don't have self-esteem because you accomplish a lot. You accomplish a lot because you have self-esteem." Children need to know that they are loved no matter what they do, that they are valuable. "As valuable as anybody else."

The LEAF National Roadshow '89, a celebration of women who made a difference, included performances by Lillian Allen, the Clichettes, Hart-Rouge, Buffy Sainte-Marie and Katari Taiko.

PSYCHEDELIC PAST POWERS GUITARIST

An Interview with Ellen McIlwaine

The Georgia Straight, February 24–March 3, 1989

It was a while before Ellen McIlwaine realized that she was white. The daughter of American missionaries, McIlwaine grew up in Japan, speaking Japanese and attending an international school. "We were multicultural," she said during a recent telephone call to the *Georgia Straight* from her home in Toronto. "There was no us and them. It was all us."

Her musical tastes were integrated as well: Japanese classics, American rhythm and blues, and Latin music. "Trio Los Panchos was big in Japan, as were the black American recording artists [including] Fats Domino, Ray Charles and Professor Longhair. And then in the South you met the same people and found out they didn't have the same status that they had in Japan. But I always followed their music. Those are my roots."

McIlwaine, now forty-two, began playing piano at a very early age and was well on her way to developing her famous New Orleans style when her family returned to the US. For a woman who referred to white people as "foreigners," moving to Georgia at the beginning of the civil rights era presented some problems. "It was awful," she says. "I hung out with a group of people who were racially mixed, and that was a big no-no back then. We used to get pulled over a lot by the cops because they thought we were outside agitators. When people talked racial slurs I would have to ask what most of them meant. It was unbelievable. I didn't understand where all the hate came from.

"I became a history major in college, and I learned that what's in the books isn't always what happened. And I was appalled when I found out the things that went down."

But a Presbyterian college was not where McIlwaine really wanted to be. Unable to find a piano, she had taken up guitar and was playing rock and roll in the basement of the boys' dormitory. In time, her desire to be a working musician led her to New York City. "People hung out. They played together," she says, referring to the Village scene in the mid-'60s. "There was openness and an exchange of ideas. I didn't feel discriminated against. They were mostly all men, and I still didn't feel any difference. That came later. I felt quite accepted and encouraged."

Although younger than her contemporaries, McIlwaine played club

1987, Toronto: Slide guitarist Ellen McIlwaine in all her glory at a record release party and concert. *Looking for Trouble,* her seventh album, was released that year on Stony Plain Records. She closed the evening with a Jimi Hendrix cover.

dates with Muddy Waters, Elvin Bishop, John Hammond and others. She was particularly encouraged by the young Jimi Hendrix, who asked to sit in on her sets at the Café Au Go Go. "He was really nice to me. He was a very sensitive guy, and the main way he communicated with the world was through his music. He listened to everything everybody played. He never put anybody down. It was a real pleasure to play with him. I watched him write 'The Wind Cries Mary,' and I learned from him how to use my guitar and my voice like two guitars."

McIlwaine, who will be playing the Railway Club March 1–4, 1989, is now legendary for her powerful, dual-action performing style. She's recorded eight albums, including a concert at Carnegie Hall and two Canadian-made releases. *Everybody Needs It*, recorded in 1982 with Jack Bruce, won the award for Best Rock Album in the US from the National Association of Independent Record Distributors. The state of Georgia has honoured her, and Atlanta declared the first day of spring Ellen McIlwaine Day.

A passionate musician, McIlwaine plays with wit and wisdom as if guided by ghosts from New Orleans's Storyville and the psychedelic past. "It's a hard thing to come through," she says, reflecting on life in the late '60 and '70s. "A lot of people ended up abusing drugs and alcohol. But I've heard of a lot of wonderful recovery stories. I feel like I've been fortunate in my own recovery from alcoholism. We've come a long way as artists and musicians. The more responsibility we take, the better it is for us. You don't have to be high to be creative. In fact, it gets in the way."

RIP: June 23, 2021

A LIFE FULL OF SHARP SHOCKS

An Interview with Michelle Shocked

The Georgia Straight, February 24–March 3, 1989

It's been less than three years since Michelle Shocked was discovered playing guitar at a folk festival in east Texas. Two successful albums later, this outspoken woman lives alone on a London houseboat riding the wave of a media storm.

She's been interviewed by every major music magazine in the Western world, analyzed, idolized and packaged as political feed-and-seed for those seeking greener pastures. Her personal life has been documented in minute detail, in sharp contrast to the privacy laws surrounding other performers. Her strong opinions and extreme candour when talking about her own life not only feed the folklore machine but, remarkably, strengthen her career.

"I feel like it's my right to do that," Shocked said during a recent telephone conversation from West Germany. (She's sharing the bill at the Commodore on March 1, 1989, with the Cowboy Junkies.) "I think my idea was to tell the story of my life. One ambition I had was to stimulate people's imagination to the possibilities. I feel like [my life] is very much a modern-day feminist testimony because there were certain things that I was deliberately attempting to challenge. For example, the idea that it's dangerous for a woman to travel alone, hitchhiking with no money. That, of course, was inspired by all the *On the Road* stuff. But you can read Jack Kerouac for yourself and you know what's wrong with the picture. There's no woman in it."

Women's oppression is one subject that continually surfaces throughout the conversation, especially when she is talking about some of her more painful experiences. On the subject of leaving home: "For years I thought I'd run away from home, but the truth is, I'd been kicked out. I just rebelled too often too loudly and I was given an ultimatum that was completely unacceptable for somebody who was really chomping at the bit for her independence and freedom."

On being committed to a psychiatric ward by her mother: "The percentage of women that are incarcerated in those hospitals as compared to men is really disproportionate."

On being raped while travelling in Europe: "I really compared the experience of being raped to the feeling of someone, say from the South, where I come from, being lynched. The anger, the rage that you go through while you're experiencing this degradation. Unfortunately, with most lynchings you die with that rage."

On her experience in a separatist women's commune in Italy after her attack: "It was not a sanctuary at all. It was like a whole new set of problems. Those women were trying to survive in a very misogynist society on very strong terms, and the consequences were very extreme poverty."

Compared to Bob Dylan on the strength of her debut album, *The Texas Campfire Tapes*, Shocked was declared the female anti-hero of the '80s before she'd even spoken a word. Her press has been consistently generous. Still, it's worth wondering whether Shocked has had time to catch her breath and define herself, or whether that process is ahead of her.

Controversy did catch up with her last year when she released her second album, *Short Sharp Shocked*, featuring a photo of Shocked being carried away by two policemen. The cover design, identified by fans of the hardcore band Chaos UK as being a dead ringer for a previously released Chaos album, caused some "embarrassment," but Shocked survived the publicity generated by the headline "Right On Folkie In Punk Rip Off Drama." The Chaos UK album, titled *Short Sharp Shock*, features a picture of vocalist Mower in the grips of two policemen during a demonstration in London. Shocked told England's *NME* that she had seen the Chaos UK cover but only after the artwork on her own album had been completed. In the same story her management said, "The phrase 'short sharp shock' is very common. It's a case of great minds think alike."

Coincidence or the work of extraterrestrials, Shock's cover has little to do with the collection of melodic story-songs inside, a fact she easily admits. "Enamoured" with a '60s philosopher who "put the idea in my head that it was the medium itself" that was important, Shocked decided to use some reverse psychology. "Knowing that the cover was going to be used as an advertisement, I felt like I could just use the vehicle of the record to sell the record cover, which is the opposite of most people's logic that the cover is supposed to help sell the record. Now I'm able to talk about the issues around that arrest and what that arrest itself represented."

In 1984, Shocked was charged in San Francisco with conspiracy to commit a misdemeanour for protesting against a corporation responsible for producing Agent Orange. (The company gave money to both political parties during the recent presidential campaign.) What the arrest represented was Shocked's first time "in the thick of it." Reputed to be a squatter activist and "knee-jerk anarchist," Shocked reveals that those terms are more concepts than reality, and that she simply hoped to deflect attention *away* from herself and toward the issues behind the image. "It was when I was first introduced to the hardcore scene that I realized that you can have the maximum impact by what you say between the songs. That gives you a lot more freedom with the actual music."

If squatter and anarchist are not wholly appropriate to Shocked, then the term *feminist* certainly is. Shocked follows the women's movement axiom that the personal is political. This is very apparent in her stage raps and interviews and to a certain extent in her music. "I consider [my songs] to be much more in the Texas songwriting-storyteller tradition. I consider them stories and, in that case, to be political because stories pay a great amount of respect to people's intelligence."

But she is first and foremost a folksinger from the plains of east Texas, who sang into a stranger's tape recorder one summer night and found herself with a hit record in England as a result. In time, Shocked may be more comfortable with the contradictions inherent in her celebrity status. Living on her houseboat, she says, is helping her feel like she's being consistent. "It's a drop in the bucket, [but] I can prove that they are wrong: this whole thing about my generation being a bunch of yuppies, that we turn from political commitment as soon as we get our piece of the action. I say wrong. Really committed people will continue to be so."

ESTHER BEJARANO

SONGS TESTIFY TO COURAGE

The Georgia Straight, April 14–21, 1989

"I'm sure that I would not be on the stage anymore if I were to know that everything is okay in our world," Esther Bejarano told the *Georgia Straight* during a recent telephone conversation from her home in Hamburg, West Germany. "But we have very big difficulties here in western Germany. I'm sure you have heard about the last vote. The Nazis are coming back again."

Bejarano was referring to a recent election in West Berlin where the extreme right-wing Republican party won eleven seats in the city parliament, a win that gained them two seats at the federal level. Although neo-Nazi parties are officially banned in West Germany, the federal leader of the Republican party was an officer in Hitler's SS during World War II. On election day, ten thousand people protested the election results and federal chancellor Helmet Kohl called the Republican win "a clear warning signal to us all." Unofficially, neo-Nazis are alive and well.

But so is Esther Bejarano, who will be performing at the Vancouver East Cultural Centre on April 20, 1989, with an all-women band led by her daughter Edna. Esther is a survivor of Hitler's extermination camps. In 1943, after her parents and sister were murdered, Bejarano was taken by cattle car to Auschwitz-Birkenau. Although certain death awaited her, when it was learned that she had musical abilities, she was chosen to play accordion and flute in the women's orchestra. This decision kept her alive, but she was forced to play on the platform while the trains arrived and the guards chose which prisoners would be sent to hard labour and which would go to the gas chambers.

Because Bejarano had a Christian grandmother, she was eventually transferred to a labour camp at Ravensbrück. The next time she held an accordion in her hands, it was given to her by an American soldier. Liberated by the Soviets and the Americans, Bejarano played while survivors and soldiers danced around a blazing picture of Adolf Hitler.

Bejarano, sixty-five, now plays music to a generation with little or no knowledge of the Holocaust. "The pupils are not taught in the school what happened then," Bejarano said. "When I am making a concert and I tell about my story, they tell me, 'Oh, I never knew.'" Bejarano is a leading member of the International Auschwitz Committee, an educational organization. One of its projects has been to pay for students to visit the camp at Auschwitz.

Unfortunately, young people's ignorance exists despite the number of former SS members and Nazi collaborators living openly in West Germany and around the world. Bejarano recalled the story of Arnold Strippel, an SS officer who ordered the hanging of twenty children between the ages of five and twelve who had been used as living subjects for Nazi medical experiments. Strippel, now seventy, was never tried for his war crimes and is now living in Frankfurt. "He has doctors who say that he is not able to go to trial," Bejarano said. "There are so many murderers from this time running around here in western Germany. They have big pensions. Much more than the people who have been in the concentration camps. That's the reality, I tell you."

Thankfully, Bejarano's songs tell of another reality, one of people surviving on courage and hope. The songwriters are dead, but the words that formed in their heads or on scraps of paper while imprisoned in the concentration camps or barricaded in the Jewish ghettos have survived. They were whispered while comforting a motherless child, while honouring the dead and dying, or sung loudly to bolster spirits withering from starvation or torture, and to celebrate those who escaped to join the partisans. For Bejarano, who feels "solidarity" with many suffering people, including the current immigrants to Germany, the black people of South Africa and the Palestinians, these songs are alive as long as people continue to resist.

"I suffered so much that afterwards, I said, Well, I have to live life and I must bring up a family so that I can help to make the world a little bit better. But when I saw that there are Nazis in the streets, I said somebody must tell the people. We are the only people still left who know what happened then."

Through the retelling, Bejarano said she herself gains strength. "It's my opinion that I have to do something against [fascism] and therefore I'm not so sad. It is my wish that my children can live in peace."

RIP: July 10, 2021

COUNTRY RAISED, COUNTRY BLESSED

An Interview with Teresa Trull and Cris Williamson

The Georgia Straight, May 12–19, 1989

"It's been so crazy since this record came out," says Teresa Trull from her horse ranch near Martinez, California. "So when I get up *here*, I go out and work a horse, go for a ride, hack weeds or mend a fence. There's always a million things to do. When you're trying to help a foal survive, your life slips into perspective."

The album *Country Blessed*, a collaboration with singer Cris Williamson, sold out its first pressing within ten days. "I'm out here in the boondocks with all these horse people and I have all these cowboys taking tapes and playing them for other people. I haven't had a single person not love it."

For Trull and Williamson, who will perform at the Vancouver East Cultural Centre on May 14, 1989, recording an album with country roots was a return to fundamentals. "Cris and I are similar in a lot of ways," Trull says. "We both were raised in the country and spent an enormous amount of time in our childhood alone—hers in Wyoming and South Dakota, and mine in North Carolina in the woods. And we both made this trip back to that original lifestyle that made us really happy."

The two women are both widely respected on the independent music scene in the US and are favourites of critics. In the 1970s, they helped pioneer a phenomenon known as "women's music," which was to the early women's movement what civil rights music was to the '60s. Their treatment of previously unexplored topics and their support in the creation of an alternative music network brought many issues to the fore and paved the way for the freedom of expression that newer female artists now enjoy.

"I think women of talent have always been there," says Williamson from Lexington, Virginia. "It's just that they had no place to go with it. Now I think there's a place for them to go and I think we've helped."

Williamson's success includes twelve albums, two songbooks, three sold-out appearances at Carnegie Hall and performances at almost every major concert hall in the US. Her first independent album, *The Changer and the Changed*, sold 250,000 copies by word of mouth. "I'm an independent person," she says. "I'm forty-two. It would be pretty difficult for me to have anybody tell me, 'This is what you have to do.' My nature—stubborn—is what leads people to me. That's the source of my strength."

For Trull, *Country Blessed* is her fifth album. She performed with the likes of Sheila E., David Sanborn, Joan Baez and Ferron and toured with Bonnie Hayes and Huey Lewis. She also has a reputation as an independent producer, with nine albums to her credit.

But her return to horses was an unexpected gift. "A woman who came to see my show turned out to be the manager of probably one of the richest Arabian horse ranches in the world. I told her it was a dream of mine to own an Arabian. Her young son was having difficulty learning to speak and I taught him to sing a song. She was really appreciative and the next time I came to town she wanted to do something for me. So she gave me that dream."

Trull now manages an Arabian horse ranch, is learning animal husbandry and breeds thirty-five birds—a way of life that has enriched her music, she says. "Cris came [out to the ranch] to rehearse and right when we got in from the airport the vet was rolling in. I had to run out and do five-hour surgery on a horse's ear that had been bitten off. As we were sewing it back on, and Cris was holding the lamp, I said, 'See, Cris, this is what the record is all about,' and she said, 'I know.'"

QUIETLY CHRISTIAN POP

AMY GRANT'S SPIRITUAL SONGS REACH OUT
TO A SECULAR AUDIENCE

The Georgia Straight, September 9–16, 1988

Talking with Amy Grant is a bit like talking with my sister in Nebraska. Our first subjects were at once familiar. Motherhood. Career. The drought in the Midwest. Unfair taxes for farmers. As time passed, I wished we had some iced tea.

Amy Grant has had an extraordinary career. At twenty-seven, she has already won four Grammys, received numerous Dove Awards from the Gospel Music Association and sold millions and millions of records—all this within the distribution circles of Christian music, and without airplay on mainstream radio.

Grant signed her first recording contract when she was fifteen years old with the Christian label Word Records. A remarkable young songwriter, she had been discovered a year earlier sweeping floors and demagnetizing tape heads at a Nashville recording studio. This year, she released her eleventh album, *Lead Me On*.

Although primarily influenced by popular music in the '70s ("It had more of a folk flavour to it back then," she says), her range of styles has included rock and roll, soul and the one-woman choir. It is her message that lingers on—a message not so different from those of other concerned individuals who are guided by their political or social beliefs rather than by God.

This month, Grant will end her hiatus with her newborn son and begin a thirteen-month tour to promote *Lead Me On*. Her work will bring her to Vancouver September 12–13, 1988, when she will be performing at the Queen Elizabeth Theatre. She talked to the *Georgia Straight* a few weeks ago about how her music evolved and where she thinks it's headed.

CK: You didn't grow up surrounded by church music or singing in a choir, yet at fourteen you were writing the kind of songs that interested Word Records. Where did you get your inspiration?

AG: When I started writing, there were lyrics to express every experience in my life except for what was then a new-found spiritual revival. I was a

Christian, a new Christian, and just totally bowled over by this whole new relationship with God. And I thought, Why is nobody writing about this? So I wrote music to fill the gap in my own musical repertoire.

Were you recording while you were in high school and at Vanderbilt?

Yes. You know, it's funny when I read the press. I think, "Good night! This child didn't have time to grow up." But you make time for things that you love to do. I started recording my first album halfway through my junior year in high school. But that was my activity. You know what I mean? There was no press involved. There's wasn't a lot of hoopla. I wasn't touring. Even in college, the first platinum album that I released didn't come out until the spring of my senior year. So I was out of school and really pursuing music full-time before I had a major album.

The title song on *Lead Me On* is very moving. Did living in Franklin, Tennessee, contribute to that song?

Well, it did draw from the Civil War and from slavery. The street that I live on is not too far from the site of the Battle of Franklin. A whole lot of Confederate soldiers died there. I don't know the specific date, but the South was falling hard and fast. In the field right next to our house is the tombstone of a slave. I guess there was a whole little slave cemetery, but people have run cows through there and all the tombstones have been knocked down except for this one. The tombstone is very tall and slender, and it would have fallen down a few years ago except two little saplings grew up and encased the upper corners. Now, it is frozen at a slant, but upright, because of these trees.

You've lived in the South all of your life. Were you influenced by black American music or spirituality?

I think more from the women that I've worked with. For five years the trio that I sang with on the road was two black women and one woman whose dad was black and her mom was white. But I feel like my greatest influence as far as black gospel music came from Donna McElroy, and she'll be back on the road with me again. We're great friends, and I really enjoy working with her.

Do you think popular music is closer to acknowledging its debt to black artists, including gospel singers?

Oh, yeah. Rock and roll came out of that.

There are all kinds of stories about black artists who have "crossed over," bringing their message with them. Do you see any movement like that within the white gospel community?

I don't know. I really don't. I think that what black gospel had going for it was that it was a music *movement*. And I don't think that white gospel has that going. There's no specific movement. The music is very diverse; it's basically just all kinds of music. The reason they call it "contemporary Christian" is because of the lyrics. I do think that maybe artist-by-artist acceptance will be gained, but it will just be on the basis of individual songwriting. On the whole, the music is not some force to be reckoned with.

Has your Christian audience been supportive as you move out into the secular population?

I think there have been mixed reactions—understandably so. Any kind of underground music, whether it's bluegrass, or punk, or Christian music—anything that doesn't get a lot of radio support—it gets its strength and its fuel from an underground following. When I first started broadening my music base, I did get a sense of people saying, "Wait a minute. We've hung in here when nobody was playing your stuff. Don't abandon us." But I got some really good counsel from the people around me, and whatever criticism is coming, the best response is time. So, I realized when I kind of felt like, "Oh gosh, this thing is a grass fire, there's just no way to put it out," that I'm just going to live a few more years, and a decade or two decades from now it will be evident what my goals were and the kind of songwriter and communicator I wanted to be. It's something that only time will bear out.

Do you think that the scandals with the evangelists have hindered this music?

I don't know what the ramifications of those particular scandals will be on the music industry. I was home pregnant when all that was coming down, and I felt like it was a great year to be off the road. I never really felt that marketplace was necessarily receptive to the kind of music I do anyway.

Am I right in assuming that social issues or human issues are really important to you?

Oh yes. Yes. More so the older that I get. You know, growing up in the US, we're just so isolated. And I grew up in a great family. But as I've gotten older, I think that our cultural response is to insulate ourselves. I feel like it's the cultural response of the church to be separate. I feel like it's the cultural response of the yuppie movement to remove ourselves from hunger and pain. I feel like it's the cultural response of America to be a one-language country, and everybody has to meet us on our terms because we're the biggest and most powerful.

And you know, you grow up in that and you don't question it, and then all of a sudden your horizons are broadened and you study history and you begin travelling and you think, "Gee, no wonder Europe is so mad at us." We're the big, bull-headed, *duh … America*. Especially in light of the simple message of Christianity. It's incongruous with my cultural experience.

That is the war inside of me. That's the polarity that I fight against every day. You know: "The first shall be last and the last shall be first." And here I am going down all the roads that my culture says [I should] to be a singer. And I'm doing it. And I'm going, "Oh gosh, what am I doing?" I wake up in the morning and I look in the garage and I've got a brand new Dodge Caravan, and I put on my black cowboy boots that make me feel like somebody, and I start embracing all the props that I've grown up feeling like I have to have to feel like somebody.

You often write about the strength it takes to be true to oneself. What kind of values do you want to instill in your listeners?

I really want my songs to bring life to people, and to renew hope. That sounds kind of nebulous and sort of like a Miss America pageant answer—no offence to Miss America—"I want to bring hope to the world." I don't mean it in a silly way like that. I mean in a real sense we do operate on two levels. Everybody does. There's the flesh part of you and all of its needs and appetites and wants, but also everybody has a spirit side, too.

I think the opening song on this album, "1974," was the best that I had been able to articulate it, when I realized that I was part spirit and determined to find truth and meet the needs for that part of myself. Obviously I feel that need is met in God. But even artistically, good music can make somebody feel good. You know, it moves the soul, it really does. No matter what you buy into.

You once said that you thought you were so popular because you were so ordinary.

I remember feeling that.

Do you still feel that way?

Yes, I guess I do. I *like* ordinary, honestly. I'm very comfortable with ordinary, and I guess I still feel that way. I bet there are things about me that have changed because of what I do, but I hope it's not some huge growth or something. I hope I haven't grown a tail.

BLUES PLAYER BLESSED WITH A STYLE OF HER OWN

AN INTERVIEW WITH KATIE WEBSTER

Kinesis, February 1987

Nightshift column, *The Georgia Straight*, February 6–13, 1987

When Kathryn Thorne was thirteen, they called her Big Mama Cat. "At that time, I was quite heavy and I would do dances and splits and I would stand up on top of the piano stool and play." After her marriage at fifteen to Earl Webster, they called her Katie. And after just a few short years as a session pianist, some musicians called her by the wrong sex. "So many guys before they met me thought that Katie Webster was a man. They thought that the name was just like 'A Boy Named Sue' because they said no woman plays the piano like that. I have run into some guys that don't even want to come onstage after my performance is over. They say, 'Put me before her; do not put me after her because she will make me work myself to death.'

"I don't categorize myself as just a blues singer or boogie-woogie pianist, because I do so many different types of music: jazz, gospel, blues, urban blues, folk music. Plus, I do Stevie Wonder–type songs, Fats Domino, Dinah Washington. But I do them my style, because I was blessed with a style of my own."

Katie's career began in the 1950s in Beaumont, Texas. "My father was a minister and my sisters and brothers were all in the church singing gospel, and I wanted to play rhythm and blues and boogie-woogie. I knew that if I stayed at home during that time there was no way. So I left home [Houston] and went to stay with an aunt of mine in Beaumont. And with her I could march in the drill squad with those little short dresses on, and stuff that I couldn't do at home. But I was very conservative about not wanting anything to happen to me that would embarrass my parents. So I went to school and finished school. I took the music that my mother wanted me to take, and when I went home I would play the classics for her, and I would play the gospel music for her. I know so many beautiful gospel songs I was raised up singing."

On the weekends she worked as a session pianist in the Goldband studios in Lake Charles, Louisiana. Although not always credited, Katie played piano on over five hundred records before she was eighteen years old,

1985, Vancouver: Katie Webster brought her boogie-woogie piano style to the main stage of the Vancouver Folk Music Festival, and shared weekend workshop stages with Barbara Higbie, Margret RoadKnight, Teresa Trull, Bob Lenox, Erwin Helfer and Angela Brown. She was on the road as a teenager with Otis Redding until his death in a plane crash. She was too pregnant to fly.

including cuts by Clifton Chenier, Smiley Lewis, Lightnin' Slim, Lonnie Brooks and Dolly Parton's first recordings. "I would be doing my homework in the back of the station wagon while I was going across the state line, because I would play on the weekends and go to school during the week."

In 1964 she put herself in the position to be discovered by Otis Redding. He was so impressed with her that he asked her to leave with him that night. She said, "In the morning," and she travelled with him until his tragic death in an airplane crash in December 1967. At the time, Katie told me, she was eight months pregnant with her second child and "was too big to fly," or she would have accompanied him.

Despondent over his death, Katie did not perform for some time. But when she began again, she opened for B.B. King, Bobby "Blue" Bland, John Copeland and Etta James. Her repertoire grew to include over three thousand songs. In 1974 she took another break from her career to care for her ailing parents. "Even though my mother and father have passed away now, I will never forget their teachings." After their deaths in 1978 and 1979, she returned to work and hasn't stopped.

In Katie's thirty-year career, she has made sixteen tours of Europe, released numerous 45s and half a dozen albums, married twice (Earl Webster was killed in Vietnam) and raised five daughters. Recently she received the 1986 Performer of the Year award from the Bay Area Women in Music organization.

Although Oakland, California, is now her home, she is rarely there. Her current tour will bring her to the Savoy in Vancouver on February 9, 1987, for two sets beginning at 10 p.m. The following night Katie will begin a five-night run at the Alhambra Hotel in Victoria.

Katie's first and last visit to Vancouver was in 1985 at the Vancouver Folk Music Festival, where she was an overwhelming success.

RIP: September 5, 1999

RITA MACNEIL'S
SIMPLE TESTIMONY

The Georgia Straight, March 20–27, 1987

When Rita MacNeil was a young girl, her mother used to put a broom in front of Rita's face and have her pretend it was a microphone. "She had an incredible belief in my singing," Rita says.

However, in her later years her mother preferred "Green, Green Grass of Home" and "The Happiest Girl in the Whole USA" (which were popular at the time) to the original material Rita was writing. "I wrote a song about my mother long ago. It's on the first album. The line 'The dream she had and the life she led were all lived for others' was true. She always wanted me to sing." Sadly, her mother died, Rita says, "before she heard my music evolve and change and grow. And I felt very bad about that."

For anyone who has spoken with Rita MacNeil or heard her in concert, this kind of testimony is her trademark. But there is no sadness in the way she talks about her family, her life in Big Pond, Cape Breton, and the lives of those she has met along the way. Rita sings about ordinary people in a way that makes them extraordinary.

It's not surprising, then, that her upcoming five-day run at the Vancouver East Cultural Centre (March 24–28, 1987) sold out even before it was advertised. (An extra show has been added at the Orpheum on March 21.)

Rita was one of eight children born to a Cape Breton housewife and her carpenter husband. Her mother played the violin and often took walks in the hills just to whistle. Her father wrote poetry. (Her song "Old Man" is written about him.) Although Rita was a fan of the compositions of Stephen Foster and of live "kitchen music," she was not a performer. She was certainly not a songwriter. She was a "shy, country girl," and it wasn't until she left high school and moved to Toronto that her outlook changed.

The tale about the night in 1971 when Rita MacNeil went to her first women's liberation meeting has been well told. It was on that night, after being moved by what she heard, that she wrote her first song. "It was quite a thing when I found I couldn't speak very well on the issues, but for some reason I could write about them." "Need for Restoration" became a classic and, encouraged by the women's movement, Rita continued writing.

1985, Vancouver: Interviewed and photographed at the Expo Centre, MacNeil sang into an open space with the odd passersby. A year later she would achieve unimaginable status when Canadian audiences met her at Expo 86.

In 1975, Rita released her first collection of original songs, *Born a Woman*. The album was a perfect mix of songs that expressed her compassion for all, and others that voiced her concern for women. Historically, *Born a Woman* was the first album of what can loosely be called "women's music" to be released in this country. It made women proud, as Rita wrote, "to be among the people we were warned about."

I am convinced that, had this album received widespread distribution in the United States and Canada, Rita would have taken a place ten years ago alongside Joni Mitchell and Ferron as one of Canada's most compelling songwriters, and with Bob Dylan, Joan Baez and Holly Near as the cultural recorders of our time.

As it is, Rita is doing very well. Her subsequent releases *Part of the Mystery* (1981) and *I'm Not What I Seem* (1983) increased Rita's fans tenfold, although she still remained outside the attention of the masses. But the popularity in Atlantic Canada of her latest independent release, *Flying on Your Own*, inspired A&M Records to initiate a licensing agreement and re-release the album on their own label.

Rita's career wasn't hurt any when she became a main attraction last summer at Expo 86, playing to packed houses in several venues for five weeks. "It changed me in a lot of ways to have that many people come to the shows and show that kind of real interest in what I was singing about. That touched me deeply." Also touched was *Vancouver Sun* columnist Denny Boyd, who wrote passionately about Rita MacNeil's talents.

Due in part to her empathy with the miners in the Maritimes, and to her performance with the Cape Breton miners' choir, Men of the Deeps, who perform her song "Working Man," Rita has become popular in the mining areas of Wales. She plans to tour the region in July.

Rita lives in a converted yellow schoolhouse in Big Pond with her sixteen-year-old son, Wade, and her daughter, Laura, a college student. But her recent fame keeps her touring. Can she explain her special gifts? "No. But whatever I'm doing, it's working."

⊙

In 1985, a year before her resounding success at Expo 86, I sat with Rita MacNeil outside a concession stand during her break from performing at the Expo Centre in Vancouver. Her audience was transient, and at times she sang to an empty plaza. This conversation was published in Herizons *magazine in the October/November 1985 issue under the title "A Symbol for Women"* and is referenced in part in "Rita MacNeil's Simple Testimony."

CK: Tell me about your home.

RM: Cape Breton Island itself is quite beautiful. The little village I live in has about 175 people. It's right on the Bras d'Or Lakes and it's just a gorgeous place to live. It's very inspiring. It gives me a definite sense of peacefulness. Unfortunately, the area itself as far as employment is very economically depressed. But I think I stay there because it's such a place of inspiration and such wonderful people.

And your children ...

They're really neat. I really love them. I hope I did all right by them. I think so. They're very independent. I always treated them very individually. I think I gave them a lot of respect as far as not treating them as possessions. I learned a lot through the women's movement about raising my children. I learned a great deal. I learned how to treat them like individuals because of it.

So, it's true then, that you went to a women's liberation meeting in Toronto and then went home and wrote your first song, "Need for Restoration"?

Yes. It's the very, very truth. I always loved music, but I could never stand up in front of an audience without falling apart. So, it was quite a thing when I found I couldn't speak very well on the issues, but for some reason I could write about them. I certainly received an awful lot of confidence to keep speaking the way I needed to, through my music. I know lots of times there wasn't often work for me, and lots of women would get together and create a situation where I would be hired so that I could get some money. I've lots of fond memories. Learned a lot. Took a lot with me. Left some behind.

I understand your mother was a great inspiration to you.

Well, she always believed in my music, and I wrote a song about my mother long ago. It's on the first album. The line "The dream she had and the life she led were all lived for others" was true. She always wanted to see me sing. She used to stick a broom in front of my face to get me to pretend it was a microphone. She had an incredible belief in my singing.

I could never—I always felt guilty because when I first went home, she was dying, and I wanted to tell her about my music. I can remember she was in the hospital: "Oh, Rita, for God's sake, you've got to stop singing that stuff you wrote. Why don't you sing something like 'Green, Green Grass of Home' and that song that was popular (she loved it then), 'I'm the Happiest Girl in the Whole USA.'" She said, "Now there's a song you should be doing." So, I was always very sad she died before she heard my music evolve and change and grow, and I felt very, very bad about that.

What do you want to say to people in your music?

One of the songs I wrote a little while back is called "In the Spirit" and it speaks about the Native Indians [sic] in the Maritimes. It has quite a punch to it. Quite. It all depends. Now, today, I'm singing love songs, because I felt a lot of love for someone. It all depends, you know. I think I'm just trying to communicate and sometimes things really feel strong inside me, whether it's about rights or wrongs, or love.

What would you say have been the three biggest influences in your life?

The women's movement would be the first. Moving back to Cape Breton was the second. I'm still waiting on the third.

RIP: April 16, 2013

LILLIAN ALLEN SAYS HER PIECE

Based on an interview with Lillian in her home in Toronto in 1987,
and on a follow-up phone conversation.

The Georgia Straight, May 8–15, 1987

Although its roots are in Africa, dub poetry owes its life to Jamaica, and to a woman named Louise Bennett, who broke form in the 1930s and began writing dialect poetry in Jamaican Creole. She wrote as people spoke, not in *proper* English, as was the tradition. Her talent for capturing this rhythm launched a career that took her and her poetry around the world. She was, and still is, a serious, hard-working cultural ambassador. Her work inspired national pride.

Now, fifty years later, dub poetry has emerged as the artistic language of Jamaica. As the Caribbean sister of rap music, dub sprouted from the legacy of Miss Lou (as Bennett was affectionately known), was seasoned by the rap deejay "toasters" in the '60s and was brought to a boil in the '70s with the popularity of reggae music. It left the Caribbean on the tongues of Jamaican immigrants and came to Canada in the form of Lillian Allen. And it will come to the Vancouver East Cultural Centre beginning May 12, 1987, when Allen begins a five-night stand there.

Last year, Lillian won a Juno for Best Reggae/Calypso Recording. Her album *Revolutionary Tea Party* was her first full-fledged recording project. Winning on her first try illustrates the powerful effect of dub, Lillian-style. And credit must be given to the Juno selection committee for choosing an album that really *says* something.

Revolutionary Tea Party is *not* milquetoast. The title poem encourages people to analyze, strategize and work together to get more control over their lives. The song "The Subversives" describes women who have broken from their traditional roles to make a life in the "underground." And "Nellie Belly Swelly," the most tragic poem on the album, tells of the rape of a thirteen-year-old girl ("In her little tiny heart / Nellie understood war").

But *Revolutionary Tea Party* also includes the humorous and pointed "I Fight Back," Lillian's signature poem, as well as "Riddim an' Hardtimes" and her famous "Birth Poem." "Mi pregnant in mi belly / And mi head full of jelly / An' mi vamit in mi sleep / An' mi tired an' mi eat." A true story.

The album was produced by Parachute Club's Billy Bryans and features the contributions of other Club members Lauri Conger, Juli Masi and Lorraine Segato. Bryans, Dave Gray, Terry Lewis and Quammie Williams are the major musicians, with guest appearances by Sherry Shute, Elaine Stef,

Ringo Junior, Screecher Nice and the Toronto All-Girls Subversive Chorus.

On the first night of her appearance here, Allen will read without accompaniment, but she will perform with a full band the rest of the week.

Born in Spanish Town, Jamaica, Lillian was the youngest daughter in a family of ten children. "My grandmother had eighteen children. I had lots and lots of cousins." She immigrated to Canada in 1969 when she was seventeen to escape the economic restrictions of Jamaica. But she also came to find "new worlds, new ways of thinking, new ideas and new people." She planned to attend university and become a lawyer.

"I got into Canada quite easily," she says, on the phone from Toronto. "I came at the time when they were looking for more people, when they wanted workers. I fit the bill. I was nice and clean and well-spoken, and had the pioneering spirit. You know, the one that moved mountains. They accepted me and welcomed me. Officially." Unofficially, it was another matter. As Lillian writes in her poem "I Fight Back," "I came to Canada / And found the doors of opportunities well-guarded."

"There was nothing that reflected or validated my existence," Allen says. "For the way society was set up and looked, I didn't exist. That was quite a shock. It was hard to get jobs. And it took me a while to realize that it was because I was black. I had never had the experience of racism. I was completely naive and hopeful."

Unable to find reasonable employment to support her dream, Lillian worked as a babysitter eleven hours a day for fifteen dollars a week. Other

1987, Toronto: Dub poet Lillian Allen performs at an evening organized by Mayworks, an organization which encourages and celebrates working people in the arts. She was accompanied on this night by multi-instrumentalist Rachel Melas.

low-paying jobs followed. Eventually Lillian decided to try New York City. She lived with relatives, and studied communications and black American literature at a community college. When she was offered a scholarship, she attempted to legalize her status. She was refused and was given ten hours to leave the country. "The thing with racism is that it's blind to any other factor except colour," Allen says, "so it doesn't matter if you're a pimp or a doctor, or you were born in Nova Scotia or Buckingham Palace."

Lillian returned briefly to Jamaica and went to work for the Ministry of Education, but in 1974, an even more determined Lillian Allen returned to Canada. She enrolled at York University and studied creative writing. She founded an annual Third World Cultural Festival. She began writing plays, short stories, poetry and songs. She joined the reggae band Truths and Rights as a resource person, education coordinator and writer. And she had a daughter, Anta, now five and a half years old.

In 1982, Lillian published her own book of dub poetry, *Rhythm an' Hardtimes*, which sold an impressive seven thousand copies. She also recorded an album with Clifton Joseph and Devon Haughton called *De Dub Poets* and released a spoken-word cassette, *Live in Concert: The Portrait of Lillian Allen*. "I do write non-dub. I write all kinds of stuff," she says. "Right now I'm working on some electronic poetry. But I think dub is one of the more satisfying ways for me to express my ideas and it's probably not only because I can bring in a number of my cultural and historical influences, but because I'm at the forefront of what it is. So, I am actually creating it as I go along."

At the forefront, but still relatively unknown, Lillian was introduced to a national audience on the Peter Gzowski show in 1984. That same year, Lillian filled in at the Vancouver Folk Music Festival, where she'll appear again this year.

"I think the great task in life is to keep expanding. The more you know, the more you need to know. The more you do, the more you need to do. The more you see, the more you need to see. Those people that I would say are the most whole and beautiful people that I've met are people who continuously challenge themselves and continuously broaden their scope and their fields."

Allen is currently at work on material for a children's album, and an original play about immigrant women in public housing was produced by Groundswell in Toronto. "I'm striving for an integrated, balanced life," she says. "There are times when I push the boundaries here and there, but basically I'm trying to have it all. You know, have the connections. Do the dishes. Watch the TV. Listen to the radio. Play with my kid. It will beautify my art. Because that is life."

AN INTERVIEW WITH KOKO TAYLOR

Rubymusic column, *Kinesis*, April 1986

Cora Walton's childhood friends nicknamed her Koko because they couldn't pronounce her name. When she married musician "Pops" Taylor back in 1953, they decided Koko was the name they'd put on her records. Since that time, she's been called a few other things: the hardest-working lady in show business, Chicago's premier blues growler and the queen of the blues.

Koko was raised on a farm outside Memphis but grew up singing in the clubs of Chicago. Among her fans were Muddy Waters, Howlin' Wolf, Junior Wells and Willie Dixon. She played with all of them at one time or another. It was Willie Dixon who wrote and produced her first big hit, "Wang Dang Doodle," for Chess Records. The song was a million-seller in 1965, prompting the first of a dozen European tours for the young star.

Koko stayed with Chess Records until the early '70s when the label folded. In 1975 she signed with Alligator Records. The company called it "the best decision we ever made." They were right. Since that time, Koko has won every major award the blues has to offer. Her most recent honours came at the 1985 W.C. Handy Awards in Memphis, where she won Entertainer of the Year, Blues Vocalist of the Year and, for the sixth time, Contemporary Blues Female Artist of the Year.

The *College Media Journal* voted her recent album *Queen of the Blues* Best Blues Album of '85, and in 1984, after five previous nominations, Koko received a Grammy for Best Blues Album of the Year. ("I've waited twenty years for that one, and I was real pleased to get it.")

But of all the titles she's received, it's "the hardest-working lady in show business" that sticks in my mind. Koko spends ten months out of the year on the road. She and her husband and her four-piece band, the Blues Machine, travel throughout North America in an '83 Dodge van ("We all comfortable in there; there's just six of us"), eating at Denny's restaurants along the interstate ("That's my favourite place to eat") and, in the case of her November trip to Vancouver, driving on some of the most treacherous snow-covered roads she'd ever seen.

Sponsored by the Pacific Blues and Jazz Festival, Koko Taylor performed November 29 and 30, 1986, to packed houses at the Town Pump. I spoke with Koko on Saturday afternoon while the band watched the football fame. We began with a favourite topic—her family.

KT: I've got one daughter and two grandkids. My little granddaughter is twelve and my little grandson is six years old. And he's just like I was when I was his age. He wants to be a musician. He's trying hard to play guitar. Right now he's trying to play drums. He's trying to sing. [Laughs.] Oh man. I remember when I was growing up, when I was his age, I would be just singing away, you know.

CK: You had the choir, didn't you, to help you get started?

I grew up singing gospel. Going to church. Just like he's doing. And every day when he come from school, he gets that guitar and goes to playing and trying to sing "Wang Dang Doodle." [Laughs again.] I remember I used to do the same thing every day. Me and my sisters and brothers, we would go to the field or wherever we were doing our daily chores, and we'd be just playing and singing the blues, and listening to the radio and stuff like that.

How old were you when you went to Chicago?

I was about eighteen.

Did you go there to be a singer?

No. I didn't have no idea I was going to be a singer. I have always loved singing and listening to other singers, and whatever music is going on, that's what I liked. I used to sit in with other people, you know, other local bands, and all of this was for my own enjoyment. It was something I enjoyed doing. No money involved or anything. And it was Willie Dixon that heard me and got me my first recording for Chess Records in Chicago.

Did you have any idea that "Wang Dang Doodle" would become such a big hit?

No, I sure didn't. Let's see, he wrote this tune for me, "I Got What It Takes," which is re-recorded now on Alligator Records, and I did "What Kind of Man Is This," a tune that I wrote, and "Honky Tonk." Those were my first recordings and didn't nothing really happen. It was just a recording, you know. Then after that I did "Wang Dang Doodle" and it went to the top.

That must have been kind of a shock.

It was a shock. It was a surprise, and it was really unique. I couldn't believe—I had to pinch myself. Is this really me? I just couldn't believe it, but when that happened that's when I formed my own band, the Blues Machine, and I've been going strong ever since. It's been good times, bad times, rough times, and even now it's still rough times, but ... you know.

Well, how do you feel about that? On one hand, they tell you you're the greatest blues singer in the world; on the other hand ...

It's no flower bed of roses just because they say I'm the greatest. They didn't give me a million dollars when they told me I was the greatest. [Laughs.] It didn't increase my salary none. I'm not getting rich out here. I'm a long way from that. And, it's hard work travelling up and down the highway, travelling for miles and miles.

One thing you've been able to do that a lot of women never get the chance to do is produce your own records.

Yeah, I help out with that a lot. With ideas, with selecting tunes, help arranging, getting the music and stuff together. That's also a hard job. But I've been managing pretty good.

When you put together the Blues Machine, what were you looking for in a musician?

I was definitely looking for a special kind of musician. Someone that loved music, loved blues, as well as I did. Now if I meet a musician and he say, "Now I can play your stuff but I really don't like blues, but I can play it, I'm really into jazz," then that's not my musician. That ain't my man at all. Because I figure he's got to be into the same thing and want to do what he's doing to put his best foot forward. He's got to support me. Support the blues.

Have you always had a lot of say in your own career?

No. When I was with Chess I didn't have no say at all. All I did was just perform. Just sing. And it was always somebody else that did the arranging and took care of what had to be done.

Was that a problem then?

It wasn't a problem, but I do find that now that I have a little say-so into my own music, I can get into it more. I'm more comfortable with the tunes that I'm doing because these are tunes that I selected. It makes it more comfortable. Easier.

Are you still writing?

Not a whole lot. I am doing writing but I don't have a lot of time to devote just on writing because I spend most of my time concentrating on what I'm going to do in clubs or in concerts.

When you sing songs like "I'm a Woman" or "You Can Have My Husband, but Please Don't Mess with My Man," do you find you get a strong reaction from the females in the audience? "I'm a Woman" is a great song.

I feel that way. And that's one of the reasons I feel proud of myself that I'm able to do this because it's like I'm saying something or doing something for other women that maybe they don't have the nerve to say. [Laughs.] It's like I expressed something or said something to their man. "I couldn't say that, but she said it for me."

Do you still like being on the road as much as you are?

Yeah. I enjoy being out here. I gets tired but I do enjoy it. Matter of fact, if I didn't like what I was doing I wouldn't be out here at all because like I said before, I'm not getting rich, and it's not something easy. But it is something enjoyable. I enjoy it. That's the one thing that keep me out here. I'm doing what I enjoy doing.

Has there been any particular time that was more difficult than any other?

There has. Like I said, it's been rough times. There's been times that—uh—it was difficult. Like trying to get airplay and stuff. It's kind of difficult right now with me. It's kind of annoying, too, that blues entertainers, we always the last ones on the list. We get less recognition, less airplay, less money, less everything. And yet we work just as hard and put just as much into it as a rock singer or any of those people.

What do you do when you have time off?

Well, when I'm off and I'm home, I'm right back to housewife, grandmother, daily chores. After being on the road so much and so long, when I'm home I spend most of my time trying to get things caught up—like laundry. Really, I've got a pile of clothes here right now that needs to go to a laundromat. But I don't have the time to get into that now.

When you're home, whose music do you listen to?

I don't have time to listen to nobody now.

RIP: June 3, 2009

ETTA JAMES

Surviving with Soul

Kinesis, "Women in Music" issue, July/August 1985

When Etta James walked out onstage at the Town Pump this past May, the woman standing in front of me started to cry. And when Etta began singing "Tell Mama," shedding tears was the only proper response; that, and an overwhelming need to scream and applaud. It was an evening suspended in time, when images of other female singers influenced by this great woman flashed through my mind, Janis Joplin being her most obvious protege. By the end of Etta's first performance, there wasn't an inactive body in the house. Everyone was on their feet stomping and clapping and returning her peace sign. I felt much the same way when I watched her on television last summer at the opening ceremonies of the 1984 Olympics when she sang "When the Saints Go Marching In" backed by a full gospel choir.

Etta left home in the early '50s to join the Johnny Otis Revue. She was fourteen years old. The sum total of her previous singing experience consisted of membership in a three-part harmony group called the Creolettes. Their only venue had been the street corners of Los Angeles. But their original song, "Roll with Me Henry," an answer song to a popular ballad of the time, became Etta's first hit record. She was fifteen when the song was recorded, and not much older when she won the audience at New York's Apollo Theater.

In time, she would be named as a major influence on Janis Joplin, Christine McVie, Koko Taylor, the Rolling Stones and Rod Stewart. She would also record thirty-three albums, earning the title Queen of Rhythm and Blues. I was the emcee and photographer the night Etta performed at the Town Pump. I talked with her at length in the days leading up to her concert.

CK: Do you have a sense of yourself as a living legend, as living history?

EJ: Everybody else does. Yeah, yeah, you're a living legend. I think the more they're saying it, the more I start looking around and going, "Oh, am I." To me I don't seem like it. I'm just an everyday average singer hanging by my fingernails.

What do your kids think of you? Do they realize that you have a very specific place in music history and that you are important?

1985, Vancouver: Responding to the crowd and to my camera, Etta James rocked and rolled the Town Pump. With a four-piece band behind her, no one stopped moving.

You know, I really don't know. I don't think so. I think they don't look at me like that. A reason is because you don't see on television, when they show the history of rock and roll, when they show the history of this and that, or the evolution of music, you very seldom see Etta James's name. I think my kids at one point are a little disappointed, and maybe not at me. You know what I'm saying. A little disappointed.

And as they get older—my one boy is seventeen and he definitely knows, and one is nine; both of them are musically inclined—they have the attitude, well, they don't say it, but you can see it on their faces: Well, Mom, don't worry if you didn't get a lot of awards or if you're not walking on the stage for Grammys or if they never mention your name. One of us will go get something. Do you know what I mean?

I don't have any hard feelings. I *have* feelings. I have little sad ones, you know. Sometimes when I see things and my name's not mentioned, but I have to look at that, too, that there may be a reason.

Well, historians generally tend to be men, and they generally tend to be white, and they seem to just write women out of history. They write a lot of white women out, but they particularly write a lot of black women out.

Well, like you said, they write women out, period. Right? And I try to get away from that. I know there was a girl that wrote an article, it was one of the best articles I'd ever seen on me. It was called "If ... Etta James." It was so bad. If Etta James was younger. If Etta James was thinner. Suppose Etta James was white. You know what I mean. I try not to have that in me even though I know that Janis Joplin came along and in two years she was a superstar and she was doing the same thing that I had been doing for twenty years at that time. But she liked me. And she admitted that she always thought she was a third-class Etta James. That's what she said to me, and to some other people.

But I don't know what to say because how many of these other chicks aren't written out? They don't write Aretha Franklin out. They don't write Gladys Knight out. I could go on and on. I can't think right now. Then there are people like Tina Turner who didn't get mentioned too much at one point, but Tina Turner didn't have as many records as I had, so there are mixed feelings there, you know.

I had heard a story once about how Janis Joplin used to come to wherever you were singing and stand off to the side of the stage and sing along with you.

When she was a little girl ... in Tulsa, Oklahoma, there used to be a bar room called the Big Ten Ballroom. And at that time, the black people and white people couldn't go to the same dance together. The place belonged to a white man. I don't know whether Janis was related to him or what, but she was on that land.

We would get there around four or five o'clock in the afternoon and when we would get all our equipment in, we would rehearse. There were two doors that led to the back of the place, and I'd always sit in the doorway and open the door because it was so hot. And it led right out into the back and on into the club and into the dressing room. And this little white girl used to come, and then I would say she must have been twelve or thirteen years old, and she would come and sit in the dressing room and would talk. I always just thought she was somebody's little daughter or something.

We'd go there two or three times a year, and every time we'd play there, she would be there, hanging out in the dressing room. She was the only little white girl around. But she was so young she was beyond the point where the guys were hitting on her, so they never had to worry about that part.

Now, how I found out she was Janis Joplin was, in 1969 or '70, I went into a studio to record. I went into a studio where Sly Stone was cutting records and we were doing some joint stuff. I was going to rehearse and I had a closed session. I had put a sign on the door and all of a sudden when I looked up, there was this little lady sitting over in the corner looking like a hippie, right, with shaggy hair and all the little velvet and the little hippie-looking stuff. And she had a little bottle of whisky in her hand.

I walked over to one of the guys in the band and I said, "This is a closed session." He said, "Oh, the sign is on the door," and I said, "Well, what is she doing in here?" He said, "Sh-h-h-h Etta, don't you know who that is?" And I said, "No, I don't. What does that have to do with it?" I thought he was going to say, "Well, that's the owner of the studio's daughter." And I said, "No, I don't know who she is." And he said, "That's Janis Joplin." I said, "Janis Joplin, well, who is Janis Joplin?"

See, I didn't start listening to white rock or blues or any of that until I went away to rehabilitation. That's how I listened to it because I was in a basically white program, and all the kids were younger than me and they were the ones who would come in and say, "Etta, did you write this song, 'I'd Rather Go Blind'?" or "Janis Joplin sings like you." And that's how I started because they had record players and rich families. They would bring them all the latest records and they would play them and that's how I know the Bob Dylans, and the Stones, and Rod Stewart, and ZZ Top. That's how I learned about them. I never listened to any of that.

I was a real R&B fan. So when the drummer said to me, "That's Janis Joplin," and I said, "Who is she?" She's one of the biggest rock singers there is. I had an all-white band then, and they were all excited and all. She saw him talking to me and she knew I was jamming him about her. So she walked up and she said, "I'm sorry. I didn't mean to send anybody through any changes. Hi, I'm Janis Joplin." And I said, "Yeah." And she said, "I just love you. You don't remember me. I'm the same little girl that used to come and see you in Tulsa." And then it brought it all back to me. Then I remembered I didn't get to see her anymore after that. Maybe one time. But then shortly after that ... you know ... what year did she die?

Nineteen seventy. Did you feel any sort of kinship with her even though ...

Yes, I did. Well, the thing was, I knew that if she was hanging in there that she really liked my singing. It was so weird, like that's that same little girl that was in Tulsa, you know. And here she is Janis Joplin and these guys are all excited over her. She was the queen of rock and roll. Truthfully, I think my really closest thing with her was after she's gone, you know. That's usually the story, isn't it? They're more valuable to you or they mean more to you after they're dead. I'm saying now that I wish I would have been able to be around her, to be able to really talk with her. You know what I mean?

How do you feel about R&B and rock and roll revivals? I'm asking because I don't understand the concept of reviving something that is still alive.

Yeah, that is something. Well, you know, now I don't do those. But if somebody tricks me in some kind of way and books a gig on me and gives me my money, I'll go and work as anything. Revivals, too, if the money is right. But basically, I don't like to work anything they call "Oldies but Goodies," or "The Reincarnation of ..." I don't like that because I've been here all the time. I never left. I've been singing just as hard. I never went into retirement like all those lies that are in the magazines that I quit show business for a while. I never left.

Didn't somebody once say you were dead?

Yeah, that too. Matter of fact, I heard the guy on the radio say it. The late great Etta James. Called me the late great Etta James. I thought, Well this fool.

It seems to me that performers, especially white women like Cyndi Lauper and Madonna, get away with more these days, and Prince gets away with a lot.

Don't they. Oh, they get away with so much. When I came out, my record got banned from the air in 1955 because I said "roll with me Henry." But you know, Cyndi Lauper and Madonna, well, I don't know about Madonna, but I hear that Cyndi Lauper is a very smart, very intelligent chick, and all this is a premeditated, calculated act of hers, you know. And this chick is investing her money. She's not a drug addict. You know what I mean. She's really smart. They say so. She's just a clown. A little clown. I like her. I like, ah, well don't get me wrong. I don't like her singing.

I like Madonna, I think she's cute. But I went over to Universal studios in the music department and they were telling me about Cyndi and Madonna, and they said that those voices that they use, that's a prepared voice. In other words, that's a special voice they conjure up in their throat. It's like you have a nasal [imitates Cyndi] "Girls just want to have fun, whoa oh."

You mean it's not from the gut.

No, it's not. Well, it wasn't meant to be. I just look at them and they're young people and they're just fishing around and trying to find new bags.

Prince, he's the same way. He had a good *Purple Rain*, was swinging and all that, and the movie, and now he comes out with an album that's just like rotten buttermilk. Know what I mean? It's like he's run out of things to sing about.

That's the one thing that never bothered me even with disco and all the rest, and I didn't have a hit record, but I always knew that the music that I sing is real, you know. And it's from the gut and it's from the feelings and soul and everybody has feelings and everybody has soul. And if you're singing that way, you're going to reach somebody and they're going to feel it. It's just like you're sitting and listening to somebody sing and you get chills, you know, down your arm. That's what that is. That feeling ... oh, you know.

Willie Nelson, he gives me the little chills because he sings just so. His pipes are not that beautiful. His chops are not that great, but it's just the way he says his words. Like Ray Charles, you know. He's not the greatest singer in the world, but it's the way he sings the songs.

You said once, "If you give up today, tomorrow's when it's going to happen." I think about that a lot.

I just have a faith that's down in me. You just don't give up. You've got to hang in there by your nails, by your cuticles, because that's the way it goes.

You know, I heard Henry Fonda say one time that he had never gotten any Academy Awards [until his final film in 1981]. You figure a man as great as him, and they said, "What do you have to say, Henry?" and he got tears in his eyes—this might have been for *On Golden Pond*, I'm not sure—and they said, "What can you say to the people? This is your first award, after all these years of putting your life on the line, working these movies, going downhill, wanting to kill yourself, wanting to live again, got kids to raise, going crazy, wanting a life." He said the one thing I'd like to say is, "It's not how good you are; it's how long you can hang in there." And I just always remembered that. Hanging in. And he's right.

I got a thing that history repeats itself, and if you can keep yourself healthy, if you can go through all those changes that you go through in your life, and keep living, and keep holding on, things will come back around, and when it comes back around, you'll be more ready and more able to handle whatever comes your way.

So I have a feeling that things are going to come back around for me. Like you said, I'm a legend, I guess. And they are going to have to come and get me as long as I'm alive to document something. They're going to have to come to me to ask me something. So as long as I can—I got off drugs. I came through alcohol. I came through all that trip, and now I know what I want to do. I don't know everything about what I want, but I know what I don't want. And that's really important. I just know that it's going to happen for me.

What stands out in your life as your greatest achievement—besides surviving?

I guess the Olympics. To me that will always be a great thing. Imagine, *me* out of all my career, just standing there before that many people, in my hometown, singing for the world Olympiad. That's going down in the history books if this town shakes and goes to the ground. So that takes the place of all the Grammys, and the American Music Awards, and all the other little things that I might sit and feel sorry for myself about, sometimes. The Olympics, and I did a thing in December called "Beyond War," which means as much to me.

It's a documentary and it will be shown this summer on NBC. In December I represented the United States and I sang to Russia by satellite from San Francisco. Shanna Vaninski, who is a Russian folksinger, sang to me. I wrote a song called "Beyond War." Matter of fact, the song was called "We Are One" at first, and then I decided to change it. Now this is before the USA for Africa.

We were trying to get peace. We gave the Beyond War Nobel Prize to the Russian surgeon general and the American surgeon general. So while other people were doing other things, we were really busy doing that. It was so great for me to be able to write a song called "Beyond War, We Are One World" and sing to the Russians. Those people—you know, we were looking at them by satellite and they were looking at us. I had the San Francisco Boys Choir singing behind me. That was so fabulous. I just can't even explain.

I was with the Olympics and that was a world thing, and now "Beyond War." That's really the kind of thing I would like to be remembered for, you know, besides my regular worldly kind of rhythm and blues singing.

I'd like to be a singer that would go all over the world and sing for a reason. What I mean—I sing for a reason now. It helps people, brings them out of depression. Or I relate to them on their depression. But I just want to do something a little more meaningful in the way of—I don't know, maybe I've got a save-the-world complex or something.

Tell me about your idea to form an International Rhythm and Blues Association.

The big thing is forming an organization that will prevent things that have happened in the past. I want to promote entertainment awareness, preserving certain music, giving the people their roses while they are alive. Helping. Having. We want hospitalization, a burial plan and things like that for people. It's just like when Little Esther [Phillips] died, she didn't have any hospitalization, didn't have a burial plan. They buried her in somebody else's grave. We just now got a headstone for her the other day.

There are a lot of things we want to do. We want to have festivals; we want to figure out some kind of schooling. We want to get some kind of stuff going with UCLA for a foundation that will give scholarships. We want to be a hotline. You got clubs that bring entertainers into town and end up closing their clubs and the entertainer is stranded. They have no way. Maybe we can stop some things. Maybe we can teach some people how to read a contract. Maybe we can help them in whichever way we can, but we don't have a Rhythm and Blues Association and I think we need one.

It's a shame. Even after the man got the headstone the other night, he comes to me and tells me, "Oh, now we need a grave that Esther was in, that's not her grave." And I said, "Well what are you talking about now?" Well, they want to take her out to some big-time cemetery, you know, Forest Lawn or one of those. And I said, "Look, Esther wasn't no Forest Lawn girl."

You know, that's what we need. We need some entertainers that are involved directly in this business, who love this business and who will look out and run the business, coming from the entertainers' part, not coming from the system. We know what we need best. We can understand best. It's like you. You understand. You ask the questions that need to be answered.

We want to get something going to preserve that music. What's happening to our music? What's going on around here, really? What's happening to our music? It is like you said, is it going to be a revival? Have we got to call this stuff dead and raise it from the dead? No. No. No. It's supposed to be here. It's an art form. So we just want some kind of—I do, I want something, and I know that nobody can start any more mess than me. I don't mean mess. You know what I'm trying to say. I'm a big mouth, and I'm a feminist, and I just think we need this association. And we need some chicks. You know women will get out and hustle something. You better get women behind it.

We're going to draft every chick I know all over the country. We're going to send them letters. They're going to be sitting on the board of advisory. They will make themselves available for this, for one reason or the other. There are chicks all over who want to be involved, that will help. Let the women do it. Let us show somebody. Mostly we got women. We can do it, and boy, will that make the guys mad. When the hens get together, boy, they don't want to mess with one of those hen parties.

For people who have hung in there so long, give them their awards. Give them something. Give them some show of appreciation. Here's Richard Berry. You know, Richard Berry who made "Louie Louie" one of the greatest songs that has ever been recorded. The most often recorded song in the world. Here he is living in this little house on Fifty-Fourth Street. Can hardly walk. I want to hurry up and get this thing together just to call him in and have a big show and give him an award. Him and a few more people that I know that deserve them. Don't wait until they die to give them their roses.

Richard wrote many songs. The thing is, now the people will find that out because the twenty-seven-year period of all the songs that people wrote, that we wrote and sold as youngsters that didn't know any better, and gave away for twenty-five dollars or something, now they're coming back. All the publishing rights are coming back.

They never thought we'd live this long. Most of the entertainers are dead. The ones who wrote songs twenty-seven years ago are dead or drunk or something. Now the ones that are living, all of the songs that we wrote are going to revert back to us and then we have the right to assign them like we want, and then we get paid retroactive. Isn't that great?

So that's the kind of stuff that I'm talking about. Richard Berry wrote many hit records for many people. He just was very poor and needed every little dime he could get. So he'd go over and write a song for somebody and say, "Give me fifty dollars, and goodbye." That's the way it went. It wasn't that we were ignorant.

I think to our kids sometimes they think we were ignorant black folk, you know. And that's the point that I would like to make to my kids. That I wasn't ignorant black folk. I was just young, and anxious, and I didn't finish school. I didn't know how to handle my business. And these are the things I'm thinking about. This Rhythm and Blues Association will be able to help young people, also. Entertainment awareness coming straight from the pros. You know what I mean. So, I think that's the deal, schlemiel.

RIP: January 20, 2012

PATSY LIVES

An Interview with k.d. lang

Rubymusic column, *Kinesis*, December 1984/January 1985

Radio Waves, Vancouver Co-operative Radio program guide and magazine,

January 1985

If you've ever been to a hootenanny or spent time dancing to the music of Wanda Jackson, Lorrie Collins and Patsy Cline, you may have some idea what it's like to be in the presence of the phenomenon that is k.d. lang. She brought her truly western experience to Vancouver in October, and between the Savoy and the Railway Club, k.d. and her band, the reclines, mesmerized hundreds of people who waited in long lines to see her.

k.d.'s music is in keeping with the aforementioned queens. She shakes all over in the style of Wanda, hoots and hollers like a teenaged Lorrie and croons with the wisdom of the great Patsy Cline. All this and more in the body of a twenty-three-year-old native of Consort, Alberta.

"It's a beautiful little hamlet. (Pop. 650.) The school is right across from my front yard. There's a big water tower that says Consort, Alberta. And the main street is paved. You know when we got it? It was 1967. Expo. That's why we paved the roads. Expo was only halfway across Canada. Somebody might have dropped in."

k.d. is the youngest of four children born to a teacher and a pharmacist. All of the children studied classical piano. k.d. also wrote songs.

"You know what? About 1972, when I was in love with Anne Murray, let's see, I would have been eleven years old, I wrote some lyrics on foolscap paper. You know those long pieces of paper ... with purple felt pen. And it was a real nice little political song about love and let's get together and let's make this work, and at the bottom I put, 'PS: You have my permission to use these lyrics.'"

Anne never wrote back, but k.d. went on to become a "model student" and athlete of the year "many years in a row." Then came the night of the big fire.

"In Consort, somebody had arsoned the curling rink and skating rink, which was a huge scandal. To replace it we held a hundred-dollar-plate supper, and Judy LaMarsh stayed at our house. That was one of my life's highlights. I think she blessed me with celebrity-ism."

k.d. left Consort when she was seventeen to study music at Red Deer College. "Actually, it was a performance business course. And I studied the music business and contemporary performing. It wasn't a very good course. I learned more from my fellow students than anything. I did study classical voice there." But it was her musical theatre experience in Edmonton that introduced her to the music of the woman who would become her primary inspiration.

"There was this country music musical about this woman who wanted to become a country western singer. And I played her dream, which was a country music star. The playwright, Ray Storey from Toronto, said, 'Stand there like Patsy Cline,' and I went, 'Oh, Patsy Cline.' My siblings had been telling me about Patsy Cline, so I continued from there. And after hearing her music, I got some original albums and it just hit me. I mean Patsy and I are ..."

k.d. will tell you that Patsy Cline lives inside her body. The name of her band confirms this fact. (What would Patsy Cline be if she were reincarnated? A recline.) But contrary to previous press, k.d. was *not* born on the day Patsy died, and her love for Patsy's music is anything but frivolous.

"I totally understand her music. I totally understand her soul as she sang. I can't explain what it does for me. Every time I hear her voice, it just melts me. And I know we're from the same something." As for country music in general, "the most important thing is the human emotion. And that's what country music is all about. No matter what the topic is, the main thing is you're hurting or you're not."

k.d. and the reclines have been together for less than a year but audience response on their first Canadian tour has been tremendous. The release of their album *A Truly Western Experience* didn't hurt any. But here is the hitch: k.d.'s voice could warm a room full of the most conservative souls. But those same souls have been known to be a bit taken aback when they first set eyes on her.

Visually, she's a mixture of punk, Grand Ole Opry and just plain flash. But her original appearance prompted someone in a Calgary bar to bet $200 on whether she was a woman or a man. Her ability to be completely unselfconscious makes an uptight person stick out like a sore thumb.

"The reason I do have such a contrasting style—well, it's not contrasting because it's coherent. I'm very honest and my music is full of integrity. I deliver it straight but my delivery is just a little bit off the wall because we are living in the '80s. I am a young woman in the '80s with the '80s attitude. The '80s appearance.

"I think the main reason I do what I do is to provide a ladder for everyone. The people who don't understand the concept of being bizarre can grab on to the first rung because I'm providing them with music that is delivered in its purest form. Now for people who are bizarre but who can't grasp the music, I give them the delivery and they understand it. Actually, that's just a smart way of saying that I don't know what the hell I do.

"I've always been pretty self-confident. My beliefs and my spirituality really help. I live a very straight, clean life, contrary to popular belief. And just knowing I have the support of Patsy, John Lennon, people up there, I have no qualms about doing anything really. I feel a little bit shy during the day when I'm not onstage. But onstage, there's nothing I probably wouldn't do."

k.d. lang and the reclines will be the featured performers at a benefit for Co-op Radio, January 12, 1985, at the Commodore Ballroom. My in-studio interview with k.d. lang, on which this story is based, will be broadcast January 11 on *Rubymusic*.

HEATHER BISHOP

SIDE ONE
Stereo
45 RPM

WRC3-5234
Merjoda Music
BMI

YOU DON'T OWN ME
3:25
(J. Madara/D. White)

FACE THE MUSIC

RISE UP

SONGS OF THE WOMEN'S MOVEMENT
Can't Find Its Feet

Kurated, March 12, 2021

One of the perks of being part of a historic social movement is when that history is being written, you get to have lots of big opinions. And I formed a few while watching the documentary film *Rise Up: Songs of the Women's Movement*. As the producer of *Rubymusic*, an early women's music radio show (1981–96), and a music journalist, I have been preoccupied with researching and writing about the history of women in music. If I wasn't backstage, or behind a mic, I was in the audience. It took me multiple viewings of *Rise Up* to realize this documentary wasn't made for me.

Co-produced by the talented team of Jim Brown and Donna Korones, the film was made to celebrate the hundredth anniversary of the Nineteenth Amendment to the US Constitution, which gave women the right to vote. Told by an impressive group of musicians and activists, *Rise Up* is an abbreviated overview of the modern women's movement structured around a playlist of nineteen songs.

Speeding through History

In one brief hour (fifty-two minutes, to be exact) we're taken from the suffragettes to the civil rights movement to the early women's liberation marches. The birth control pill is introduced, the National Organization for Women is formed and lesbians fight for recognition. Next up is the battle for the Equal Rights Amendment, Phyllis Schlafly's anti-feminist countermovement and Ronald Reagan. Holly Near comes out, and women-only festivals, coffee houses and bookstores emerge.

Historic struggles are explained quickly. There's talk of being at the feet of men, of wanting a seat at the table, how women's rights are civil rights, how the women's movement offered "a cauldron of training and possibilities" and how women came out after buying their first Holly Near album, which made me laugh. But I found myself saying, "It was so much bigger than this." Eventually, I became more generous in my assessment of the film when I understood that its target audience is people who weren't there, most likely because they weren't yet born.

Songs Influenced by—but Not of—the Women's Movement

Of the songs chosen, several were very significant when released into the pool of popular culture. But with one or two exceptions, I don't think of these songs as "songs *of* the women's movement." This is an important distinction, as the women's movement had started writing songs of its own.

"You Don't Own Me," recorded by Lesley Gore in 1963, was a big hit with teenage girls, for sure. Canadian musician Heather Bishop gave it a new twist when she sang it to her early feminist audiences. (It's now used in an Armani commercial.) Aretha Franklin's 1967 cover of Otis Redding's "Respect" deserves just that, as does anything Aretha ever touched. Loretta Lynn's song "The Pill" was originally banned on country radio when it was released in 1975. Janis Ian's "At Seventeen" came out that same year and reached into some lonely places. Gloria Gaynor gave us something to dance about in 1978 with "I Will Survive." Two years later Joan Jett sang "Bad Reputation" and Dolly Parton wrote "9 to 5."

Helen Reddy's "I Am Woman" Resonated

These songs certainly set the stage in their own genres. They were signals of what was coming and in some places had started to arrive. These songs were influenced by the *spirit* of the women's movement but were not from inside. That's a different documentary. However, one popular song did find women where they lived and crossed over big time onto the front lines. It was Helen Reddy's "I Am Woman" in 1972.

There is very early film of Bessie Smith and Sister Rosetta Tharpe, and some great video from the Michigan Womyn's Music Festival (Michfest) and the 1975 Women on Wheels tour. There is concert and video footage of Joan Jett, Gloria Gaynor, Tina Turner and Aretha, and music videos for "Girls Just Want to Have Fun" and "Sisters Are Doin' It for Themselves."

Gloria Steinem, Jane Fonda and Toni Van Pelt, the president of NOW (the National Organization for Women) at the time of the filming, provide some historical context, as do musicians Cyndi Lauper, Loretta Lynn, Janis Ian, Gloria Gaynor, Joan Jett and Melissa Etheridge. The women's music movement is represented by Margie Adam, Holly Near, Judith Casselberry and June Millington, among others. Ginny Berson, a co-founder of Olivia Records, and Lisa Vogel from the Michigan Womyn's Music Festival are also included.

Rich History Is Unheard

There is a lot of rich history here along with the women who lived it. Olivia Records was a trail-blazing all-women recording company. Michfest was a cultural hub for women (especially lesbians) for forty years.

June Millington and Ann Hackler founded the Institute for the Musical Arts, a twenty-five-acre campus dedicated to supporting women and girls in music and music-related business. But you don't get to hear about it. Unfortunately, for the most part, the questions asked of these women are limited to what they thought of this particular list of songs.

"You Don't Own Me" is referred to as a wake-up call. "At Seventeen" is called seditious; "9 to 5" is an anthem exposing workplace sexual harassment. "Girls Just Want to Have Fun" becomes "multi-racial, multi-generational, feminist fun," and Tina Turner's "What's Love Got to Do with It" is now an example of speaking truth to power, an early example of #MeToo. (Ironically, the songwriters intended the song for a male voice as its subject matter is sexual encounters without emotional attachments. I suspect because the song, recorded by Turner in 1984, became the title of the 1993 biopic on her life, it is used in *Rise Up* as an example of a woman standing up for herself by leaving an abusive relationship, which she famously did.)

About the Producers

Jim Brown is a prolific, Emmy Award–winning documentary filmmaker who specializes in music biographies and concerts. His work goes back to the remarkable 1982 documentary *The Weavers: Wasn't That a Time*. Donna Korones is a major player in women's music. Her client list has included Linda Tillery, Margie Adam, Holly Near and the late Ronnie Gilbert, whom she married in 2004. Previously, Korones, Brown and Heather Smith (who also worked on *Rise Up*) produced the documentary *Holly Near: Singing for Our Lives*.

The Greater Story Remains to Be Told

I watched *Rise Up: Songs of the Women's Movement* as part of a fundraising drive for PBS, which may have added to my frustrations. (I got so tired of hearing the word *empowering*.) But here's what I think. Someone was in a hurry. It's as if they pulled together whatever they could find and went with it. Despite the title, *Rise Up* can't find its feet. This is too bad as there is a greater story waiting to be told and so many songs of the women's movement still waiting to be heard. By everyone.

A WOMAN'S PLACE IS ON THE RADIO

TEN YEARS OF RUBYMUSIC

Live! From Canada, *Hot Wire*, September 1991

There are fifty-five steps from the ground floor of the old bank building to the top floor of Vancouver Co-operative Radio. The memory of that tortuous marble staircase binds souls together around the world. Once you have been to Co-op Radio, you never forget.

The diagonal slab of concrete in front of the station is also part of the legend. Known officially as Pigeon Park, this small area once served as a resting place for seniors and the tired traveller. Now, it's the gathering place for drug dealers and those attracted to the life. Because of this I welcome winter. It is easier to move past a handful of covered heads, too cold to say a crude word, than it is to handle the summer crowds. I've had many anxious moments standing in front of the door waiting for the night operator to buzz me up.

In my youth, it was nothing for me to make my way through the broken bottles, blood and urine to the bright yellow door of the station. But as the elderly were pushed out and a more desperate type took their place, my safety became an issue, especially during my two pregnancies when my vulnerability was obvious. In short, during my ten years of bringing women's music to the airwaves, I have been verbally abused, physically assaulted, generally harassed and urinated on. Twice. Now I find myself strangely relieved when I come around the corner and find a paddy wagon, an ambulance or the Salvation Army band. Their presence guarantees my uneventful entry.

"You're listening to Vancouver Co-operative Radio, CFRO, 102.7 FM, and on a variety of cable frequencies throughout British Columbia and northwestern Washington. Good evening. I'm Connie Kuhns, and this is Rubymusic."

It is a privilege to do this program.

On May 15, 1991, I celebrated my ten-year anniversary as producer and host of the longest-running women's music program in Canada. In ten years, my own life has changed and changed again, but my Friday nights have remained the same. For two hours, beginning at seven thirty, regardless of what has happened in my life or in the world, I am alone in the studio. I am alone with the potter over on Saturna Island, the two

CO-OP RADIO · 102.7 FM
PROGRAMME GUIDE · AUG. 1981

Rubymusic: A Half Hour of Music by Women Artists

Interview with host Connie Smith

RUBYMUSIC WENT ON THE AIR ON CFRO ON MAY 15. THE FOLLOWING IS AN INTERVIEW WITH CONNIE SMITH, RUBYMUSIC'S CREATOR AND HOST. PROMOTED AS 'ONE HALF HOUR OF MUSIC BY WOMEN ARTISTS', WE BEGAN THE INTERVIEW BY ASKING SMITH TO DEFINE WOMEN'S MUSIC.

SMITH: Women's music is anything and everything that a woman writes, plays, or sings.

CFRO: Then what is feminist music

SMITH: Feminist music is usually written with an analysis in mind. The songwriter has reached certain conclusions about her life and adheres to political or personal guidelines; guidelines set by her own consciousness or by a group. Often this music is generated by women owned and operated recording companies — Olivia for example. Most popular lesbian music falls into this category. But for the purposes of Rubymusic, I don't usually differentiate between the two. It's ALL Women's music as far as I'm concerned

CFRO: You did a show called Blue Notes. Isn't blues rather humiliating music for Women

SMITH: On the contrary. Blues and Jazz contain some of the most aggressive strong-willed lyrics to Date. Just listen to Billy Holliday's 'Baby get Lost', 'No More', 'Ain't nobodys business if I do', 'Now or Never'. These are all excellent examples of a woman asserting herself. It's true blues can hurt. But then so does asserting yourself sometimes. Blue Notes was a finely tuned show. I included Gwen Avery's 'Sugar Mama', Holly Near's 'Get off me Babe' and Joplin's 'Little Girl Blue' with the Holliday material. It was a very strong program; one of my favorites

CFRO: what do you think of country and western music as it pertains to women..

SMITH: Country and western music is also underrated. Its lyrics are unpretentious, honest, and completely to the point. Aida Pavletich (L.A. Free Press) once said, 'The themes may be trite, but they are the values that people kill for.' I don't agree that the themes are trite; but it's true that Country and Western songs cover the most basic details of a woman's life. As with Blues, the field is replete with women songwriters literally shouting out women's reality.

CFRO: Who do you think are the outstanding country songwriters

SMITH: Dolly Parton has written some excellent material and in some circles she is recognized as an accomplished songwriter — not as a woman of large proportions. Loretta Lynn (a another songwriter I respect. 'Don't come home a'drinkin (with lovin' on your mind)' is the only song of its type that I know of — not a trite theme at all. And 'One's on the way' Exemplifies perfectly a country woman's ambivalence towards a big city womens movement she can't understand. Complimenting this material is the Feminist genre of Country and Western. Willie Tyson, Woody Simmons and Terri Garthwaite for example. Then there is the new breed: Carlene Carter with her new wave album cover, Juice Newton and Tanya Tucker. Tanya brings a sexuality to the stage not previously seen in country music.

CFRO: Why do you think country and Western wasn't acceptable at one time..

SMITH: It wasn't sophisticated enough; too working class perhaps. There was prejudice towards the country accent as well as an unwillingness to listen to some basic truths. Country and Western women inundated their music with songs of Divorce, Abortion, Adultry, Alcoholism, Passion, Revenge. They said what most people were embarrassed or afraid to say, which doesn't exactly make someone popular.

CFRO: Has anything been overlooked as far as pop music is concerned..

SMITH: Absolutely. 1964 produced one of the most feminist songs in popular music, Leslie Gore's 'You don't own me.'

Vancouver Co-operative Radio
337 Carrall Street
Vancouver, B.C.
V6B 2J4

women with the baby up in Whiskey Creek, the teacher and her husband in North Vancouver, the Americans down in Port Townsend and a young woman named Chip.

My desire for a program that would discover, promote and analyze music by women was completely inspired by the musicians who burst out of the women's movement in the early 1970s and gave women's music a name. I sat in the front row at the LA Women's Building when Teresa Trull made her first performance for Olivia Records. I attended the California NOW (National Organization for Women) convention in 1975 where Cris Williamson and Margie Adam stopped their concert so that we could recognize and support the women from the California Institution for Women who were being returned to their cells. I was transformed under that full moon at Michigan in 1978 when Sweet Honey cried out, "Every woman who ever loved a woman, mother, daughter, sister, lover, stand up and call out her name." The music of Mary Watkins and Linda Tillery was on my turntable constantly. I played *The Changer and the Changed* until it was alive in my head.

I have been a convert, a foot soldier and hopefully a pioneer. For a couple of years, I was a singer and songwriter. In 1981, I wanted a radio program. Aubrey Dayman, a local artist and broadcaster, spent many hours teaching me to operate the board. I was completely ignorant of anything technical and had a lot to overcome. To Co-op Radio's credit, I was given the chance and have received their unwavering support ever since. In the beginning, however, *Rubymusic* was only a thirty-minute program. There was some doubt as to whether there was enough music by women to fill the hour I had requested. In my secret thoughts, I wasn't sure myself.

As a radical feminist, circa 1974, I had rejected everything and everyone who had gone before me. My standards of political purity were quite unforgiving. Now, as a radio broadcaster and historian, I searched for any trace of a woman's presence. For the first time, I realized how music by women had completely shaped my life.

During my first month on the air—May 1981—the term *women's music* grew to include anything a woman did. I produced a show on Olivia Records, a program featuring the music of Marilyn Monroe, Dinah Shore and Hayley Mills, a dance show with my favourite women from the clubs, and the first of many programs on "girl group" music.

By the second month, I was reeling with excitement over the release

Opposite: Vancouver Co-operative Radio proudly announced on the front page of their August 1981 program guide that *Rubymusic* was on the air. In a wide-ranging interview on women's music history (included in Bonus Tracks), and with an illustration by artist Marcia, it all began.

of an album by Louise Goffin. Louise had spent her baby years in a play-pen outside her mother's songwriting cubicle in the Brill Building in New York City. Now, a mother-daughter program with Louise and Carole King was on the schedule. Slowly, and completely without guidance, I began to dig away.

My first great find was the book *Rock-a-Bye, Baby* by Aida Pavletich. (It's also published under the same *Sirens of Song: The Popular Female Vocalist in America*.) Used book stores and old record bins provided other clues: an old *Guitar Player* magazine with a couple of women inside, a signed copy of Fanny's album *Mothers Pride*, Linda Tillery's album with the Loading Zone and a book about the female singers who accompanied Bob Hope to Vietnam.

My mother, who was cleaning offices at the time, saved boxes of demo 45s for me that she found in the basement trash of her local radio station. The labels included Chess, Cadet, Duke, Gordy, Tamla, Ohio, Spur, Newtown and Sun. Most of the artists were women. With an open mind and some critical research—substantiated in later years by talking to the musicians themselves—I learned what I had never been taught. Women had always written, recorded, produced and sung their own songs. It wasn't a question of why not, but rather why wasn't I told.

I began searching for the connections and the moments of valour. Offhand, I think of a young Janis Joplin standing outside the back door of a Texas club listening to Etta James rehearse, and how Etta joked years later (to me) that someone had accused her of trying to imitate Janis Joplin. I remember countless stories from the women in the girl group era: Martha Reeves refusing to follow orders at Motown, Darlene Love remaining outside the grasp of Phil Spector, the Chantels launching a new era in music in 1958 with the lead voice of fifteen-year-old Arlene Smith.

I also think of Helen Reddy fighting to have "I Am Woman" released—a song that sold twenty-five thousand copies a week to mainly women—and Loretta Lynn's bold move by recording "The Pill." I will always mourn the death of Tammi Terrell (who some historians say died of head injuries allegedly inflicted on her by her lover James Brown, although in the end, it was a brain tumour), and Karen Carpenter's long goodbye. But I get strength from imagining the International Sweethearts of Rhythm driving to freedom in a stolen bus, and of the busloads of Freedom Singers in the '60s in the South.

Janis may have died, but she told me to be true to myself.

I also received some support and information from musicians in my community who welcomed the opportunity to come on the air and tell what they knew. Marian Lydbrooke, a founder of one of Canada's first female punk bands (the Moral Lepers) and a native of the UK, explained in detail why punk music was important and why feminists should care. In time, Heather Bishop became *Rubymusic*'s unofficial promoter.

The Vancouver Folk Music Festival was also an endless source of talent. Margret RoadKnight, Ronnie Gilbert, Judy Small, Betsy Rose, Ellen McIlwaine, Alix Dobkin, Holly Near, Teresa Trull, Cris Williamson, Nancy White, Jane Sapp, Leslie Ann Jones and Jill Davey are just some of the women I met through that organization. This folk festival is also the place where I met Karlene Faith. As a music historian she is unequalled. Not only did she become a regular guest on my program, sharing her knowledge and enthusiasm, but she introduced me to her friends, including June Millington, Mary Watkins, Anne Rose and Judy Werle. Her connections connected me, and *Rubymusic* became more worldly in the process.

It was just by luck that I was in the right place at the right time. The year *Rubymusic* went on the air was the year the Vancouver Folk Music Festival started producing American women's music artists on a grand scale. It was also the year that Canadian women finally started getting some long-overdue attention, and there was tremendous co-operation among women working in the alternative music scene. Gayle Scott asked me to write about Ferron for a national feminist magazine. Judy Werle introduced me to Etta James. Joan Miller recommended me to an editor in Winnipeg. Marcia Meyer asked me to photograph her album cover. A friend called me about a young country singer making her West Coast appearance, and k.d. lang joined me in the studio that week.

Simultaneously, my radio interviews turned into print, and Rubymusic became a monthly music column for more than five years. C.T. Sand, editor of the *Radical Reviewer*, was the originator of the idea, and after the *Reviewer* stopped publishing, we took the column to *Kinesis*, Canada's oldest feminist newspaper. Then, in what now seems like overnight, Toni Armstrong Jr. asked me to write for *Hot Wire*. Soon, I started writing about women for a Vancouver entertainment paper, and the Canada Council gave me a research grant to learn more about women's music in Canada.

Still, it is radio that gives me the charge. I was raised on radio: KCOW, KSID, KOMA. The station in Oklahoma City was no less than a secret force beaming out across the Great Plains and into the soul of this young girl in bed with her transistor radio. Unlike other media, radio is personal. The listener comes upon the signal and what transpires is nobody's business, especially after the sun goes down.

In the beginning, my main thoughts were for the women's community in Vancouver. I knew from personal experience how one song could change a life. And to this day, my words and thoughts are directed to the Great Feminine. But I wasn't on the air long before it became clear that my audience wasn't only feminists, and it wasn't only women. I think once I fully understood this fact, my work truly became consciousness-raising, and the challenge became a joy. I remember one night several years ago when I received calls from a draft resister, a woman who followed her boyfriend to Canada and a Vietnam vet after I had played a certain song and talked about my generation's war. The vet was crying. Supported by the beauty and power of women's music and the privacy of radio, a very important integration had taken place. I live for these moments.

Because I work alone, I work without censors, committees, collectives or consensus. I am completely trusted to adhere to broadcast standards and to do a good job. My listeners expect the same. This freedom of expression has enabled me to editorialize on the massacre of the women in Montreal, the missile silos surrounding my hometown in the Midwest, the value of children and the crisis in the Persian Gulf, as well as the current happenings involving women in the music business.

After ten years of producing documentaries, interviewing musicians and writing dozens of articles on women's music, I welcome the opportunity to blend it all together. Women do not live in a vacuum (even if it feels that way), and I hope my program reflects this philosophy. In the end, I just tell stories and hope that someone cares.

I must admit that with two small children at home, these days I hardly feel like a major player. After a day of changing diapers and handling preschool business, I find I'd rather eat a bag of potato chips and watch *LA Law* than listen to a new CD or read my creeping mass of untouched music journals. But then I get an uplifting phone message from writer Noelle Hanrahan, or someone asks me to emcee a benefit, or I hear an advance cassette of someone wonderful—and I am reminded of how strength is cumulative and something that we pass along. When Friday night comes, I am ready.

"You've been listening to Rubymusic *on Vancouver Co-operative Radio. 102.7 FM. I'm Connie Kuhns. Good night."*

A BRIEF HISTORY OF WOMEN'S MUSIC FESTIVALS IN CANADA

Live! From Canada, *Hot Wire*, May 1989

The original research for this essay, as well as for the essay "Women's Music and the Mothers of Invention," included in this book, was conducted in Vancouver, Nelson, BC, Calgary, Winnipeg, Saskatoon, Toronto, Ottawa, Montreal, San Francisco, Seattle and New York City, during 1986–90, thanks to a Canada Council Explorations Grant that allowed me to travel to interview the many women at the forefront of the feminist music movement. As this essay was written for an American feminist audience unfamiliar with Canadian history, there are some similarities between this essay and "Women's Music and the Mothers of Invention."

⊙

In August 1988, a group of women in Vancouver, British Columbia, produced a one-day women's music festival. Billed as Vancouver's First Women's Music Festival, the lineup was an impressive collection of local women, including a remarkable band of teenaged musicians, two early lesbian-feminist songwriters out of retirement and a large selection of jazz musicians with national reputations. As one of the emcees for the day, I can testify as to the calibre of the talent. The festival was the realization of a dream for Artistic Director Nadine Davenport, but the organizational aspect was certainly trial and error.

Four days before the festival, the organizers still needed coordinators and volunteers. There was no fencing, stages, sound systems or stage instruments—and already a deficit of $2,100. It is certainly a testament to the determination of the dozen women who came together and worked tirelessly over those last four days to pull this festival together. In the end, however, despite a turnout of roughly 550 women and men, the deficit had grown to $3,600 and not all of the performers were paid on schedule.

Although the festival was open to the public—and this was widely publicized—some women complained about the handful of men in the audience, and they objected to the male musicians who accompanied some of the jazz women. This included a woman of some renown who began her career singing and recording with Duke Ellington.

Contrast this with Women in View: A Festival of Performing Arts, held in the same city in January 1989. Concentrating on dance, storytelling, visual and literary art and related workshops, this seven-day festival featured very little music but presented a variety of other performances on subject matters that included motherhood, the environment, lesbianism, spirituality, feminism and the experience of immigrant women from Latin America. With a paid staff and crew, Women in View received generous grants from the government and private sources. Their purpose in producing the festival was "to increase public awareness of women in the arts." The festival was open to everyone, with special discounts for students, seniors and the unemployed, and was not subjected to the same type of criticism the 1988 festival had received.

There is no definitive model for a Canadian women's music or cultural festival. Our festival image is always in flux. What an event is to become is shaped solely by the perspective of the women involved, and there are many issues to be considered: Canada has two official languages and many distinct cultures. It is sparsely populated and women are separated by mountain ranges, expansive prairies, tundra and water. Unfortunately, we may also be separated by class, race, culture and language. In some areas, women are also divided by sexual orientation. Traditionally, it has also been easier to gain access to women's culture from the US than to our own because the border is just a car ride away. In Canada, some women must travel a thousand miles to attend an event in their own country.

The first Canadian women's festivals took place in the mid 1970s in a spectacular mountainous region in the southeast corner of British Columbia known as the Kootenays. The area is a mixture of Doukhobor people, the rural working class, urban exiles, American expatriates and an active women's community. Even the provincial tourist bureau describes the area as having "a reputation for seclusion. ... Several generations of settlers have found a safe haven here from the anxieties of religious persecution or social unrest."

The first festival, held in 1974 in Castlegar, BC, was organized by Marcia Braundy for the Kootenay Women's Council, an ad hoc group of Status of Women organizations in several small towns. The two-day festival featured local and regional musicians, workshops on witchery and crafts, a film festival, square dancing and an arts and crafts fair. It was open to both women and men. The second year, the festival was held in nearby Kaslo and lasted for four days. The first two days were for women and their invited guests, and the final days were for women only.

These were historic events. It was revolutionary for women to put themselves first and to celebrate and promote each other. It was entirely new, as in the second year, to designate women-only space. Likewise was a workshop on lesbianism led by the Lesbian Caucus of the British Columbia Federation of Women. The primary purpose was to bring all rural women together for the first time. As Rita MacNeil sang "Angry

1988, Nelson, BC: In the mountains, thirty miles from Nelson, the organizers of the West Kootenay Women's Festival, gather on the stone steps of the community centre for a photo. *From the top, left to right:* Lee Sims, Sally Mackenzie, Margo Farr, Valene Foster, Marcia Braundy, Brie Mitchell.

People in the Streets," so did the Doukhobor Women's Choir sing the music of their culture.

Womankind Productions of Vancouver, with the assistance of a volunteer group, hosted the next women's festival in October 1976. The First Western Canadian Women's Music Festival (and last) was held at a YWCA camp with cabins and catered food. It was for women only, and as with the other two festivals, attendance was less than two hundred women. But again, these were the first steps taken in that initial rush of feminist awareness that changed so many women's lives.

The West Kootenay Women's Festival (as it is now called) is still being held. Its permanent home is the Vallican Whole Community Centre, a beautiful log building in the mountains thirty miles from Nelson, BC. It's still a community celebration for about 150 women, with performers from the area, workshops, a potluck dinner, auction and dance. Occasionally women attend from Vancouver, Washington or Oregon, but it is primarily for women in the area.

Toronto took the spotlight in 1979 when A Muse Inc. organized a three-day festival at the University of Toronto, which included more than forty performers, primarily from Eastern Canada. But there would not be another festival of this magnitude until 1984, when the Canadian Women's Music and Cultural Festival was held in Winnipeg, Manitoba. In the meantime, two major folk festivals became the main producers of women's music in Canada.

Although both festivals were founded by Mitch Podolak, the artistic director for the Winnipeg Folk Festival is now Rosalie Goldstein, and co-founder Gary Cristall has overseen the Vancouver Folk Music Festival since 1980. With some philosophical differences as to what constitutes "folk music," both festivals offer an incredible opportunity to hear a wide variety of music from around the world, in an atmosphere of tolerance. "I think there are some important principles around which the festival operates. I mean, in addition to its concern about women," Rosalie Goldstein told me recently. "Its concern in general is about people who live in a society that's alienating. And the concern is to bring them together— the artists, the audience, the volunteers—and give them a quality of life experience which is something hopefully they take away with them and use as a model for their lives on a daily basis. Because I really think that is how the world changes."

The Vancouver Folk Music Festival is an example of this as well. At its peak, twenty thousand people gather for two days and three nights at an oceanside park in a beautiful area of the city. The counterculture attends, as well as seniors, politicians, teenagers, students, children, professionals and a large contingent from the feminist community. Lesbians are out of the closet. And over the years the music workshops have given women a place to gather.

The feminization of both festivals came about in part because of the large number of women who volunteer each year to work. Currently exactly half of the eight hundred volunteers at the Winnipeg festival are women, and in Vancouver women lead the pack. When women's music began to rise to prominence in the US, the artistic directors took note and, urged on by women working in the ranks—in particular, in Vancouver by Susan Knutson and Wendy Solloway—began to book the first wave of feminist and lesbian performers. In his first year as artistic director, Gary Cristall, who had already been working toward better representation, sent talent scouts to the Michigan Womyn's Music Festival. He called "someone who knew someone" who eventually got him in touch with Holly Near. And in 1980, the floodgates opened. Onstage in Vancouver, in front of ten thousand people, were Sweet Honey in the Rock, Cathy Winter and Betsy Rose, Ferron, Robin Flower, Nancy Vogl, Laurie Lewis, Barbara Higbie, and Holly Near and Adrienne Torf. "Feminist" appeared alongside "Gospel" and "Celtic" in festival publicity. The festival program printed articles about women's music and songs by Rosalie Sorrels, Ferron, Holly Near and Betsy Rose. There was a workshop called A Good Woman's Love. All of this happened in an environment that included traditional folk and blues music and performers from other parts of the world. In varied proportions, it has remained this way ever since.

The big breakthrough at the Winnipeg Folk Festival came in 1982 when Heather Bishop, Holly Near, Betsy Rose and Cathy Winter, Meg Christian and Diane Lindsay, Ginni Clemmens, Frankie Armstrong and Mimi Fariña all appeared in the Big Tent. Under founder and artistic director Mitch Podolak's tenure, Winnipeg also introduced a women's theme tent, which operated from 1984 to 1986. In 1984, nearly thirty women appeared on this stage, including Toshi Reagon, Judy Small, Anne Lederman, Teresa Trull and Barbara Higbie, Heather Bishop, Holly Near, Ronnie Gilbert, Patsy Montana and the Reel World String Band. In 1985 newcomers included k.d. lang, Margret RoadKnight, Four the Moment and Rory Block. The final year was a blowout with Ellen McIlwaine, Christine Lavin, Tracy Riley, Heather Bishop, Connie Kaldor and Sweet Honey in the Rock, among others.

Despite its popularity, when Rosalie Goldstein became artistic director after the festival in 1986, she disbanded the women's stage. "I did so with the most loving care," she told me, "because I believe it's important for women to be dispersed throughout the entire body of the festival. I would not put up a tent at the festival and say, 'Here are all the blacks,' or 'Here are all the Jews'—and that's exactly what was happening with women. I don't think that's fair. I don't think it shows off women to their best advantage. I don't think that it invites people who might under other circumstances come and see that programming. It doesn't make it easy for women, whatever their sexual orientation, to put their music across. And I want that to happen in a serious way. It's what I believe in." True to her word, the opening lineup for the 1989 Winnipeg Folk Festival will feature the thirteen-piece band Women Who Cook from Minneapolis; the Mahotella Queens, a female vocal choir from Soweto singing classic Zulu jive; the Roches; and Gordon Lightfoot.

So, it is here that women's music meets the music of the world on Canadian soil. In a non-combative atmosphere, women can state their case to a supportive, or at least open-minded, audience who might never have heard the music under other circumstances. But there were still issues to be resolved. The folk festivals programmed, naturally, folk music in all its indigenous forms. But women's music was not just folk music, so many Canadian women were being left out of this musical revolution.

In 1983, a group of Winnipeg women known as the Same Damn Bunch asked Joan Miller, Heather Bishop's manager and business partner, to organize a women's music festival. She accepted the offer, and by the time the Canadian Women's Music and Cultural Festival took place in Winnipeg, in September 1984, there was a festival office, a paid staff of five, a total budget of $90,000 and $70,000 in grants. It was a phenomenal experience for those who participated, especially the forty-two musicians who performed that year along with two theatre groups. It was the largest cross-section of Canadian women musicians ever assembled.

Despite the fact that a thousand people, predominantly women, attended every day throughout the weekend, there was public criticism. Similar to the criticism levelled at the 1988 Vancouver festival, women complained that there were men in the audience. Reviewer Didi Herman, writing in a national alternative magazine, suggested that the organizers couldn't exclude men from the audience because they were too dependent on funding. She said there was a "please-keep-it-in-the-closet feeling in the air, a rather unpleasant situation for women who had experienced or know of US women's festivals, which are known to be an integral part of lesbian culture" ("Winnipeg 1984: Our Time Is Now!," *Fuse*, February/March 1985).

But this was not an American festival. This was not a lesbian festival. Although certainly lesbian women were involved in the organization, the festival was intended to be for the entire community of Winnipeg. It was intended as a gathering of Canadian female talent. And the organizers were not prepared to tell any performer what to say or not say from the stage. To what degree a performer was "out" was up to her. Ironically, letters to the *Winnipeg Free Press* complained of "taxpayers' money being spent on hate propaganda" and of "women hugging and kissing in a family-based park." But the mainstream reviewers were excited about the event, and it also received a significant amount of favourable coverage in the feminist press.

In the end, the festival changed how Canadian women musicians viewed each other. Heather Bishop told me: "What it did for all of us women musicians was just short of a miracle. It put us all together in the same place. It changed people's lives. That's a victory." And for the women who sat screaming on their blankets into the night, it was a victory as well.

The following year the festival became a non-profit organization. The performers doubled and the attendance doubled, but the organizers were left with a $15,000 deficit. They decided to hold a smaller festival the third year. This time they moved indoors with seven acts. Since there was no advertising budget, attendance was down considerably. But for those who attended, it was an intimate, fun weekend. Although the decision to host another festival is still on hold, the organization is still in operation, producing events around the city. They are also involved in the Alliance for the Production of Women's Performing Arts, which will hold its second annual conference in Winnipeg this year.

In 1988, women's music took yet another turn in what journalist and musician Susan Sturman called "the most ambitious women's music event ever undertaken in the country and possibly in North America" ("Women Centre Stage: Festival international de musiciennes innovatrices," *Fuse*, July 1988). The five-day festival was produced by Les Productions Super Meme Inc., a production company formed by avant-garde musicians Diane Labrosse, Danielle Roger and Joane Hétu. Held in Montreal, the Festival international de musiciennes innovatrices featured experimental and innovative composers and musicians with origins in Iran, China, Japan and Jamaica, throughout Europe and in Canada from Winnipeg, Montreal and Toronto.

The organizers wrote in their program guide (of which twenty-five thousand were distributed free): "We believe these musicians have acquired enough identity to be appreciated outside of all-women events. That's the reason why the festival will only take place this year. The Festival International de Musiciennes Innovatrices wants to be a place of diffusion so that the Quebec public may become aware of these styles of music and ask for the presence of these musicians in the future." Consequently, feminist and lesbian sensibilities were expressed through music, along with other sentiments for everyone to hear. Susan Sturman noted that Third World, eastern European and black North American jazz musicians were not represented, nor were the musicians from Western Canada—facts that organizers acknowledged in their brochure.

In Canada, it is hard to compete with the major folk festivals. They are established events that are an integral part of Canadian culture. They have the budgets to produce any artist they want from any part of the world. Canada's one and only women's music distribution service went out of business in part because it could not compete with the Vancouver Folk Music Festival, which has the budget to distribute a variety of women's music. We have no equivalent to the Michigan Womyn's Music Festival or the National Women's Music Festival in the US. The only annual women-only festivals held in Canada are in the Kootenays and outside Kingston, Ontario, on private land. As mentioned, the Kootenay festival is community-based and the Kingston Womyn's Music Festival, now five years old (at the time of this writing), accommodates only three hundred women.

Although there are lesbian women who desire and work toward a lesbian-only festival environment, it remains to be seen if this will ever be a national movement. It has not happened yet. Consequently, many of the debates that take place in the US do not occur in Canada on a grand scale. In fact, a clear majority of feminist performers in Canada—heterosexual and lesbian—that I interviewed do not support the exclusion of boy children of any age from any event.

For lesbians who prefer a lesbian-only festival and can afford to go, the festivals in the US have traditionally filled this need. Through the work of Montrealer Anne Michaud, the Michigan festival has become user friendly for French-speaking Canadians, and California is generally the place to go for lesbians on the Canadian West Coast. With the exception of Sisterfire, the US festivals are generally perceived as off-limits to heterosexual women, whether this is true or not.

What we do have in Canada is an incredible opportunity for women's music to be fully integrated into the country's music scene and from there into the consciousness of Canadians. Although the same prejudices exist in Canada as in the US regarding women and minorities, in the last couple of years lesbian and politically oriented performers who began their careers with support from the left, immigrant and women's communities have been nominated for, and are winning, major music awards.

I'm not suggesting that the purpose of women's music is to win awards. But because women's music did not separate from the mainstream and instead held its own alongside every other Canadian independent, there is the opportunity for music not only to change women's lives, but to change how Canadian society feels about women. Our festival history reflects and encourages this development.

MEAN AND MARVELLOUS FOREMOTHERS

AN INTERVIEW WITH ROSETTA REITZ

Fuse magazine, Fall 1985

In 1980, an album appeared on the market titled *Mean Mothers: Independent Women's Blues, Volume 1*, an apparent contradiction for anyone who believed that blues—particularly women's blues—was only of the downtrodden variety. The music inspired many to look behind what they had been told; *Mean Mothers* became the record Alice Walker listened to while writing *The Color Purple*.

Since that time, Rosetta Reitz ("as in women's") has issued a total of twelve albums (seven compilations and five single artist collections) on her own independent New York–based label, Rosetta Records. She will be releasing four more albums shortly and has another twelve in the works.

This enormous collection of lost women's music, as well as Rosetta's extensive liner notes, represents an astounding contribution to the history of blues and jazz.

She has also salvaged dozens of film clips, which have been assembled into a program called *Shouters and Wailers*, and she has presented *Shouters* at such diverse venues as the Hollywood Bowl, the National Women's Music Festival and the Smithsonian Institution. She is currently working with Greta Schiller (*Before Stonewall*) and Jezebel Productions on a documentary about the legendary International Sweethearts of Rhythm.

But as she says, not without irony, "editors think that the important blues was by men, and that the women are not a broad enough subject," so the book she has written on jazz women has yet to be published.

Rosetta Reitz was in Vancouver this spring.

RR: I've always been a jazz buff. I was one in college. But it wasn't until the women's movement that I began to question. Well, where are the *women*? Why is this a male domain?

CK: You could have wondered all your life. Instead you went in search of the answer. What motivated you?

The women's movement made the crucial difference because women were looking at every discipline to find out where the women were. I don't like to give myself that much credit because this happened to be

Rosetta Reitz with the performers of the Blues Is a Woman Concert at the New-
port Jazz Festival at Avery Fisher Hall. (standing, l to r): Koko Taylor, Linda Hop-
kins, George Wein, Rosetta Reitz, Adelaide Hall, Little Brother Montgomery, Big
Mama Thornton, Beulah Bryant; (seated, l to r): Sharon Freeman, Sippie Wallace,
Nell Carter. Photo Barbara Weinberg Barefield, wikimedia.org/wiki/File:Blues_
is_a_woman_Reitz.jpg

a field that I was interested in. I just never identified in terms of doing
anything about it because it was so clearly a male establishment. Male
dominated. Male critics. Men always gave me jazz, so to speak. I always
had boyfriends who were jazz buffs. Women didn't own it. It's a very crazy thing about the history of this country in that sense.

I assume you started out to find out why women weren't in jazz.

Right.

**How did you feel when you realized that women had been in jazz all
along?**

I felt cheated. Why didn't I know that?

And then it was six years later that you founded Rosetta Records.

Well, I wouldn't put it that way. It just seemed a very natural thing. I was
especially interested in the blues women I discovered because of the way
they confronted their lives. They weren't interested in keeping the crazy kind of false morality going or any cultural cohesiveness. They were

honest women and they were singing about their honest feelings, and I love that. So whenever anybody would come to my house, I'd say, "Listen. You've got to listen to this woman. You've got to hear this. You won't believe this." And people would get very excited and say, "Why don't you put that on a tape for me. I'd love to hear that again." Or they'd come by and say, "Play those good songs you've got." So, it got to be that it wasn't such a big step on a certain level of my getting involved because I'd been telling people about it for some time.

Did you have any idea how to do such a thing?

No. That's what took me six years. No. I just started looking around and questioning and got myself acquainted with other independent record label people and started hanging out with them and going where they went, just trying to learn as much as I could.

I would think there would be an incredible amount of difficulty, at first, finding the material you needed.

Yes, there is. I buy 78s at auctions and there's a whole system of auctions through the mail. And I go to certain places where these things are for sale. So I just keep building up my collection and as soon as I have enough that would make an album to satisfy me, I issue it.

I have my idea about what I want to do. I want to retrieve material I consider to be of great value that has been lost, so to speak. For example, that Georgia White album [*Georgia White Sings and Plays the Blues*, Foremothers, volume 3], I think she was very important, and it's hard to believe that the woman recorded one hundred songs and was the main one on the race label Decca for a period, and nobody knows who she is. So little is known about her and she's been left out of the books. That's one of the biggest problems I have—getting biographical information on these women. So, wherever I go or whoever I think might know, I ask them and then I put together these various little pieces.

Tell me about the period between 1920 and 1927.

That is an extremely important period in history. My original creative point that I claim is that from 1920 to 1927 is what I call the Women's Reign. And it's never happened before in history when a group of women had power. Now I certainly admit and recognize that their power was limited. But within that restricted area, they did have a power to be themselves and sing their own songs. That was before the producers started telling them what to do. And then in 1927 the men took over in terms of greater import in sales, so that wonderful freedom that the blues women had for those seven years ended.

Why did that happen?

History was moving, changing. I think there are many elements involved. One of the elements was a kind of backlash. A lot of people were tired of having the women—"If you can't do it, I'll get another sweet papa who can." The women had gone very far, so there was the element of backlash. But I don't think that was the major one.

You once said the blues women weren't burdened by Freud's mistake. Now, I'm amazed at how much those women knew about their anatomy.

Press my button. Ring my bell. It's something that's very interesting, I think. Don't you?

Why did so many of those women have such a positive sexual outlook?

You see, the chief thing is they didn't have to be dependent on a man; not that some of them didn't want to be, but the men weren't making the livings as much as the women were. There weren't enough jobs for men, particularly in the South. So when women don't have to be involved with their living from a man, they're much more independent. But when they're dependent on a man for room and board, they've got to do what he wants.

The women who sing the songs on *Mean Mothers* and *Super Sisters* seem so completely sexually aware.

It's because they were freer in that sense than white women were. There's this whole other thing in the black culture that's involved in this, too, and that is that sexuality is taken as much more of a natural phenomenon. One for joy and enjoyment. It's a much more acceptable part of the culture. It has been in this country. It is simply something that is not shied away from in the way it has been in the white culture. It's not looked upon as dirty. It was looked upon as a much more natural thing.

There appears to be freedom as well for women to sing about their affections for other women.

People were generally more human and more realistic.

None of this seems very blue to me. Is it safe to assume that the blues has been misrepresented? I think you've called it "an overload of victim-variety blues."

The blues has really been suffering from a bad reputation. From poor press, so to speak. The blues is really a form of music, a technical formulation. But it fits into a whole lot of systems better if it's seen as moaning, whining, crying music. There were joyous aspects to the blues. When the woman uses the blues form and sings "I baked the best jelly roll in town" or "the best cabbage in town," whatever the euphemism is that she uses, I wouldn't call that sad and blue and lonely. I'd call that a pretty wonderful view of yourself.

Why are victim blues the only kind that has been available to us?

The fact of the matter is, all kinds of blues were bought by people all of the time when they were first issued. That's what was so wonderful about that free period of women, 1920 to 1927. Women sang on the record the songs that they sang in the clubs and in the church shows and in the places where they performed. And there was a combination. A mixture.

The trouble is, when they were reissued and brought out for the white market, there was a preponderance of that victim variety. Now, it's a very difficult thing for a white producer to identify with "I'm a one-hour mama, so a one-minute papa ain't the kind of man for me." That embarrassed him. It's easier for him to identify with "Daddy won't you please come home, I'm just so alone." So I believe that a lot of this distortion we have comes from the editing by the producers, and by the writers, because I couldn't put my hands on this material if it didn't exist. I'm not making it up.

Another theme you tackle is the myth of the freedom train (*Sorry but I Can't Take You: Women's Railroad Blues*).

All the history books tell us that the train led the blacks to freedom in the North from the South. Well, the fact of the matter is, it led the men to the North. It was the men who had the jobs in the automotive industry in Detroit, meat-packing in Chicago, steel mills and coal mining in Pennsylvania. Women couldn't get those jobs, so they hated the train. The train meant their lovers were being taken away. They couldn't go get those jobs, nor could they have the free ride if they felt the feeling of adventure. In the '20s, they couldn't because they didn't permit women on the freight trains. Later, during the Depression, women dressed up as boys and got away with it. But in the '20s it was absolutely not permitted. So, the train was the enemy. Also, the women couldn't get the domestic jobs in the North because they were filled by the Irishwomen who had fled from the potato famine in Ireland in the last part of the previous century.

One very important song, "I'm going to Chicago / sorry but I can't take you / ain't nothing in Chicago / a monkey woman like you can do," was in fact accurate because a woman couldn't get a job as a domestic, so she'd be a monkey on his back, and as it was, the ghettos were so terribly crowded. People slept in half beds. They couldn't even rent a whole room. If they worked the night shift, they slept in the day, and another person who worked the day shift slept in the same bed at night. There was such crowding. Such terrible conditions. Yet the history books in the country tell us that the train was a symbol of freedom.

You have a theory that women originated the boogie piano *(Boogie Blues: Women Sing and Play Boogie Woogie).*

Oh, yeah. Well, I just feel that the women were there in the churches keeping the beat. Women at the keyboards kept that beat going while everybody was hallelujahing and stomping. And the women and children are the only ones that were in the churches primarily.

You have brought forward hundreds of musicians. What has been your most exciting discovery personally?

Well, the Valaida Snow story, I think, is terribly exciting. [*Hot Snow: Queen of the Trumpet Sings and Swings*, Foremothers, volume 2.] Her story is such a classical mythological mode of the hero searching for the Golden Fleece, the fleece being one's own freedom, one's own self, and travelling to distant lands for it. For freedom. And then her near death in the concentration camp. And her rebirth.

I'm also crazy about the International Sweethearts of Rhythm, too, because to think that they were an integrated group in the '40s. It is just so unbelievable when there are problems still today. [*International Sweethearts of Rhythm: Hottest Women's Band of the 1940s.*] I'm in touch with them, and the thing they had together with each other is so unbelievable it has lasted for forty years. They share something that was so special and rare.

Women are generally seen as accessories, and you have proven that women are contributors. Now, without these women, specifically without the singers, how do you think the sound of blues and jazz would have been different?

It would have been very different, because the women, for example Bessie Smith, Clara Smith and Ida Cox, chose the musicians they wanted. And they told them concretely—faster, slower, no, I want this. Ethel Waters, for example, used to pound on Fletcher Henderson to get him to play the sound she wanted. Well, what does that mean? It means that Ethel Waters affected the way Fletcher Henderson played. Then Fletcher Henderson went on to become a very important band leader and arranger. This was when Ethel and Fletch were travelling for the first black label that ever existed, called Black Swan. When Ethel described to Fletch what she wanted, that's what he had to give her.

When Bessie Smith and Ida Cox were running revues, they were the ones that hired the band and hired the chorus line. They had power. They weren't victims. And if they weren't getting what they wanted, they had the power to fire the people and get people who would give them what they wanted. No question about it.

I heard Bessie Smith had Louis Armstrong working for her.

No, that really isn't true. What actually happened, on a couple of recording sessions, Columbia suggested that Louis come in and she went along and was agreeable. But after the second session, she wouldn't take him again. He just got too pushy and she got Joe Smith back, her regular.

If you had had this music when you were growing up, do you think your life would have been different?

If I had heard a woman sing about "if you can't do it, I'll get another sweet daddy who can," it would have been a revelation to me. Absolutely. If I had had that, someplace in my background, I wouldn't have lived through the dark '50s in the way I did. But on the other hand, there are some other women my age who did have it and what did it do for them? I don't know. It's a very long question that kind of requires a certain kind of elaborate discussion. I think it would have changed my life.

RIP: November 1, 2008

THE WINNIPEG FOLK FESTIVAL *Presents a Series*

Women in Folk Music

Ferron
mon.
nov. 23

Connie Kaldor
wed. dec. 16

Cathy Fink
tues. jan. 26

Heather Bishop
wed. feb. 24

Tickets: **$24** for
4 concerts, **$7** each
on sale at A.T.O. (downtown only)~
Action Committee, 209-388 Donald~
Mary Scorer Books ~ the Womens
Building, 3-730 Alexander~
Liberation Books, 160 Spence St.~
Folk Festival Office ~
for information call 453-2985

All Concerts begin at 8 p.m.
Planetarium Auditorium

TESTIMONY

HEATHER BISHOP

SET TO TOUR STATES

Rubymusic column, *Kinesis*, May 1987

Live! From Canada, *Hot Wire*, November 1987

Last month, Milwaukee's Icebergg Records added Canadian singer-song-writer Heather Bishop to their catalogue. This distribution deal, combined with a renewed work permit, allows Heather access to that great American market: a well-developed concert circuit populated by record-buying women who appreciate Canadian talent.

Certainly part of Heather's appeal on both sides of the border is that she is *Canadian*. She's a prairie woman who illustrates her album covers with hand-drawn pictures of her grandmother. She's a family woman living with six other women on a quarter section of land in homes they built themselves. She's a friend of children, touring the reserves and small farming communities of Manitoba two months out of every year, performing for young people. Although these are not exclusively Canadian attributes, Heather has a way of exuding hometown pride. She is glad she is Canadian. She has a Canadian identity. She tells stories about cold weather and muddy roads. And she reminds Canadian women that there is a music culture in this country that is uniquely their own.

On the other hand, Heather grew up greatly influenced by American politics of the '60s: Vietnam, civil rights, women's rights. And her musical influences (with the exception of Nina Simone and Connie Kaldor) link her directly to the political sector of the American West Coast women's music movement that produced the woman-identified singer-songwriter.

Unlike her US counterparts, Heather did not have the option of a thriving women-only concert circuit, although she had the support of women's communities. Heather developed into a blues and folk singer on the stages of integrated folk festivals across this country. From the Sun Dog Festival in Saskatoon to the Year of the Child tour that included Old Crow, Yukon, to the Conference of Women from Mining and Mill Towns in Terrace Bay, Ontario, Heather Bishop accomplished an unusual feat. She took her repertoire of blues covers, folk songs, children's songs, pop tunes, political stories and lesbian originals to the Canadian people. And they didn't back away. After twelve years in the business, twelve years of outreach, Heather is now considered a *Canadian musician*.

Heather's influence on the women's communities in this country has been substantial. She has performed at lesbian and gay conferences, benefits for sexual assault centres, conferences on rural women and mental health, women and the law, women in trades and women in international food production, and women's music festivals. She has appeared at universities, women's centres, coffee houses, bookstores and transition houses. Her fan mail is poignant. She has made a difference in the quality of women's lives.

With the exception of her third adult album, *I Love Women Who Laugh* (Heather has recorded two albums for children: *Bellybutton* and *Purple People Eater*), Heather predominantly sings covers. And not obscure ones, either. Heather's knack for the popular song has led her to cover songs written by Billie Holiday, Nina Simone, Joan Armatrading and Randy Newman.

Many of her selections have already been huge hits: "Fever," "Cry Me a River," "You Don't Own Me," "Am I Blue." She also revived a collection of unlikelies including "Please Don't Let Me Be Misunderstood," recorded by the Animals in 1965, and "(Ghost) Riders in the Sky," which was made popular by the Sons of the Pioneers and the Ramrods.

In a recent conversation, I asked Heather why she records songs that have already had maximum exposure. She answered, "They are such great songs that they warrant doing." She's right. And whether or not you think Nina Simone recorded the definitive version of "Sugar in My Bowl" or only Diana Ross can sing Billie Holiday, there is something going on here.

For a lot of good reasons, some of them economic, most women are not sitting around charting the advancement of women in the music business, reading *Billboard*, *Rolling Stone* or *Hot Wire* or spending food money on highly priced albums. For some, owning a radio is as good as it gets. For others, music is just not part of their lifestyle. For still others, popular music has gone into the political dumpster. (Blues is sexist, girl groups are stupid, folk music is whiny and rock and roll is male oriented.)

Heather Bishop is in the business of music education. Because of the songs she covers, women are learning a bit about their music history. They are being introduced to songs they may have never heard. Or if they are familiar, such as "Please Don't Let Me Be Misunderstood," they hear them in a new way.

I Love Women Who Laugh has the largest collection of Heather originals. The title track may be the most popular, but "Yukon Rain" is the most brilliant. It stands up easily as one of the top twenty Canadian love songs. (Ferron's "Ain't Life a Brook" and Joni Mitchell's "A Case of You" would be in this same category.)

There is no "Yukon Rain" on Heather's latest album, *A Taste of the Blues*, released on her own label, Mother of Pearl Records. However, the perks are these: a revival of Billie Holiday's "Tell Me More and More" with instrumentation circa Janis Joplin and the Kozmic Blues Band, a powerful and original rendition of Carolyn Brandy's "Spirit Healer," a very grown-up version of Lesley Gore's hit "You Don't Own Me" (with one small lyric change) and a live-wire interpretation of Gary Tigerman's cleverly written song "Seduced."

A Taste of the Blues was produced by Dan Donahue (who has produced all of Heather's albums) and in supporting roles are Connie Kaldor (listen carefully for her comedic asides), Suzanne and Annette Campagne and Ilena Zaremba. Her band on this album is: Greg Black, drums; John Ervin, bass; Janice Finlay, clarinet; Walle Larsson, saxophone and flute; Marilyn Lerner, keyboards; and Glenn Matthews, congas and percussion. The album was engineered by Dave Roman.

Heather will be in Vancouver this month (May 1987) performing at the Children's Festival. Then, after a two-month holiday on the farm, she'll begin her American tours.

EMILY EXPERIMENTS WITH MUSIC

Rubymusic column, *Kinesis*, April 1985

CK: Basically, you were alienated.
E: Yeah, very.
CK: Still?
E: Still. Hopefully it will stay that way.
CK: Hopefully forever.

I felt a kinship with Emily right away.

My first introduction was through the cassette she released in 1984. It was called *I've Got a Steel Bar in My Head*. She designed the cover and hand painted each individual cassette. The song list was written in ink, "and I had to label the sides of the cassette myself. (Oh, these things. Cottage industries.)"

I didn't understand all of her lyrics, but I liked the way her music sounded. And then there was the title song. I understood "Steel Bar" perfectly. I sang it to myself when I was alone. ("It's catchy. Can't get it out of *your* head. I've got one in mine.") "Steel Bar" reminded me of Frances Farmer and I was convinced that Emily was talking about brainwashing or lobotomies or something similar. But when I finally met her, she described the writing of the song in terms more appropriate to an Excedrin headache. Oh well. But she said I could interpret it any way I wanted.

When I think of Emily, the word *compact* comes to mind. She performs from a table and she doesn't take up much room. Her equipment consists of a cassette deck and two small Casio keyboards. With the exception of the vocals and keyboards, the rest of the instruments have been pre-recorded and mixed on her porta-studio. She uses a drum machine, a beautiful wood bass guitar and a variety of sound effects. She used to play the bass onstage, but it broke one night while she was playing it with a drumstick. These are the risks one takes when being an experimental musician.

An Emily performance is a joy to behold. She has a solid grasp of the absurd and a great sense of humour, and one can always tell when a song is *completely* over, because she takes a drink from her beer.

"I've always been a loner. I get it from my mother. She's the same way. They live in a nice house in suburbia, but she doesn't go out with the tea club. She stays at home. Our family has always kept to themselves."

1985, Vancouver: Experimental musician Emily Faryna found support living in a house occupied by Mo-Da-Mu Records. It was the summer of 1983, and their encouragement inspired her to create her own music.

Emily Faryna entered the world in 1963 in Edmonton, Alberta. She is the youngest of six children, five girls and a boy. When she was in the fourth grade, her family moved to Richmond, BC.

"My sisters had records and I'd listen to theirs. And then there was the radio. I never really got into what was popular on the radio. We used to have grade seven sock hops but I just thought it was garbage. I was listening to old Moody Blues, Kraftwerk and Jethro Tull. I never liked— what was that song, 'Mama's Got a Squeeze Box'? That was a great hit in grade seven." When she started buying her own records, she bought the Clash and the Stranglers.

In high school, she wrote short stories and prose. "We were told a lot what to write. But my stuff was always about the dark side because I really didn't like high school at all. I had long, feathered hair. Got my mom to buy me jeans. It still didn't work. Nobody wanted to be my friend. So one day I came to class with a safety pin in my ear.

"When the hardcore scene first popped up in Vancouver, I really fit right in. It was great when it was in the small little halls and everybody was going nuts. It was the first time I had a feeling that I belonged. I was totally an outsider in high school because I wasn't cute. I was kind of a hairy, gawky girl. I was just not cool."

After high school, Emily spent two years studying to be a sculptor at Emily Carr College of Art. She left in 1983. "It just didn't work. I was doing nothing by the end of it but still getting good marks. I wanted to be in a band. While I was living at home, somebody gave me a little Casio. So I used it to make recordings, from cassette deck to cassette deck. Then I got a big Casio. Then a porta-studio."

There were other influences as well. She had left home and moved into a house occupied by Mo-Da-Mu Records. It was a stimulating time, and she started to experiment with her own music. During the summer of '83, she was offered her first job.

"Somebody offered me a gig at John Barley's. I was working with this guitar player and he said no, he didn't want to do it. So I did it by myself. I played just with the Casios. No tapes or anything. I had three songs. I'd never been onstage before. But I got up there."

That same year, she produced and released her first cassette, *PLAY-THING: The Conquest of the Human over the Chaos of Nature.* ("I don't know why I called it that.") She used a variety of musicians and then mixed in sound effects and her own vocals. She made a hundred tapes. "I didn't know what to do with them so I mailed them to obscure addresses in Europe." She supported herself by working in a print shop.

Since she was a perfect opening act for Mo-Da-Mu bands ("One person is less expensive, very portable, quick sound checks"), she continued performing. She also did artwork for the band 54-40. She designed their posters, their logo and their most recent album cover.

Emily has been playing around the city for over two years and her music continues to change. "'Doomed to Fail,' 'Steel Bar' and 'My Wife She Loved the Butcher' are very verse, verse, verse, chorus, verse. Except for 'Steel Bar,' which is repeat, repeat, repeat, repeat. I'm trying to break away from that. I want to get a new approach that is less predictable and poppy. And some of the songs I've been working on and the sounds that I'm getting out of the instruments are not pleasant. But I like it." She also has a new cassette in the works.

"I don't see my music and the things that I say as 'political' because I'm not citing specific cases and accusing. But I have a personal politic. I'm interested in people relating to other people *as people*. And not as corporations and countries and huge governments. It really does bother me. I can see the world run totally differently and working a lot better.

"I think people have to be more responsible for themselves. They just can't go along being happy, happy and blind. I'm just starting to wake up to a lot of ugly realities and I'm not just going to sit around."

SINGING FOR OURSELVES

An Interview with Eileen Brown/Maura Volante

Rubymusic column, *Kinesis*, June 1985

I have in my photograph album two pictures of Eileen Brown. They were taken over the May 6 weekend, 1977, at the Pacific Northwest Women's Music Festival in Olympia, Washington. She is one of about twenty women who have relocated to the roof of a building on the Evergreen campus. If I remember correctly, we were all up there because we had been kicked off the lawn by the university officials. Evidently, rows of bare-breasted women playing conga drums on the grassy knoll was somewhat incongruous with the rest of the student body. In the photograph, Eileen is wearing white drawstring pants with rows of beads and shells around her neck. She is slightly sunburned. And she is singing.

I first heard Eileen on the steps of the BC parliament building in 1976 at the Women's Rally for Action, and later on the steps of the Vancouver courthouse. Her strong, melodic unaccompanied voice was the musical equivalent to the powerful speeches the women of our community were writing during those early years.

Eileen was also a regular at the Full Circle Coffee House on Eighth near Main, and I seem to recall one infamous night when someone pulled the plug on her and Bells because an unruly crowd of women, fresh from the WAR (Women Against Rape) demonstration, wanted to dance to records.

Eileen and Bells is another story. They sang together for a couple of years, travelled across the US and back and took their music to Europe. By then, Eileen was playing fiddle, and with Bells on guitar and mandolin, they entertained non-English-speaking audiences with such original hits as "Lesberadas"—*in a wild western town, passing liberated garlic around, Lesberadas, renegades, nozama, amazon.* "Nozama is amazon spelled backwards, right? And occasionally when passing the hat, someone would say in English, 'Oh, that was interesting.'"

Eileen returned to Canada in 1979. She became involved in a relationship, moved into a house full of women and started parenting a three-year-old child. She changed her name to Maura, and later to Maura Volante. The combination of names signified her connection to water and to the three stages of a woman's life: maiden, mother and crone.

Her music changed, too. She stopped singing in public for a time but continued to sing for recreation. She experimented with free form. When it was time to step out again, she wrote music to Cyndia Cole's poetry. She

Whether singing traditional songs or her own compositions, Maura Volante's a cappella performances (a.k.a. Eileen Brown) were rich and melodic. She was a valuable contributor to rallies and festivals, highlighting those messages, universal and true.

and Luna Nordin sang while Chantale Laplante played piano. They called one performance "New Weave."

Later Maura was given a conga drum, and after a move to Denman Island, she played briefly with two other people who were interested in learning her songs. ("I say 'people' because they weren't women.") More recently she sang and played drums while Frannie Ruvinsky performed a dance about the death of a lake destroyed by uranium mining.

Now Maura commits her time to *Kinesis* and Vancouver Co-op Radio. She also teaches singing workshops, encouraging people "to open up and actually let a sound come out, and to enjoy the feeling of making that sound. To enjoy their own voices." She calls the workshops Singing for Ourselves.

I'm not as familiar with Maura's music as I was nine years ago, when she was one of a group of women who were our first freedom singers. And until we talked in preparation for this story, I knew little of her life before the women's movement.

The first record she ever bought was "The End of the World" by Skeeter Davis. She went to a Catholic school in Ontario and survived because she sang in the choir. She became "really" interested in music when she heard Joan Baez, Joni Mitchell and Buffy Sainte-Marie. And she was the emcee for the Vancouver Folk Song Society, a position that required she sing "The Wild Mountain Thyme" at the closing of each variety night. (The what? "The Wild Mountain Thyme." Will you go, lassie, go, and we'll all go together.) The rest of the story, she can tell you herself.

CK: Do you sense that our community has a musical history?

MV: Yes, I do. And I think that a lot of women who weren't there might not know that, because it was mostly live stuff that wasn't recorded and not all of us carried through to become stars. So, a woman coming into the city now wouldn't realize how many performers there were of women's music back then, who later went on to do other things, or who are doing music in different ways. I think that Ferron is the only one who emerged out of that to become well known. And incredibly well known. More so than we ever would have imagined at the time.

Why did you make the break from traditional folk music?

Gradually, I began to feel more limited by that, as I was coming into a feminist consciousness, and I was searching high and low for songs that had strong women characters in them. But then, when I came out as a lesbian, it seemed like 99 percent of my repertoire was suddenly irrelevant because it was all about men. Whether the women were strong or not, their lives revolved around men. So I didn't have very many songs to sing. Then I started learning songs by contemporary women, and some by women who were in the folk scene, like Malvina Reynolds, who was writing feminist songs, and Hazel Dickens and Alice Gerrard. So, I was still in the folk milieu. It was while I was doing that kind of thing that I first performed for the women's community.

When and where was your first performance?

Late '75 or early '76. It was at Simon Fraser University at a benefit for Press Gang put on by Womankind. They had about ten performers and then a dance. And since I was going to sing "Hang in There," which they thought was a good ending song, they put me at the end. So, for about an hour before the end of the performances, there were these crowds of women waiting to dance. So, I got up there, my first performance in the women's community, and I had to cut it short and only do two songs. I felt it to be a very restless crowd. But I also felt that there were women who were listening.

I remember you singing everywhere.

There were always benefits, coffee houses, and there would be people ...

yourself, Ferron, Jane Perks, myself ... I mean we all kind of shared the bill, and we were all just sort of starting out and finding our way.

What did music represent to you when you first began to sing? Was there a message that you wanted to share?

In the beginning, if you were going to be a singer, you had to be a star. That was the model. But now I've come around to seeing that the way I'm going to use my singing is going to be different from that star model. When I got very politicized in the women's movement, I felt that singing was something I could use to get a message across. I felt very much like that. That was why I was singing. It was what I had to offer.

I've never been a singer who could sing stuff that she didn't agree with. Well, back in the early days, I could sing stuff that was not very meaningful to me. But it wasn't offensive at that time. Gradually more and more in the mainstream of music became offensive to me or so meaningless that I just couldn't relate to it.

So that's been a problem for me. A lot of people have suggested to me, "Oh, learn a few pop songs and you'll get along." I can't do it, you know. I'd rather sing as an instrument without any words. So, I'm really what some people would call hung up on the content. Content is extremely important to me.

What were your early themes?

Women awakening to a consciousness is one of the things. I always went for the positive and hopeful. But somehow it seems like it was easier then to do that. I don't know. It seemed simpler then. Some of the songs I wrote around that time, like one that I called "Ocean Song": "I'm going to jump back into the ocean, until the earth can be a home again ..."

"I feel like a magic potion ..."

Yes, that's kind of a naive song in a way because the ocean is just as polluted as the rest of the world. And it probably was then, too. But I was just feeling very hopeful and positive. Another song is "Music Makes Us Strong." That was one of the first ones I wrote, and it was to a traditional tune.

What are some of the lyrics?

I am a travelling woman—I can't remember how it goes. [Begins to sing.]
> I am a travelling woman
> And I'm learning how to live.
> Building up my strengths
> giving what I have to give.

I always have been singing
since before I learned to speak;
It helps me find the peace of mind
and wholeness that I seek.
And music makes us strong
Oh, music makes us strong.

Basically, it's the same sort of stuff I'm singing now, in a way.

Then what is different? You?

I don't know what it is that's different. Now, I feel like it's going to be a struggle all my life. And that we are not going to achieve exactly what we want in my lifetime. Yet I have to keep being aware of all the shit that goes down in order to not be like an ostrich. At the same time, when I go out to sing, I don't want to get everyone really down.

I appreciate new wave and punk more than I did a few years ago. I think it has a lot to say, and I think it's really important to sing from your anger. But that's not my style—to sing of the anger. My style is just more ... well, okay, there's a lot of crap around and we have to find ways to feel positive about ourselves.

I think back then I felt more hopeful and I felt that we were on the verge of something really wonderful that was going to change everything overnight. Now I don't feel that it's going to change overnight. But I still feel that we have to remain hopeful in order to live through it. In order to keep on going. I think that's the difference there.

I think that without music and art and dance and theatre in our political work, it is lifeless. It's dry, cold, and it's dead. We really need that stuff, more than the speeches. Especially as the struggle goes on and on and the speeches sound the same. Year after year. When the speeches start and women turn to their neighbour and start to talk, or go get a coffee or something ... I've seen it happen. So, to me, it's very important to have music as part of the political work we do.

AN INTERVIEW WITH ANIMAL SLAVES

Rubymusic column, *Kinesis*, July/August 1985

Animal Slaves: Elizabeth Fischer, vocals and keyboards; Rosco Hales, drums and percussion; Rachel Melas, bass.

Recordings: *Animal Slaves* (EP), 1984; *Dog Eat Dog* (LP), 1985.

Itinerary: Currently touring across Canada. Final destination the Pyramid Club, New York City.

Mental Health: Encouraging.

Musical Capabilities: Staggering.

Financial Status: Unknown.

Last Words: As follows.

Elizabeth Fischer: This particular group which is the Animal Slaves, as I see it, has been around since—when was it—1982. Oh yeah, there was this other band called Animal Slaves for a little while beforehand, with me trying my wings. However, it was not very memorable and it's best left forgotten.

CK: What is the meaning of the name?

EF: I had this idea at the time, which had to do with the words that I was writing, that I really wanted to explore the passionate side of human nature and talk about things that weren't necessarily pleasant. Things that I felt were inherent in every human being, which is the animal side of one's nature. And that is how it became Animal Slaves—in my mind, anyway. Everybody thought I was jumping on some kind of fucking bandwagon or trying to be a punk band or something. But it really wasn't that at all.

Well, the first band I was in was kind of like that because it was a bunch of guys and they all played as much as they could and as loud as they could, and I tried to scream on top of that. But it wasn't meant to be like that. I didn't imagine it to be like that.

Your personal history. I think that "Eye of the Hurricane" may be an example of roots because it sounds like rhythm and blues.

I've always really liked rhythm and blues and I've always liked blues. To me, it's like I've always wanted to die and be reborn as Otis Redding.

1985, Vancouver: The photos of Animal Slaves were taken late in the day in their windowless basement practice space. I shot two rolls of film, which later had to be recovered by the good women at ABC Photocolour because I didn't use enough light. But Ross Hales, Rachel Melas, and Elizabeth Fischer were in fine form, full of genuine affection.

You grew up in Hungary. What did you listen to?

It's the birthplace of the blues, man.

Hungarian funk, I think you once called it.

I was raised on gypsy music. My father really liked gypsy music and he had a real close friend who was a gypsy and a traditional violin player. I was raised with all these stories about this guy and what a fabulous guy he was, and I really like gypsy music. I like that kind of feeling. I like it because it kind of plucks at your emotions.

When did you leave?

I left Hungary when I was nine.

Why?

Oh, you know. Your average Hungarian refugee type thing. We went across the border, you know, with flares and guns going off. Trudging across the border. And then we went to Austria and explored refugee camps in many countries.

I went to Argentina and then came back to Austria and lived in refugee camps for about nine months, and then went to Sweden and hung around there for about four years. But my father had a real hard time getting a job in Sweden, and he was a real proud Hungarian-type guy. So he wanted to get out of there real bad. So we ended up going to Canada and we lived in Montreal, and he was real happy there.

What kind of shape were you in when you got to Canada?

Well, I was kind of smaller. I was younger. Well, what kind of shape. We were poor. I mean we didn't have anything. We left Hungary with a change of underwear and a piece of jewellery that got us back from Argentina, which was really nice.

Could you speak English?

No. I spoke a bunch of languages, but English wasn't one of them.

You must have had incredible adjustments to make.

Yeah. I really hated it.

When you came here, did you have an original ambition or some sort of dream?

No. I mean, I was fourteen. I did not have an original dream. I knew that I was strange because I'd been strange all my life. So, I was mainly exploring the strangeness as far as it would go. I've always wanted to be different from everybody else. I didn't have an ambition. I still don't really have an ambition. I just do things.

> I'm learning to live; I'm learning to live somewhere. I'm learning to give, I'm learning to give something ... I don't need your money or your sweet delights. I'll lock the windows; I'll put out the lights. I'm too old to cry, I'm too tired to fight. I'll learn to live in black and white.

Rosco Hales: What was I looking for when I left Kamloops? Well, I was young and fairly stupid at the time and I hadn't really learned as much in my life as I have now. I wanted to be as good a drummer as I could, and to make a living from playing music. It wasn't until I'd gone to Cap College for three years, and gone out and played for just over a year out in the real world in terms of the bar scene and what's required to make a living as a musician, that I realized it's hopeless. It's not what I wanted to do.

I did, in fact, go out and join a cowboy bar band, only to find after about six months, this has nothing to do with my relationship with music.

The Animal Slaves is really different. To me, it's really special. It's sort of what I'd always wanted to do. It's most definitely what I want to do now. First and foremost, it's really creative for me as a drummer.

Part of leading up to joining the Animal Slaves, I had some friends who were more involved in the arts community as opposed to the music community. They started putting ideas into my head that I had never really considered, living a fairly safe, protected life as I had, coming from a very traditional suburban Canadian–North American upbringing.

These people got me thinking about a bunch of things. Politics in particular. And although I don't profess to be any sort of political wizard, it made me aware of the fact that I had a certain responsibility, at least I decided myself I had a responsibility, to live life in a particular fashion and interact with people in a particular way.

The Animal Slaves, for me, is the first band that I felt represented any sort of strong politic. I never played music with a strong politic in the past. Obviously it was political what I played in the past, but it was all fucked-up politics. It wasn't good politics.

CK: What are you learning about yourself being in this particular band?

RH: Oh boy. About myself. The big thing that I've learned in this band is just how easy I've had it in the world. And how easy it is for a white male to have it, particularly in this culture.

Because of that and of all the advantages that exist for people of my type, somehow it struck me as being awfully unfair. I guess I single-handedly can't change that overnight, but I can certainly help to influence hopefully other men to respond to women and the world around them. White males of this society just have it too easy. It's too good.

> Our leader's fat jowls are wobbling in the glow / He's mouthing scriptures lit from below / As the stinking breeze whips the waves / Our leader in ecstasy raves / Heaven and Hell / And the might of the just / Such is the power / Of his lust.

Rachel Melas: I played cello for a long time when I was a kid. Really badly. And then I met some blues musicians here in Vancouver—I hitchhiked out here when I was about fifteen—and they said, "You should play the bass." So I did. I went back to New York and I got this sixty-dollar bass and started playing it.

CK: When someone sits down and writes the history of Vancouver music, you will go down, of course, as the best Jewish lesbian bass player on West Fourteenth Avenue.

RM: Between Main and Cambie; that's about a four-block radius.

But you'll also go down as a founding member of the Moral Lepers, which was a very significant band. Was that experience significant for you?

Yeah. It took about a decade off my life in sheer aggravation. We were a freak show so everybody thought we were fun, you know. We played some good music, too.

It always takes one person or one group to break ground and make it easier for other people. But they become a target for everybody's fears.

Well, we were a little bit scary, I guess, for some folks.

But do you think I'm overestimating ...

I hope so, because it really annoys me that more women don't go out and do it and get themselves a guitar, a bass or some drums, or whatever, and play quite loudly and aggressively. A lot of women around do mellow material, you know, but I guess the Moral Lepers were probably about the most aggressive and original all-women's band I ever heard.

Are you satisfied now, being with the Animal Slaves?

Up to this point, it's probably about my best creative outlet in certain respects, because I can play whatever I want. I can play the best bass that I can, and I'm not limited by "Oh, we're playing this kind of music, so you can't get too outside," or whatever.

In the band, we don't want to be self-indulgent. And I don't want to be self-indulgent. But I'm not really capable of being self-indulgent in a lot of ways musically. I don't think my chops are up to total wanking, or bass solos or anything like that. I just try and do the best I can. I can only do the best that I can in the Animal Slaves. There's basically no limit.

Messages. Content. The themes on the first record—people talking platitudes, easy solutions, too much social protest, no action. Does this sound familiar?

Coffee cup warriors with character references.

On *Dog Eat Dog* the things that stand out are "You can't fool me, I can think for myself, and no matter how you try to pacify me, you can't take away my secrets, my soul. And in spite of everything you have done to the contrary, you can't take away my life." What can I conclude—this is a test question—what can I conclude from this as being the overall philosophy of the group?

Well, we all work for ICBC.* (Insurance Corporation of British Columbia)

RIP: Elizabeth Fischer, October 15, 2015

TRUE TO HERSELF

AN INTERVIEW WITH RONNIE GILBERT

Kinesis, "Women in Music" issue, July/August 1985

There are many things I want to tell you about Ronnie Gilbert. Here are the facts. She was a member of the Weavers, a very successful folk group blacklisted in the US in 1952 by the House Committee on Un-American Activities. She moved from New York to California the next year and gave birth to her daughter Lisa. Later she became a single parent.

During her time with the Weavers, Ronnie recorded a solo album, *Come and Go with Me*, and after the Weavers disbanded in 1963, she recorded *Alone with Ronnie Gilbert*.

In 1964, she joined Joseph Chaikin and the Open Theater, an opportunity she described to me as being similar to "offering a little kid a brand new bicycle and a pair of roller skates and a telescope and a microscope set—everything all at once."

Theatre is still her favourite subject. She continued to work with Chaikin in the Winter Project, with Harold Pinter and Peter Brook in Paris and London and with Meredith Monk and Elizabeth Swados. This past year, she directed and read a radio play with Chaikin based on moments of crisis in an individual's life. The project was important to her, as Joseph Chaikin is recovering from a stroke.

In the '70s she became involved in primal therapy and went back to school to get her degree in clinical psychology. She immigrated to Canada in 1974, after "this guy came down on a motorcycle with his scarf flying and a toque on his head," looking for a counsellor for his community in the Slocan Valley. She fell in love with the Slocan and built her house there. She helped form Theatre Energy, working in Vancouver with Tamahnous, but she eventually ended up back in New York with the Winter Project.

Her association with Holly Near began when Holly dedicated her *A Live Album* to Ronnie. They sang together for the first time during the filming of the documentary *The Weavers: Wasn't That a Time*.

Ronnie recorded *Lifeline* with Holly in 1983, and *Harp* with Holly, Pete Seeger and Arlo Guthrie in 1985. *The Spirit Is Free*, also released this year, is her first solo album in twenty years.

What is difficult to describe to you is her generosity, her commitment to aiding in the reconstruction of this place we call home and her ability to wrap you up in her big strong arms and say, "We can all change.

It's easy. Watch me."

Ronnie will be appearing this year at the Vancouver Folk Music Festival in July (1985). Our conversation took place in May of this year.

CK: The first thing I want to ask you about is your mother. I credit my own mother with the fact that I had a political consciousness at a young age. You've made comments along similar lines.

RG: What's her background? What's your background?

We lived in western Nebraska near the southern tip of the Pine Ridge Indian Reservation, in a segregated town. I can remember one Thanksgiving, when I was about eight years old, a woman from "Indian Town," as it was unfortunately called at that time, came up to me on the sidewalk and asked to speak to my mother. She had come begging for toys for her children for Christmas. My mother took me aside and explained to me why this mother was in this situation. And, even though we didn't have much, she asked me what I was prepared to give. That's one example.

How amazing! What a wise mother you have. My mom came to the United States as a very, very beautiful sixteen-year-old, with black eyes and a history of having survived World War I—practically on the streets of Warsaw because both her parents were dead by the time she was twelve years old. *Her* mother was an unlettered person who insisted that she be taught to read and write. So my mother had a smattering of everything, Yiddish, Polish and Russian and German.

She was a very cherished child because she was the child of her parents' old age, or what went for old age in those days. Indeed, she survived. Her nearest brothers and sisters were old enough to be her parents, and most of them were gone from Europe by then, so she was kind of left there, and she somehow managed to survive.

She was a dressmaker by the time she was twelve or thirteen years old, having worked from the time she was nine, or something like that. She came here and went right into the factories of New York, which is what those young Jewish girls did in those days, if they could do so, or even if they couldn't, they went right into the sweatshops. She also came with some understanding of unionism—it was beginning to flourish then in Europe—and she joined the International Ladies Garment Workers Union.

She was a rank-and-file activist and I grew up with those things in my ears. You know, collective bargaining, stop the machines and all this stuff. It was really from my mother, who was a feisty little fighter all her life, until now, when she finds herself without hearing, without very good sight. She's just sort of lost in this dumping ground for old people, and the place that she lives in is not bad. In fact, it's considered to be the model. But it is such—I don't know what to call it. It is such an inhuman kind of situation.

Our lives are so different these days. I don't have a home to offer her, you know. I'm a gypsy. I travel wherever I work, and wherever I work is home and so on. And what they need desperately is a place where they feel surrounded by people who know them and care. They do the best they can at this place, but there's no real one-to-one stuff that goes on.

She's living a very isolated, emotionally isolated life right now, in spite of a lot of people who care a lot about her. But it's just not right. It's not right. And as you know, our beloved president, in the wisdom of his age, has decided that old people don't need as much money as they've been getting from the government. So they're cutting back like crazy. Operational expenses are hard to come by in places like that, so it's hard.

But that's the way it goes. God, they're helping us to live longer and longer lives, you know.

But poorer and poorer longer lives.

Poorer and poorer and longer and longer, and it is really on my slate for a big fight.

When you were sixteen, you went off and joined the Priority Ramblers. And the story is, you got voted in by a slim margin.

[Laughing.] How did you know that?

On one of my Weavers records.

I'll be darned. Well, I suspect that was probably true. I was a very, very shy sixteen-year-old. And the person who took me under her wing was Jackie Alpert, who was Jackie Gibson at the time, who sang with that group. She now has a disc show up in the Albany area, and has for years. She's an extremely knowledgeable person about recordings and groups. She's retired from her secretary job now. She's of age to retire. And I'm hoping that she will get more and more actively involved in music because she is really a fantastic resource.

But she was a few years older than me and she sort of took me under her wing, and we used to sing together a lot. She played guitar, kind of, you know, sort of um-pa-pa guitar, and we would sing together, the two of us. She sort of eased me into that group. I don't think they were terribly impressed by me, but she did the job.

Where did you get the self-confidence to join a group like that? Also, weren't you going around collecting money for Spain?

For the Spanish refugee children. Yes, that was really my first political action. I was very moved by the Spanish Civil War, I remember, very deeply moved by it.

I guess it was I was coming into an age of awareness when you begin to look outward, when a child begins to look outward, and I—ha! My mother used to bring the left press into the house, so I would read about it and she would talk about it, and she was active in political organizations. It was part of our conversation. So I was moved by that situation and certainly by the idea of kids being dispossessed from their homes, having to run as refugees.

There was a lot of that going on in the world around that time. There was the Japanese invasion of China, a little bit earlier, I think.

And the idea of a population being bombed was the most horrendous thing. Just think that in a relatively short time, the space of a lifetime, less than a lifetime, we've come to take that so for granted. But in the 1930s, it was the most horrendous thing. You remember Picasso's *Guernica*, the great mural. The power of those horses and people. That had an enormous impact. But that's what was going on and nowadays it's nothing. So what if people by the hundreds and thousands get killed. So what.

When I was a little girl and I was learning to draw perspective in school, at the end of my railroad tracks, at the end of a road, there was a whole period when I was drawing mushroom clouds.

It's sick that the world should frighten children like that.

Do you remember exactly what it was the Weavers did that made you un-American? Was there ever any one thing?

We were very, very active, each of us individually, as a group maybe even less so, but as individuals certainly, in various kinds of left activity. That is talking in a very broad kind of term, which is to say singing for union meetings.

Pete [Seeger], I think, sang at the Peekskill concert with Paul Robeson. You know, the Peekskill riots, a small shameful episode in recent United States history. We made a record called the *Ballad of Peekskill*, which told the story of what happened there. And we made no secret of our longing and our belief that peace was the biggest priority of the world. At the time of the Korean War, when all the jingoistic stuff was happening, the razzmatazz for war, we were among *many* people who said, "Hey, sit down and talk this out. Don't start shooting."

So we didn't run with the mainstream, that's for sure. But the thing that was cited when Pete went before the committee was the song "Wasn't That a Time," which Lee Hays had written with Walter Lowenfels, who was a left-wing poet.

Now, interestingly enough, the committee would not allow the song to be played or sung. Pete offered to sing the song for the record. For the congressional. And they would not let him do it. So the song was talked about as this subversive, anti-American song.

And what it really was, was made up of quotes from American history. Wasn't that a time. "Wasn't that a time to try the soul of man," from Tom Paine. Every verse was sort of an encapsulated little bit of American history. So that's the thing that the committee thought to point to. Mostly the House [Committee] on Un-American Activities. Had they allowed it to be read into the record, it might have been a whole other story.

The thing that is so ironic about all of that, and comparing it to some of the things that happened during the Vietnam anti-war movement, is that it's a very American thing to protest. If we assume that we are all raised with the Bill of Rights, and we are all raised to believe that we are all equal, what you did and what people did during the Vietnam War was a patriotic response to the fact that our ideals had been betrayed by the American government.

I've taken to talking about political music and political singer-songwriters from the stage now. And also during interviews. In a very different way, I like to point out that we come from a very old tradition that goes back centuries. That it isn't just the Weavers and the Almanac Singers, or Bob Dylan, but that all over the world, as far as we know, as far back in history as we know, there has been, in one form or another, troubadours, whose honourable business it is to bring to the public the dissenting view.

Certainly the Irish bards were political singers; the troubadours were in fact political singers. The calypso singers were political. The reggae singers are political singers. I mean, we're a very long and honourable tradition. This ain't nothing new.

I remember how I felt the first time I heard the music of Holly Near, and the first time that I heard Cris Williamson. And it seems that even after what I called my years of consciousness, even after civil rights and the anti-war movement, my awareness as a woman in this culture was the very last thing to gel. Was it that way with you?

Oh yes. I think for me the real, I should say, the major, rebirth of my life, I think we all have many of them, but I think the major one was the coming together of those ideas and that consciousness. It's changed everything for me. It colours everything I see and think and do and experience. And I think it's no accident that it's the last thing that came about. It's the most hidden thing overall in our society.

And ultimately the most important.

And ultimately the most terrifying.

You knew Holly for, I think, six or seven years before you made *Lifeline*. At what point did you decide that you were going to record and perform again? Was there something in particular that motivated you, or a moment that you felt, "Now is the time"?

I guess it was sort of a combination of curiosity—I was intrigued with the possibility when it was presented to me—and a kind of ambition. I don't know. I really don't have great ambitions for stardom. Those went by the wayside a long time ago.

But I'll tell you what the major thing was. When Holly and I did our first tour together, somebody had the bright idea, which at the time I thought was kind of a Mickey Mouse idea, to put together a historical look at Holly's and my life in light of what was happening in the world during the time from my youth and childhood, through hers and into our adulthood. And I thought, Oh wait a minute, this is rather presumptuous. After all, we are not historical figures. I was very reluctant to do this.

Some people at Redwood were very excited about it and insisted on it and begged me to reconsider. Amy Bank, I think it was, sent me a first draft of this program and said, "Sit down for twenty minutes and just put down a few things. Everybody is going to want to know about these things." I thought, Baloney. Anyway, I looked at it and I started writing, and I didn't stop writing for days. I just was writing and writing and writing, looking at this and thinking about that. It just brought up a whole lot of stuff.

I still felt that this was ... I can't even think of the word for it ... there was something egocentric about it. I really didn't feel like it was a good idea. They took it and made a program out of it, and it was a smasher. Everybody wanted it.

And I began to get a feeling, a notion, an inkling, of how desperately women want to know something about their history. About what happened *before* the women's movement. What happened *before* the time that they remember and the time that was accounted for by something a relative said. And I realized how the threads have been so cut, and that is what really awakened the interest in me.

Then, during these tours with Holly, seeing—well, I would have expected the response to her, I mean everybody's got that response to her, but I was shocked, literally shocked, at the response to me. At first, I said, Okay, it's a response to Holly and me and the two generations. In other words, I was having my consciousness raised as we went along with this.

So when it was suggested to me that I do a record on my own, I was sort of pleased with that notion. And then realized that I was going to have to go out and tour and promote it alone.

What was it like in Madison? Your very first solo?

I was terrified. I didn't know what was going to happen. I was terribly terrified. It was fantastic. The response from the audience was so amazing. The warmth, the welcoming. It was like being a prodigal child returned to family.

Well, that's what it is, though. Bringing back someone who was lost to us. Even though you were out living a life, there is something that you represent that was lost to us because things aren't written down. How did you feel when Bernice Reagon called you and Holly the most powerful white radical women singers of your generations? That's a huge compliment.

That's a huge compliment. Indeed it is. Especially from Bernice Reagon. Well, I don't know what to say about that. [Laughs.] All I can say is that it is a huge compliment and I hope I can live up to it.

I don't know what I'm getting at here, but one of the songs you recorded with the Weavers was "Follow the Drinking Gourd," and then twenty years later, you and Holly record "Harriet Tubman." Somehow this is significant.

Well, aside from the historical import, Harriet Tubman (Moses was her nickname) led hundreds and hundreds of people to safety. Well, not exactly to safety, but at least to freedom via the Underground Railroad. And in a way, I feel that these songs that we sing are like signposts. Guideposts. They're like Harriet Tubman. They're like the people who lead other people through to a kind of freedom.

I think in a lot of ways the consciousness of this country is enslaved. By not just one little thing, but by a kind of combination of historical things, you know. This is the country of the great individual, right? We're the individuals, and that is wonderful in its way, but what we may have lost by it is the sense that we really live in a world of other people. And that as long as other people aren't free, none of us are free.

It's been proven over and over again if you are among the oppressors of a people, what you do, what you have developed, is a very sick kind of personality. Even from a psychological point of view, it's a very bad place to be. And if you are a victim and you think of yourself as a victim constantly, you're also in a very, very bad place. So, we hope that the songs that we sing are means of throwing a light on these things, and

I feel that that is a kind of freedom from slavery. Maybe that is why that particular song feels so right to me.

Fred Hellerman said in an interview that it is hard to feel heroic when you have no choice. You either be true to yourself or line up with the scum. You added that there is a great pleasure in doing what you believe in.

Well, you can quote yourself. For the love of it and the fight of it. That's why I do it.

RIP: June 6, 2015

COUNTRY WESTERN SINGER, SONGWRITER AND SINGLE MOTHER

An Interview with Terilyn Ryan

Herizons, vol. 3, no. 5, July/August 1985

"Neither one of us likes to eat very early. We might have a bowl of granola, then I'll nap a bit while he's playing. He's very good at playing by himself. I get back up at nine o'clock and he usually watches *Sesame Street* and all the children's TV shows in the morning. So I closet myself in the washroom and work on material. Write a tune. Just to get my practice time, because he is very well occupied. Then we go have lunch, go for a walk, go to the park, or the movies, or roller skating. If I can get him into a daycare, then I will for a couple of afternoons during the week, which gives me more time with my music.

"For the last two years that we've been on the road, I've been running my record, so I've been making long-distance phone calls, writing letters, doing promotions and booking myself. We go for supper around five, then I start getting ready for work. I take him over to the sitter's at seven. Go down and work. Pick him up and bring him home at the end of the night."

That's just one day on the road with Terilyn Ryan, country singer and single mom.

This September, Terilyn will finally come in off the road. Her son Larkin will be of school age so it will be time to settle down. She'll unpack her van, move the toys and books and sewing machine inside and probably write a song about the change.

There have been times when the two of them have had a semi-permanent place to hang their hats (or in the case of her son Larkin, his little stocking cap), but their real home has been the country music circuit from BC to Alberta, and their family includes the cousins, daughters, sisters and wives of club owners who care for Larkin on the nights Terilyn is working.

She was born in 1954 in Bowness, Alberta, a town annexed by Calgary but still country enough to have horses grazing in backyards. Her dad was a janitor who became the labour representative for CUPE (the Canadian Union of Public Employees)—"He was always running for MLA

Terilyn Ryan

no time for lovin'

1986, Vancouver: When Terilyn Ryan became a new mom, her new release "No Time for Lovin'" was perfectly timed. A child on the kitchen counter eating soggy cereal and toast was natural to the scene. It was an easy shoot. The eggs and coffee were cold.

[member of the legislative assembly] of the NDP; unfortunately they're the wrong party in Alberta"—and her mother was the head of the cash office at Safeway. There were three brothers before her and a sister after, as well as several foster children who grew up beside them.

"At home we listened to country music ever since I could remember. Mom played the accordion and had an offer to be a singer in a band back when she was sixteen. But in those days singers were held in a different light, so she had to refuse. It wasn't until my older brother got his own records that I heard anything different. He was playing the Beatles, the Animals, the Dave Clark Five. And I liked it all. Still, I was really into

Tammy Wynette and my all-time favourite was an album by the Carter Family. I bought a few 45s and a couple of albums. One album was by Connie Francis. I didn't know who she was but I liked the cover and it was on sale."

When Terilyn was young she sang in a trio called the Bow Valley Belles. They entered talent shows and worked the Stampede breakfasts. She also sang at the supper table, walking down the street, in restaurants and in movie houses. "It seemed subconscious in that I never really noticed. To me it was always the right time." In high school, she was head of the drama club, president of her high school class and captain of the cheerleading team. She worked weekends folding laundry.

She graduated when she was sixteen and went up to Fort McMurray, alone. She wanted to be on her own and to experiment. At seventeen, she moved on to Edmonton, where she applied for her first job as a singer. The manager of a rock and roll band hired her and put her on the bus to Prince George. She stayed with the band for two and a half months. Based on this brush with rock and roll, she reconsidered her decision to be a singer. "I had a lot of fun pretending I was Janis Joplin. But I ran into some health problems and lost all my confidence as a singer. So I quit music."

Well, she didn't exactly quit altogether. Instead, she enrolled in the drama department at the University of Calgary. She also studied saxophone and guitar and supported herself by working nights as a cocktail waitress.

During this period, she met her husband, a country musician down from BC's Kispiox Valley, looking for work. When things didn't turn out for him, he returned to the Kispiox. As for Terilyn, after two years, she was dissatisfied with school. "I loved the performance side but the academics didn't really hold my attention." She left school, organized her own western puppet show and went on the road. "We were very well received and had endless bookings but as I didn't have a good business mind at that time, I moved on to waitressing." She waitressed in Alberta, crossing paths for the next two years with her husband, who was riding horses and playing country music.

"I always seem to end up waitressing at various periods of my life. I even like waitressing because of the communication with other people. Wherever I worked I was called the singing waitress by workers and customers. Sometimes I even got requests. My music was just always there. I made no point of it."

In the summer of '73, she moved to the Kispiox. She was overwhelmed by its beauty, by the tolerance of the people and by their music. That summer she found in northern BC a valley rich in counterculture, a haven for American war resisters. "It's a very magical place." It was a complete change of pace for Terilyn. She received a lot of encouragement from the community and she began to play her guitar and write her songs.

> I've always been a dreamer / my dreams will never end.
> People always push you / they'll always try to bend
> you to the way they do it / the way that they see;
> I've always been a dreamer / my dreams they live with me

In 1974 she joined her husband in Calgary. He played bass, and they became a duo, working on his material and learning the country standards. In 1975 they attended the Country Music Awards. "It was quite exciting. I wore a formal and did my hair, acting like a country singer. At one of the parties, people were jamming and somebody asked me to sing a song. I was terrified. My husband wasn't in the room, but I went for it anyway. Two weeks later, back in Calgary, we got a call from Bryan Fustukian, who had heard me. He wanted us to join his band."

Together they joined the Hair Trigger Cowboys, an Albertan band notorious for churning out country musicians. But there was a hitch. Her husband got paid. Terilyn didn't. "I was the flower in the band. You're supposed to stand there and try and look good and make everybody smile. I sang about three songs lead and as much harmony as possible. So I just did a lot of learning in the group." After eight months, a decision was reached between Terilyn and her husband. She would leave the group and he would stay.

"After I left the Hair Trigger Cowboys, I was terrified really. I knew very little guitar. I knew nothing about being a musician. I had no equipment. I had a classical guitar. No pickup. Nothing. I tried to be a waitress, but it was really strange. There were no jobs. It was in February and everybody who had jobs was hanging on to them. I had the songs that I'd written, and I had composed them on my guitar, and I could really play them. So I thought, I'll go down to the agency and play a couple of my songs with all the energy I have and see if they'll book as a single. So I went down to the worst agent in town and he booked me."

For the next four years Terilyn travelled throughout BC and Alberta via Greyhound Bus Lines. She played the northern circuit, the southern circuit and all points in between. If the bar had a name like Silver Spur, Wild Country or the Ranchman, Terilyn was there. She made a good living for herself singing her own songs and the country classics. In 1979 she decided to form a band. "I just bought a PA for the band. Speakers. Just starting to get the members together. Then the day after my speakers were delivered, I found out I was pregnant. I immediately got a day job as a telephone solicitor and continued singing at night. I worked until three days before I had my baby."

It's not the way we choose it / Change with the times
Sometimes we skip the water / Sometimes we toe the line
Sometimes you're down and out / Sometimes you're satisfied
But you feel so good / Because you know you've tried.

When Larkin was born, Terilyn moved back to the Kispiox with her husband. "The Kispiox is a good place for a kid to grow up. We could make a living on the circuit from Prince George to Prince Rupert. Community dances." But it didn't work out, and after a series of unfortunate incidents, she and her husband separated. In the aftermath, the country music circuit was there. And Terilyn knew it by heart. She was well liked in the communities and they welcomed her and her new addition. Larkin became part of that larger country music family.

In 1982 Terilyn moved to Vancouver and released her first record. And she did it the way she had done everything else. On her own. "The first single, I did everything as well as have the nervous breakdown. I paid for everything and folded, cut and glued every little record cover. I wrote all the promo. I sent it to all the stations. I did all the follow-up, all the phone calls, everything. A thousand of those little beasts. But it was worth it.

"I originally started this project as a birthday present to myself, that once a year I could spend money on recording and in ten years I'd have an album. And I could give it to my kids. 'I was a singer, you guys. Listen to this album.'"

Terilyn's first single was written with a crayon on the dashboard of her car on the way to Seattle. It was called "One Hour Away." The B-side, "Blue Mountain Skies," was written during her days in the Kispiox. The record received airplay on thirty-five stations in BC.

Last year, Terilyn recorded her second single, "Lovers and Love" and "I Can't Help Myself." This time, she was playlisted on over one hundred stations nationwide. She was nominated for Female Vocalist of the Year at the BC Country Music Awards and she received an honourable mention in the 1984 Canadian Songwriting Contest.

In January, Terilyn finally formed that band she wanted. She called it Line-Driver, a term reserved for a trucker who knows the shortest distance between two points, the most direct route. And until September, she'll be out there on that route.

THE LAST SHALL BE FIRST

An Interview with Jane Sapp

Kinesis, December 1984/January 1985

This interview took place during the Vancouver Folk Music Festival in July 1984. Journalist Punam Khosla sat in with me during the interview. Her questions are identified with her initials.

Jane Sapp is an expert in folklore and history of black music. She is also considered one of the leading voices in the performance of Afro-American traditional music. She is an extraordinary singer, songwriter and piano player.

Jane's style is a composite of blues, gospel and other folk forms. Her themes are working people, children and dreams deferred. She gives her music to the black community, whose courage, creativity, dignity and fight for freedom and justice has been unrelenting.

In addition to her musical commitments—her first album, *Take a Look at My People*, was released in 1983 on Flying Fish Records—Jane has developed several cultural programs and community action projects. Currently she is the cultural director of the Highlander Research and Education Center in Tennessee. Jane's personal philosophy is that the time has come for the last to be first. This was a welcome message for those who attended the Black Women's Lives workshop at the Vancouver Folk Music Festival this summer.

CK: Tell me about the Highlander Research and Education Center.

JS: Highlander started in 1932, so it has a fifty-two-year history of struggle for social change in the South. Of course you can imagine in the '30s and '40s there were very few places where white progressive southerners could have a space to fight for what they felt was just, and to fight for a true democracy. Highlander was one of the institutions where people in the South could do that. It was also an institution where black and white people could come together and talk about ways to fight for social equality.

Highlander continues today to fight around those same kinds of issues. Of course, the times have changed so the fight is a little different, but many of the issues are the same and Highlander still continues to be a place where people who want to see real democracy in the South can come together and talk openly and strategize openly about how that can begin to happen. Highlander has always had the philosophy that grass-

1984, Vancouver: Jane Sapp introduces a song from the stage of the Black Women's Lives workshop at the Vancouver Folk Music Festival. Sharing the moment are dub poet Lillian Allen (*left*), storyteller Jackie Torrance, and singer and musician Almeta Speaks. (Ms. Torrance retells African-American folk tales and other centuries old stories.)

roots people and local people can, *on their own*, come to understand and analyze their problems and begin to mount an effort to change things. I think Highlander has been an important institution and continues to be.

When you were a field researcher, what kinds of stories were you trying to uncover? Where did you work?

I spent nine years in west Alabama and northeast Mississippi doing cultural work. I don't always like to think of myself as a field researcher, but I do like to think of myself as a cultural worker. I think what I was trying to do was to get people basically to tell their stories. Looking at people's historical and cultural experiences is a real important resource that folks have in terms of understanding past and current realities. So I thought it was real important to at least get those experiences documented. I wanted to get people telling it and, in the telling of it, thinking about the validity of their own life experiences and what those experiences mean.

In Langston Hughes's book *A Pictorial History of Black Americans*, there are very few women included. Have you found these women?

More women than men, in many ways. You know we hear so much about the civil rights movement and the men who were at the forefront of that movement. Although I have a tremendous amount of respect for people who gave their lives and gave their blood, sweat and tears for that movement, there are many untold women's stories about the civil rights movement that have not yet come to the forefront.

It's not only Fanny Lou Hamer, but it's *all* the Fanny Lou Hamers. And there are so many that we just don't know about because their light did not have the opportunity to shine as brightly as others.

But they are there—the women who sacrificed in so many ways. Women who gave up time ... gave up space in their home ... gave up food. Women who went around and knocked on doors.

I've heard real moving stories about women who felt that although they were not sacrificing their children, they certainly understood that the teenagers who were involved in many of the sit-ins were taking great risks, and the women were right there supporting them.

I even talked to a mother who lost a child in that movement. Her child was just run down by a group of white men from southwest Alabama. But she understood full well that was the risk she was taking. She said that there were many risks and sacrifices that we have to take for freedom and she still continues to fight and struggle even though she lost a daughter in that struggle.

There are countless stories like that and that's not a story that we hear every day and a story that's in the books on the civil rights movement. Her continuing effort to fight for a better life in that county is not one that's publicized. But it certainly has been documented through some of the efforts that we made when I was in Alabama and Mississippi. There are women out there who are doing all kinds of things, who are real true freedom fighters, and I hope through the work that I'm doing their stories can get out. Because they are very powerful stories, rich and inspiring stories.

What you did yesterday, the Black Women's Lives workshop, and this morning's Oh, What a Morning! (gospel workshop) has never happened here before.

Oh, that was a powerful experience yesterday on that stage. And I hope it continues to happen. We could have all been put in different places, as we have been. But put in the same space to address black women's lives and experiences made it a much more powerful statement. I think you saw it again this morning.

I think that the black church has been one of those places where, again, unfortunately, black women have not been recognized for the leadership role that we play. But we do, and it's a far stronger role than men play. Most of the people who are attending church every day are women. It's women who get out and raise the money. It's the same old story. We're the ones who are out there as the foot soldiers, but who are actually the leaders, but just don't get the recognition.

PK: I wanted to ask you about culture in the church. It seems to me that the most misunderstood aspect of black culture is its relationship to the church. I'm thinking in terms of a left perspective.

It was wonderful to have the church experience because it gave me so much. That was where I learned what faith was all about. You have to understand that for many, many years, the black church was the only institution we could go to. It was the only institution we could go to and pour out everything. So political stuff got poured into the church. Sacred stuff got poured into the church. Family stuff got poured into the church. Community matters. All of this. It was the one depository where people could go and take care and manage themselves and have a very profound emotional response to their realities. So I don't knock that.

To a certain extent I think that the church of today doesn't serve the same kind of role as the church of yesterday, but I would give nothing for that experience. It's not about a religious faith or a religious commitment. It's about a commitment to keep on keeping on. Because that was the phrase I constantly heard. And I heard it poured out of the songs: that in spite of suffering so much, people were still willing to hang in there for the long haul. So I was given that view of life. Somehow you have faith. You have faith in each other.

Don't ask me about sermons. I don't necessarily remember the sermons. I remember the songs. I remember how people responded to each other. I remember all the discussions about how you take care of so-and-so because their house burned down. Or somebody lost a member of their family. How you mobilize to be there. To get food. What I learned was how a community takes care of itself and the ways in which a community begins to survive.

I think it has given me a tremendous source of strength. Just remembering those people, and remembering the kind of faith and the kind of hope that I saw, makes me feel like I have a lot of faith and a lot of hope. It doesn't have anything to do with religion. But it has to do with just feeling that somehow if you continue to hold on, as the song says, that if you just keep holding on, if you just keep hanging in there, if you just keep staying in there, somehow you'll find the way to make things better for yourself.

If there's nothing else I learned, I learned that from the church.

On the other hand, I think that black people are very spiritual people. I think when you start talking about a political movement you have to look very carefully at the culture of the people. You cannot impose a political movement that does not fit the flavour and the recipe and all of the seasonings of that group of people. If you snatch religion away, then you snatch something very profound away from the black community. So, you can't come with a political movement telling black folks that they have to let go of this church that for four hundred years helped them through some really tough times unless you have something really, really powerfully dynamic over here in its place. But until that happens ...

We are spiritual people and even I don't want to let go of that. I think it is important to be spiritual. And I don't think spiritual means mystical. But in many ways, I think it means dialectical. It means that you are able to pick up and relate and interrelate and interconnect things both intellectually and emotionally. And I think that somehow all that stuff worked together for us. So I don't see you cutting one of them out. Because if you do, you cut out some of the life in us.

We are spiritual people. We should admit that straight out, so any sort of political movement for us is shaped by us. It has to be born of and grow out of who we are as people both politically and culturally.

PK: What is the political situation in the South right now?

In a sense, the question is not "What is the political situation in the South?" but "What is the political situation in the country?"

I think there is a movement towards the right. Ronald Reagan is making an attempt to dismantle many of the kinds of progressive social movements that have been made in the country. And I think that is real clear. I think that people in the United States need to realize that we are not talking about social welfare programs. We are not talking about some economic security. We are talking about some pretty profound political directions in the country for the next eight, ten, whatever many years. This is the long haul. We're not electing a president. We are electing some very profound political directions for the country.

PK: Given the nature of your music and your social position as a black woman, do you have any strong feelings about playing to a primarily white audience?

Well, that's a real heavy question.

CK: British Columbia may be perceived as a white province with a white musical sound. There has been no civil rights movement in

Canada similar to what happened in the United States in the '60s. I think it could be difficult coming into this environment.

There are two ways I look at my singing. If I were telling a story that my family already knew, we would be just sharing and bonding with each other around stories that we've told many, many times. And we know that when we tell those stories we can laugh and it will give us strength to hear the story again.

On the other hand, I might want somebody to know about my family. The kinds of stories that we tell and a sense of what we're like. What we had to go through. And I think there's validity in doing that. And I'm ready to tell that story wherever to whomever.

So, I look on an audience in Vancouver, I won't have the same bonding with this audience as I would if I were singing to my family because then it would be more ritualistic. We would be coming together to gather strength from the ritual of coming together. We might sing the same songs we've always sung, but that's what the ritual is all about. People coming together. Bonding together. Getting a sense of strength. A sense of direction. A sense of hope. A sense of joy. And a sense of going through all of the spaces that we go through together *as a people*.

When you're not singing for the family, then you're sort of telling other folks what your family goes through. You hope they understand. If they don't, it's okay because the joy is really in the telling of it.

And occasionally when you're doing a concert and you're not doing it for your family, you reach a level where you realize that there is a bigger family out here. There is a family of people who share the same kinds of concerns. There is a family who wants to fight around the same kinds of issues. A family of people who want to understand and who want to help. And who have also experienced the same kinds of things. So when that moment comes, when you realize that indeed we are a big family out here, it is a good moment. So, yes, it's all the things you said, but it is all that other stuff, too.

A Pictorial History of Black Americans *by Langston Hughes, Milton Meltzer and C. Eric Lincoln first appeared in print in 1956 on the eve of the civil rights upheaval. It is now in its sixth edition under the title* A Pictorial History of African Americans. *Langston Hughes died in 1967.*

SPECTACLES
(GIRLS WHO WEAR GLASSES)

An Interview with Rebo Flordigan and Jan Luby

Kinesis, December 1984/January 1985

Girls Who Wear Glasses have 20/20 vision. It was the Dorothy Parker couplet that inspired their name as well as their mutual ability to make spectacles of themselves. Jan Luby and Rebo Flordigan are very funny women. They also have a bundle of talent.

Both women have musical and show business upbringings. Jan was on the road with her vaudeville parents until she was seven, at which time they settled in Coney Island. From there, her life became a mixture of soul music and Motown. Rebo began her training when she was five and grew up playing jazz, rock and soul in the clubs in Minneapolis. They found each other in California and put their abilities to work.

Their act is a blend of comedy, song and dance with the focus on fun, although these women have a way of blurring the lines. One minute we could be waving our arms and singing about chickens, the next minute sitting quietly, stunned by the lyrics of "Cutting Me Down." I'd say Jan and Rebo have discovered safe and effective uses for the funny bone.

I talked to them last summer (July 1984), at the Vancouver Folk Music Festival, and between posing for silly pictures, this is what they said.

Rebo on Rebo

RF: With all four children in my family, it was mandatory that we start piano lessons at the age of five. And mandatory that we pick up another instrument at the age of eight. Also, that we sing in the church choir for twelve years and be in the band or orchestra at school and go to music school for four hours every Saturday morning from first grade to tenth grade. It was what was expected of us. It was what we did.

I'm very appreciative of it now. I quit piano lessons in, I think, tenth grade, when I started writing music (and because I would sit there during rehearsals rubbing my fingers and getting nervous until my hands would start to bleed). So I stopped taking lessons and started writing music. And then all of a sudden all my training made sense and I was very happy that I had the knowledge that I had acquired.

As for Minneapolis, I see Minneapolis as an oasis in the Midwest. Minneapolis to me is just one of the most beautiful cities in the world. It

1984, Vancouver: Girls Who Wear Glasses Jan Luby (*centre*) and Rebo Flordigan (*right*) were true vaudevillians. Born into show business, they understood how to use their lightheartedness to make a point, and since we were all wearing glasses, it was easy for me (*left*) to get the message. Photo: Sharon Knapp

just has tons of stuff going on. The winters, of course, are a drag, but the culture is wonderful. The people are wonderful. Lots of lakes and trees. I'd love to live there again someday. I was sad to leave it.

All about Jan

JL: My father was a comedy juggler and my mother was an acrobat and dancer. My mother danced until she was thirty-two and then she got married and started having babies. She stopped dancing and started assisting my father with his act. She'd do a standing split with open-toed shoes with a knitting needle in her toes, and he'd spin a ball on her toe. Or he would balance a glockenspiel on his chin and she'd climb up on a little stepladder and play it while he was balancing it. Stuff like that. But before that she and her sister had a sister team. The DeLeon Sisters.

The Meeting

JL: There's this family of vaudevillians on the West Coast and Rebecca married one of them. And I was partners with another one of the vaudevillians, so I met Rebecca through other vaudeville people.
RF: Four summers ago, July '80, is the first time I ever laid eyes on Jan and about six months later I ended up in Santa Cruz where she was living. She brought her guitar over to the friend's house I was staying at and we

sort of played a few songs for each other. The month after that, March, she helped finish writing "Schizophrenic Love Song." And we did it in a vaudeville show together in Santa Cruz. After that it seemed a couple times a year we would get invited to do a vaudeville show and we would pull out this "Schizophrenic Love Song" and do it over and over again.

JL: Basically, we were friends and occasionally we'd pull out this song and do it. We didn't get serious about playing together until last fall.

The Message

JL: I've done a lot of political benefits and sung a lot of political songs; I've written them and done other people's stuff. And around last year, or maybe the year before, I was playing in Santa Cruz, where people are pretty politically aware. And I'd look at the audience and look at my song list and the next one would be some really political song and I'd say, "You guys don't need to hear this." Then I'd play something fun instead.

Yet, I played an air force base in Alaska and played some of my most political stuff there. And I got a lot of really good feedback from the young guys. People like that need to hear it.

RF: We only have one basically political message in our music and it comes out in the last line of our introduction song. It starts out where I talk a little bit about my life and Jan talks about her life and then we come together and we're singing stuff at the same time and it must be obvious to the crowd that we're very different. She's sort of urban and I'm kind of this midwestern hick. And at the end, the last line is we can still be who we are and still live in harmony. Everyone is different and without all those different kinds of people, the world would be pretty dull.

Girls Who Wear Glasses will be performing at the Vancouver East Cultural Centre, December 13–16, 1984.

RIP: Rebo (Rebecca Hanson) Flordigan, May 10, 1997

FERRON

Herizons, vol. 2, no. 8, December 1984

There is nothing more disarming than looking out of the darkness to a brightly lit stage at a performer blinded by the light and having her gaze pierce that darkness like a cat staring straight into my eyes. It is an intimate experience. There is a singer holding a guitar, surrounded by monitors, amplifiers, cables and other people. But the mechanics of this production are lost on me as I find myself at home with strangers, all of whom are thinking, Ferron and I are the only ones here.

I feel obliged to say that I am not an emotional homebody. But I will leave this concert knowing more about myself than I did before. And I am not alone.

Ferron's effect on people, either through her live performances or through her recorded music, is legend. In the past few years, thousands of people have come to hear her sing. Ferron has appeared at every major folk club in Canada and the United States. She has sold out concert halls at Harvard, Smith, Oberlin and UCLA. She has performed at countless women's music festivals and at the New York Folk Festival two years running. At the close of this year, Ferron will be onstage at Madison Square Garden when New York's famed club Folk City hosts its twenty-five-year reunion. Sharing the billing with her will be, among others, Joan Baez, Peter, Paul and Mary, Judy Collins and Bob Dylan. Ferron will be the only new talent showcased.

The *New York Times* called Ferron "one of the most powerful lyric voices to emerge out of the post-folk genre known as women's music." *Rolling Stone*, when reviewing her most recent album *Shadows on a Dime*, designated this "Canadian-born lesbian … a culture hero." And the *Boston Phoenix* declared Ferron "the future of rock and roll." Herein lies the secret of Ferron's music: for anyone who dares to listen with a full heart, Ferron's lyrics can bring even the most apprehensive soul past prejudice and fear into the open, into an honest and emotional world that precludes sexual differences.

For Ferron, her music is her personal way out of a great silence.

"I realized that the problem in my life and in a lot of people's lives is that there is too much silence. It's so silent that you could go crazy. And I did. And nobody knew. So, it was my intention that if I ever got a chance to talk, that I would talk. I wouldn't hold anything back."

Ferron grew up in Richmond, BC, an agricultural suburb outside Vancouver. She came from poor people. Her mother was a waitress and her father was a truck driver "who was always looking for work." She was the oldest of seven children and there was never enough food.

Ferron lived in the isolation of her room. Here at a very young age she began playing her mother's guitar and "finding this vibration they call singing." Before words she found it through sounds. Ferron had a stutter. She couldn't even say her name.

When she was fifteen, she left school to work in a factory. Other jobs would come. A waitress. A cab driver. But she continued playing guitar (she now had her own) and she filled a notebook with her compositions.

"Although I didn't understand money, in a real direct way I understood oppression. And by the time I was able to go onstage, I just had a lot of empathy for all the common people. You don't have to be totally gifted and struck by God in order to stand up in front of people and say your piece."

Ferron found her first audience in the coffee houses of Vancouver's early women's community. After her first performance in 1975, she began to play at benefits and small gatherings around the city. The women's community could not support a singer financially, but they needed music that would make them feel whole. Ferron gave it to them. In spite of the encouragement, she remained shy and rarely talked during her performances. "I would just sort of sit there and mumble away at these songs and walk out and wonder what I was doing there."

In 1977, at the urging of a growing number of supporters, Ferron recorded her first album on her own label, Lucy Records. It was very much a homemade project, using only two tracks. But like most things homemade, Ferron's album had a sensibility that could not have been manufactured. It was a beautiful acoustic record, which, if re-released, would stand on its own. Because of financial restrictions she could press only a thousand copies. She sold them all from her basement suite.

The following year, Ferron released a second album. This time she was joined by a few Vancouver friends and musicians. She called it *Ferron Backed Up*. As with her first album, she and her supporters could afford to press only a thousand copies. Both of these pioneer albums are now out-of-print collector's items.

Despite the sale of two thousand records, life went on pretty much the same. Ferron continued performing in Vancouver while working at a variety of jobs. More people regarded her as a unique talent, but she was completely without guidance. She knew only about her music and nothing about the business. Gayle Scott changed all that.

"I feel personally that I could have just stayed where I was and I could still be there and still have the same feelings (if it weren't for Gayle). It makes my heart pound when I think of it. Because I had no idea what the country was—let alone reading the map. And Gayle did."

Gayle Scott first heard Ferron at the Vancouver East Cultural Centre in the summer of 1978. She immediately recognized Ferron as someone "who had a lot of talent and deserved a wider audience. And a person in need of some very careful management and direction."

Gayle had grown up in Hollywood. She had worked in advertising, film and commercial production. And she was very familiar with the "ways and means of stardom and the high price most people pay." At that time, she was running her own commercial production company (she was the first woman in Vancouver to do this) and she was already applying her own style of human ethics to her work. She was just what Ferron needed.

Gayle did not take on the management title immediately. Instead, as Ferron's friend, she encouraged her to come out of herself and be more relaxed onstage. She made suggestions. She assembled promotional material. In Ferron's words, Gayle inspired her and gave her self-confidence.

In the two years that followed, Gayle's passion for the work grew, and eventually she gave up her production company to become Ferron's manager and business partner. She also raised $25,000 to take Ferron into the studio to record *Testimony*.

Ferron's third album was a breakthrough. *Testimony* made several critics' top-ten lists, and it paved the way for her first major North American tour. The album sold seventeen thousand copies through mail order and the Women's Independent Label Distribution Network, and in 1982, the record was licensed to Philo Records in Vermont to be distributed in the United States. After two years, Philo could not afford to keep up with the demand, and *Testimony* is now temporarily out of print.

The title track, written when Ferron said she was "at the lowest I've ever been in my life," has become a song of strength for anyone who has listened to it. Sweet Honey in the Rock have since recorded "Testimony" on their album *We All ... Everyone of Us*.

In 1983, Ferron and Gayle began recording *Shadows on a Dime*. During that year, Gayle raised $65,000, supervised the production along with jazz singer Terry Garthwaite and arranged a ten-week tour to follow the album's release.

Shadows on a Dime came off the press in March 1984. And to use Ferron's own lyrics, her recent effort is "the jewel on the crown." Every song is a carefully crafted, deeply felt story. Ferron has said that some of her lyrics have made people "cough and squirm" during performances. And part of her newly comfortable stage manner is to help those people relax. She understands. She coughed and squirmed when she wrote the song. But each performance and each of her albums is a remarkable mixture of pain, humour and hope. Kind of like life.

Ferron lives alone in a rented cabin on one of the BC's Gulf Islands. She has lived there for six years, while Gayle operated Lucy Records out of her home in Vancouver. Although there are no fortunes to be made working outside the commercial music industry, the women remain in complete control of their lives. (Although they do get the occasional letter addressed "Dear Sir.") For Gayle, the goal is to "make sure that what happens with Ferron's career is not a product that is being manufactured or packaged but is actually and truthfully in time with what she has to offer."

Ferron takes nothing for granted. She is honoured.

"I think one of my fears in life is that I would be invisible. And I don't mean me, my body or my image. But my feelings. That there would be a silence in my life, all my life. And consequently I would be at a distance from other people. But I have received more than I ever imagined was possible. So my silence is gone. My isolation is broken. And I feel a deep responsibility—beyond myself."

ELLEN MCILWAINE

ROCK AND ROLL LEGEND

Rubymusic column, *Kinesis*, October 1984

Ellen McIlwaine is very much a rock and roll legend. She has been wowing audiences for the past twenty years with her New Orleans–style piano playing, her impeccable and powerful slide guitar technique and that remarkable voice, which she uses like a second guitar. Her stage manner is uninhibited, warm and rowdy. To see her is to know that the woman loves her work.

Ellen has been on the road for years. She has a loyal following in the United States, where she lives. But her biggest audiences are in Australia and Canada, where she spends most of her time. She has recorded five albums, although four of them are out of print.

Considering Ellen's status—she was first on the scene—I assumed someone would have written extensively about her. This was not the case. Oh, her name is mentioned often in music books. Dozens of guitar players have been inspired by her playing, and Jimi Hendrix was one of her first fans. But little is said about the woman. I brought this up to Ellen when I began our interview at the Vancouver Folk Music Festival, where she was performing this summer (July 1984).

EM: It is strange. I can't explain it. When I started out, it was Janis Joplin, Maggie Bell and myself. Everybody else was playing folk music. And they were a few years older. Like Joan Baez and Judy Collins. So we were two different schools. We were the rock and rollers. I don't know where Maggie Bell is today. I think she's still around. Janis Joplin obviously didn't make it. But there weren't too many of us women playing rock and roll. And all of the women sang except me. I heard somewhere that Janis Joplin used to play the guitar and they stopped her.

They tried to stop me. I was told that women shouldn't play the guitar because people couldn't see you wiggle. And they told me to wear strapless dresses. It was all just crap, of course. And I didn't do any of it. But I got the reputation for being difficult because I wouldn't listen to that stuff. I wasn't impressionable and malleable and properly whatever, so ... But I *have* been around a long time.

One of the reasons that people don't write about my life is that they don't know very much about it. But I run up against stone walls all the time. I put out an album in 1982 called *Everybody Needs It*, and Jack

Bruce from Cream plays bass and does the background vocals. We sent it to *Rolling Stone* and they didn't think it was important enough to give it a review. Then *Guitar Player* magazine tried to put all the women in the world that played guitar in one issue and I was very surprised when they mentioned me. They didn't contact me or anything. But they did mention me. Then someone wrote the magazine a letter and said why don't you do an article on Ellen McIlwaine. I sent *Guitar Player* some promo and had a person call them to represent me. But they said they weren't interested.

So, I think that maybe sex does have something to do with it. For all these years, I've tried not to think that. But I really do believe that it does. And it isn't intentional. I believe that it's conditioning. I don't believe that a lot of discrimination is intentional. It's not something people are aware that they're doing.

I told Ellen, in so many words, that I thought our music history was being erased as soon as we'd written it. I gave as an example the fact that the Go-Go's are being called "the first female rock and roll band," ignoring such pioneer groups as Isis, the Runaways and Fanny. What's more, Rolling Stone called the Go-Go's "the best female rock and roll band in the world."

EM: Well, I think those things are fads. You have to look at women who play music as a life-long career—not get dressed up in their roller skates and pink hair. There's a woman on the West Coast named Addie. I don't know much about her, but I heard her play once. She's a very good standard guitar player, as opposed to slide, which is what I play. She plays guitar like *anybody* but you don't hear that much about her. I saw a little short record by a woman named Cindy Bullens. Lead guitar. Where is she? They're probably like me. Where am I? This is why you don't hear about us. Because this is not where women get our brownie points, I guess.

An individual who was present during this interview suggested to Ellen that perhaps a performer had to be "fresh and new" to be popular.

EM: Believe it or not, I was fresh and new once, too. But I didn't get any exposure. And I feel that part of the reason why is that I don't do what is expected of me. If you do what is expected of you, you will always have jobs. You will always have opportunities. If you fit your pigeonhole. If you don't, nobody knows what to do with you. And I really don't think age has anything to do with it. I'd like to point out that Cyndi Lauper is over thirty. So there you go. Let's talk about fresh and new.

I do think that if you want a band to work cheap, you had better get a band that hasn't been working very long. And if you want a band that you can tell them what to play, then you better get a band that doesn't know what they're doing. Because I'm not really likely to listen. I never did listen. And I'm sure not going to listen now. After twenty years, I don't think so.

I chose this moment to say that although more women are playing rock and roll, it's still a rarity to have one in front of us. I asked her if she was aware of the positive effect she was having on her audience at the folk festival.

EM: I think so because I want people to do it to me, too. Over the years I've gone through a lot of things. But I feel much better now. I went through a lot of guilt for a long time because I didn't want to get married. I didn't want to have babies. I wanted a man in my life, but I couldn't find a man who was willing to live with me. He wanted me to play a role. Things like that.

I thought that since I didn't want to have children, there must be something wrong with me. I wondered why I play the guitar. Everybody tells me I'm good. Everybody says I don't sound like anybody else. People even tell me I play like a man—which I think is ridiculous. You're a guitar player first. Then your sex comes into the picture. You don't play with your plumbing. I was even told that men don't like to see a woman play the guitar. Well, guess who is in the front row. Young boys. And they want to know how I do it. But like I said, today things are better. I believe it takes maturity. And it takes age. And it takes getting some respect. For the first ten years, I didn't get that much respect as a guitar player. I really didn't. People really stepped on me because of what sex I am.

At this point, our conversation moved into her childhood. Ellen is the daughter of missionary parents. She was born in Nashville in 1945, but when she was very young, her family moved to Kobe, Japan. She lived in Japan until the early '60s, when her family returned to the South and Ellen was enrolled in college.

EM: My father sent me to a Presbyterian college. I think he wanted me to meet a preacher. Instead I played rock and roll in the bottom of the boys' dorm. I hated the school. They didn't offer anything. No music. No arts. So I dropped out, bought a guitar, and two weeks later I got my first job singing in a little place in Atlanta where you put a dime in a coffee cup. *Ellen arrived in Atlanta at a time when resistance to the civil rights movement was severe. I asked her what it was like returning from Japan into this environment.*

1984, Vancouver: Ellen McIlwaine's performance on the stage of an afternoon workshop at the Vancouver Folk Music Festival shook the audience. There was a strength and commitment to her style not previously seen in women. In the afternoon shade, she was just as uncompromising

EM: It was traumatic. I was raised in a small international community in Japan. And when we came back to the States, I would sit down on the bus wherever I sat, and I didn't mind who I sat by. But I would get a lot of strange looks because it was bad back then. I had friends in Atlanta and we were multi-racial. But we used to get a lot of cops stopping us on the street and calling us outside agitators. "Where are you going? What are you doing?" "Going to the movies."

It was bad. But I find having all those years in the South affected my roots a lot. I came back to the States when I was seventeen. And in Japan I had listened to Ray Charles and a lot of New Orleans music. There was also Professor Long Hair and Fats Domino. I started playing piano when I was five. No lessons or anything. But I learned from those people. So I learned a sort of New Orleans–style piano.

When I first came and lived in Atlanta, I heard B.B. King, James Brown, Bobby Bland, Aretha Franklin (she influenced *everybody*), Tina Turner, Little Richard and others on the rhythm and blues circuit. And I feel really fortunate that I had that rhythm and blues base. Then I discovered old blues. Eventually I began to play with Howlin' Wolf, Muddy Waters and people like that.

By 1966, Ellen was living in New York City. It was here that she met Jimi Hendrix. They were both playing in Greenwich Village clubs, and one night he asked if he could play with her.

EM: I fell on the floor. And then I said yes. So I played piano and he played guitar. He always envied my voice, and I learned from him. I watched him write "The Wind Cries Mary," and all he used was a Strat [Stratocaster guitar] and a twin reverb and that was it. I watched him experiment and make up things. He was real shy. He was really nice to me. He was a very sensitive guy, and the main way he communicated with the world was through his music. Jimi was real receptive and open. He listened to everything everybody played. He never put anybody down. It was a real pleasure to play with him. And I learned from him how to use my guitar and my voice like two guitars. He didn't do it as pronounced as I do, but if you go back and listen to those early recordings, you'll hear him sing with his guitar. I took that into my life and that's how it comes out from me.

I asked Ellen if she had a historical perspective on herself and on those times.

EM: Now, I do. And as I look back—I don't want to sound schlocky, but I feel very grateful that I'm here. Because so many people that I started out with, drugs and alcohol got them. And it almost got me. But I'm here and I'm real grateful for that.

Although Ellen lives in Connecticut, she is considering moving to Toronto. Her current rhythm section, Bucky Berger and Terry Wilkins, are from that city and she already has friends there. She is also looking for Canadian representation and a record company.

This month Ellen McIlwaine will turn thirty-nine. October will also bring her twentieth year as a performer to a close. When I congratulated her, she said, "Twenty more and we'll see if I turn into a good guitar player." I love a good sense of humour.

AN INTERVIEW WITH TERESA TRULL

Rubymusic column, *Kinesis*, September 1984

(This interview took place during the Vancouver Folk Music Festival in July 1984.)

After her Saturday performance at the Roots and Traditions workshop, Teresa Trull stood off to the side of the stage to watch Ellen McIlwaine play slide guitar. At the end of Ellen's set, Teresa commented that the workshop should have been called the Screaming Redheads. Maybe so. Both women qualify as genuine wailers and rockers.

In Teresa's case, her inspiration came from her childhood gospel choir in Durham, North Carolina. Later she made the natural progression to rhythm and blues. Teresa has stayed true to her roots. But she has also found a way to mix contemporary and provocative lyrics with this indigenous American sound. The end product is the music of a white woman's soul.

Durham, North Carolina

TT: I was raised on a chicken farm outside Durham. Then we moved into town. But my grandparents kept the farm. Durham is like a small southern town. Well, it's not too small. It has about a hundred thousand people. It started out as a tobacco city. Now the tobacco industry is dying. They're moving it out. I'm fast wondering what's going to happen to Durham. But it's also a college town. There's Duke University, University of North Carolina at Chapel Hill and North Carolina State. It was a great place to grow up in because it was really kind of backward, yet there was all this liberal influence.

Teresa was in high school during the height of the anti-war movement. Within a year of her graduation, the war began to de-escalate.

TT: Nowadays on high school graduation, people go away on trips to Hawaii and Jamaica. I just remember when I was in high school everybody went away to Vietnam. I was involved in the anti-war movement but I was a lot younger. I was really influenced by it, but at that age I got involved in prison work. I belonged to this group in Durham called Action for Forgotten Women. We attended riots. North Carolina has had some major riots

1984, Vancouver: Raised on a chicken farm in North Carolina, Teresa Trull found her way back to the land and lifestyle she loved through women's music. Her album with Cris Williamson, *Country Blessed*, released in 1989, marked her return. On this day, she had just finished participating in the Roots and Traditions workshop at the Vancouver Folk Music Festival, where she had been mesmerized by slide guitarist Ellen McIlwaine.

in their women's prison, and we just happened to be the group that got to ride along. Joanne Little was in prison in North Carolina. It was terrible.

NEW YORK CITY

TT: I swore to myself, growing up in the country, that the two places I would never go to would be New York and LA. The first place I moved was to New York. This woman offered me an apartment there for a month because she was writing a script in Canada. But she got fired so she came back. Then I didn't have a place to stay. I was walking around the street with my last eighty dollars when this woman turned me on to an apartment for eight dollars a month. Now, you can imagine what it looked like.

My bathtub was in the kitchen. And I had this great toilet. There used to be a public toilet on the half floor. But they nailed up the front door with boards and tore a hole in the wall up near the ceiling with a sledgehammer. Then they stuck a ladder down there. So you climbed down the ladder when you had to go to the bathroom. (And there was always about *this* much water in the bottom.) This was my luxury pad in New York.

But I lived there for about a year. I played a lot on the street, but I also played a whole lot in upstate New York. The women's community there supported me like crazy. It was great. And I worked odd jobs. I took care of people's dogs. I painted murals. I did a lot of painting. And then I worked in a daycare centre.

From New York to Los Angeles

TT: These friends of mine who had a radio show in North Carolina sent a tape of a show I had done to Olivia Records. Then Meg Christian called me when I was in New York and asked me to come sit in at her New York concert. I was completely beside myself. I had bronchitis and I was saying, "Well I don't really think I can sing." And my roommate came over to the phone and said, "You can sing." So I went and did it. It was just great. It opened up a lot of things for me. I got a lot of jobs.

I continued corresponding with Olivia and they were horrified at my state. Actually I was pretty happy in New York, but they thought it was horrible that I was crawling down a ladder to go to the bathroom. So they hired me in their packing and shipping department for about six months. We can all pack a record faster than anybody else. Then I did an album.

Rhythm and Blues

TT: Rhythm and blues is still fighting it out in the women's community. People still really associate women's music with folk music. And here we are at a folk festival. (Which is really great.) Actually, I'm glad that people here are recognizing that rhythm and blues influences are just as old as most folk music. At least in America. Rhythm and blues comes straight from gospel. From the blues. Almost every R&B artist came out of gospel. And so much good folk music comes out of gospel. You can write off Christianity if you want to, but don't write off gospel music. It's one of the most indigenous American influences.

Teresa's first two albums, The Ways a Woman Can Be *and* Let It Be Known, *were released on the Olivia label. Her latest album,* Unexpected, *is on Olivia's new label, Second Wave.*

TT: Olivia created Second Wave for radio play purposes. A lot of times in radio, a label will become identified with a certain kind of music. For instance, Motown was primarily identified with soul music. When they started recording rock, rock stations would see the label and throw the record away. "Oh, this is soul music. We don't want it." Finally, Motown created their own rock label, Morocco.

It's the same thing with women's music. It's really identified as easy listening, or soft rock or folk. We were trying to get radio play on rhythm and blues stations, so Olivia thought they should create a new label.

We really need to start expanding women's music. In fact, all kinds of independent labels are having a really hard time in the economy. So if we could get some radio play, it would really help. And it's worked to an extent. But Olivia is really going all out with it. I'm not sure what they will be doing next, but Tret Fure's on the label and I hear tell they're going to have Alicia Bridges ("I love the night life, I love to boogie") on that label, too.

Barbara Higbie

TT: Barbara and I have been playing together for the last two years. We met at a Reno rodeo in the livestock pavilion. We were playing on the same bill. But I swear to god, Barbara and I saw each other from about fifteen feet away and instantly knew that we were spiritual friends or something. We followed each other around ragtag. I didn't even know she played piano at the time. She was playing fiddle and I just went, Gosh, what can I do? Let's see. Can we do vocal-fiddle duets? Then I heard her album with Darol Anger and I just loved it.

Later we were doing a benefit and each artist got up and did three tunes. I asked Barbara if she wanted to try and play with me. I had been playing with a lot of different accompanists. And even though some of them were the best, I wasn't getting what I wanted in terms of response. When Barbara came up onstage and we started to play, I felt like I had been kicked in the back of the head. We both had such a good time in the first two verses that in the middle of the song, we got a standing ovation. That had never happened to me in my life. We were so exhilarated. I'm surprised neither one of us spontaneously combusted.

I feel like somebody sent me to heaven and now Barbara and I will get to be a duo forever. Barbara is completely like me. She wants to communicate with people. We believe that the audience is an incredibly important part of what's happening.

There's a hard thing going on where people expect one performer to meet everybody's credentials. I want you to sing about El Salvador. I want you to sing about the women's movement. I want you to sing about lesbianism. And no one performer can do that. Barbara and I have made our whole thing to be almost on the personal level.

You don't have to have everything included in your music in order to have it do what you set out to do with it. We set about winning people the best way we know how. And by keeping our music at the highest standard we know. And then we use it. Sometimes in the lyrics of the songs, sometimes by getting people in the lobby, sometimes by turning over the money. There's a million ways to make your music support political activities without having to put a pamphlet to music. With our music, we try to convey enough spirit and strength to keep people going.

Following the folk festival, Teresa returned to the Bay Area to begin producing an album for Deidre McCalla.

BRICKTOP

QUEEN OF THE NIGHT, 1894–1984

Rubymusic column, *Kinesis*, May 1984

It is one of the tragedies of our culture that our heroines are often lost to us before we have a chance to learn from them. Such is the case of Ada Smith, a singer and nightclub hostess known most of her life as Bricktop.

It's not that Bricktop was obscure. She wasn't. She was legendary. But the people who knew her and loved her were part of a privileged world: John Steinbeck, Evelyn Waugh, Cole Porter, the Duke of Windsor, King Farouk, F. Scott Fitzgerald, T.S. Eliot. By the time I reached the age when I was taught about these men of history, Bricktop was retired and living alone in New York City. No one ever told me about her.

There was another side to her fame, equally inaccessible, but for more legitimate reasons. Bricktop was often featured in magazines distributed in black neighbourhoods. In the words of author and historian James Haskins, who collaborated with Bricktop in writing her life story: "It was a fact of existence for the average American black to be on intimate terms with the stories of those few of us who managed to burrow out from under."

Bricktop's grandmother was a slave. Her mother was sired by the master of the house and born into slavery two years before the Emancipation Proclamation. Bricktop was born free in 1894 in West Virginia. She was the fifth child delivered to Hattie Smith and her husband. They named her Ada Beatrice Queen Victoria Louise Virginia Smith, but she was later called Bricktop because of her red hair.

Shortly after her birth, Bricktop's father died. Her mother, Hattie, was thirty-seven, alone and very poor. She moved her family to Chicago, where she had relatives who were passing for white. It was her hope that they were in a better situation and could help her get settled. Unfortunately, times were difficult for them as well. But Hattie stuck it out and eventually she found a boarding house to run on the south side of town.

The south side of Chicago was like many urban black communities. It was poor in material matters but rich in culture—especially when it came to music. Bricktop grew up in this environment and became completely infatuated with the goings-on in the saloons, particularly in the backrooms where the music was made. Bricktop never considered herself a singer, yet that is how she made her living. When she was sixteen, she left home to travel the black vaudeville circuit. It was a very hard life for a young woman and a very dangerous profession. Americans did not take kindly to blacks on the road. But Bricktop survived.

After a few gruelling years in barrelhouses, she started singing in nightclubs in Chicago, Washington, DC, and New York City. It was at Connie's Inn in Harlem that her reputation solidified and her talent and personality earned her an invitation to Paris.

Bricktop arrived in Paris in 1924, and the American colony loved her. Not only could she sing, but she knew all the latest American dances. Almost immediately she was invited to exclusive parties to sing and give dance lessons. In retrospect, the idea of a black woman teaching the Charleston to affluent white Americans may seem demeaning to some. But Bricktop was a working woman. She was tough, independent and extremely charming, and these people were her clients.

It is ironic, however, that because she never lost touch with her roots, she became a kind of reality touchstone for American millionaires, artists, writers, film stars and European royalty. They followed her to every club engagement in Paris. Eventually someone suggested she manage her own club, and for the next forty years, Bricktop's was the most exclusive saloon *in the world*.

But Bricktop had other admirers as well, for she was not above using her influence to help as many people as possible. In her years stateside, she discovered a young piano player and his band in Washington, DC. She sang a few songs with him and decided to take him to New York to get work. She got him a job at the Cotton Club, and Duke Ellington never looked back.

In Paris, she encouraged a young busboy to keep writing. His name was Langston Hughes. She took entertainer Josephine Baker under her wing when she realized that Josephine had a penchant for destructive men. In this case, she was not wholly successful. She was able to give another young singer a chance and the two women befriended for life. (Unfortunately, her friend, Mabel Mercer, died recently.) However, no one could really help Bricktop when she was forced to return to New York in 1939 to escape the Nazi invasion of Paris.

After sixteen years out of the country, Bricktop found the situation in New York quite drastic. She had become unaccustomed to segregation and overt racism. At forty-five, Bricktop was broke, jobless and without respect. She managed to last five years in the city before a friend financed a Bricktop's nightclub in Mexico City. Again, Bricktop reigned supreme, but there were problems with the Mexican government and she longed for Paris, the place she considered home.

After six years in Mexico City, she returned to a Paris she didn't recognize. Postwar Paris had become as racist as New York, a gift from the white American GIs. A year later, in 1951, she relocated to Rome, where she operated Bricktop's until her retirement in 1964. She was sixty-nine years old and she was tired of staying up all night. Bricktop spent most of her remaining twenty years in New York City. Occasionally, she would make a public appearance or consent to sing, but she was tired and in fragile health. She preferred to stay at home.

In 1979, she hosted a "Bricktop Hour" at New York's famed 21 Club. It was here that she met James Haskins, the man who would later help her write her autobiography. *Bricktop* was published by Atheneum Books on her eighty-ninth birthday, August 14, 1983. The mayor arrived at her apartment and gave her a paperweight and a scroll.

It was this book that brought me to her, and in January 1984 I produced an interview with Bricktop for a CBC Radio program, *Variety Tonight* with Vicki Gabereau. What makes this interview significant is that four days later, Bricktop passed away in her sleep.

We scheduled the interview for late afternoon because she told us that she didn't like talking to people before noon. We sent a stringer to her apartment with a microphone, a tape recorder and a reel of Ampex tape. She remained in bed during the interview; she said she had arthritis, nothing more. She reminisced a bit about her friends, but mostly she was philosophical. She talked about the lessons her mother taught her and about her own creed: "If you're going to think, think about something." She spoke a lot about passion and about the men in her life. She admitted that she could not remember them all and in some cases, it was just as well.

When asked about her health, she said, "I'll live. But if I don't, I've had one of the most beautiful, great lives in the world and I'm grateful and God knows it." She died quietly, January 31, 1984, in sharp contrast to the way she lived.

FUND-RAISING

DANCE

Sponsored by the Vancouver
Folk Music Festival Society

SATURDAY MARCH 1

8:00 p.m.

Russian
Community
Centre
2114 W. 4th Ave.

Music by:
CONTAGIOUS
KITS KAT KICKERS
KEN BLOOM
FERRON
DAN RUBIN

Tickets: $5.00 Advance
Available at Black Swan Records, 2936 W. 4th
$6.00 Door

FOOD·MUSIC·RAFFLE·DANCE

Bonus Tracks

ELLEN MCILWAINE

THE BEST OF 2021 AND OF ALL TIME

Kurated, January 22, 2022

I spent the morning printing her obituaries. "Slide Guitarist with a Power Voice Dies." "Groundbreaking Singer, Writer Dies." "Fiery Slide Guitarist and Blues Singer Dies." "Blues Legend Dead." But I remembered the morning we were at the bank and she needed to deposit the cash she'd been paid for her gig at the Yale Pub in Vancouver the night before and the teller wouldn't take her money in case she was a drug dealer. Ellen kept explaining over and over (and I vouched for her) that she was a *musician*. But there was no convincing the woman behind the counter that this woman in front of her with the massive red hair and dried-up-overnight eyeliner was simply trying to make a deposit in order to meet her automatic rent withdrawal back in Calgary. It was humiliating. I also remembered how after a gig she came to visit me in the maternity ward. A couple in black leather showed up at the same time and the combination was just too much for the hospital staff. They threw me out (with my son) the next morning. A decade later, sitting in a tatami room, she taught both my kids how to use chopsticks.

Ellen called to tell me she was dying. My response was to send her some information from a friend about an immunotherapy drug and order her Marianne Faithfull's new CD. I guess I thought that if this treatment worked for my friend's husband (also a musician) it could certainly work for Ellen, and who doesn't want to listen to Marianne Faithfull read poetry when one is facing the end? I should have just said, "What do you need?" Or even, "This is fucked up."

On the morning of June 23, 2021, Ellen McIlwaine died. Her friend Sharron Toews was by her side, as were a group of friends from around the world who had come together on Messenger during her last days. Just six weeks before, she had received a devasting cancer diagnosis and began calling many of us to say goodbye. Her fight was brief and courageous. As Sharron wrote that morning, "She died peacefully and willingly."

Ellen was the master of her guitar. A virtuoso. A goddess. She fused slide, blues, rock and roll, country, reggae, jazz and the yet-undefined world music into her style. She sang from way down inside, often making unearthly yet melodic sounds in sync with her playing. She told me in our first interview in 1984 that it was Hendrix who taught her how to use her voice as a second guitar.

I began hearing her name in the 1970s. But an electrified woman wasn't something we could imagine. I finally saw her in the hot summer sun at the Vancouver Folk Music Festival. She was onstage in a swirl of hair and sweat, her rhinestone barrette catching the sun. Southern musician Teresa Trull stood off to the side with her mouth open, then looked out into the crowd in amazement. It was not unlike Mama Cass seeing Janis for the first time.

Ellen was adopted by American missionaries and grew up in Japan. She eventually returned to the American South, where she had been born, but spent much of her life on the road. Her travels took her to Australia, New Zealand, Germany, Switzerland, Austria, across Canada and the US and then back to Japan. She found musical homes in Atlanta, Greenwich Village, Woodstock, Montreal, Toronto and finally Calgary, where she was living when she died.

Much has been made of her relationship with Jimi Hendrix, and rightly so. (He approached *her* to jam, and she was with him when he wrote "The Wind Cries Mary.") But in her long life she played with dozens of the big bluesmen, including Muddy Waters, Howlin' Wolf, Johnny Winter, Richie Havens, Taj Mahal, Jack Bruce, Elvin Bishop, John Hammond, Jeff Healey, Paul Butterfield, Buddy Guy and Junior Wells, with special relationships with Margret RoadKnight, Sue Foley, Patty Larkin and Cassius Khan. Any musician who ever saw her play or shared a stage didn't forget.

Ellen did what came naturally and her music became heavily influenced by what she had heard on Japanese radio and in the international community where she was raised. "There was no us and them," she told me. "It was all us." She scored a play and two films using Egyptian and Lebanese traditional dance music and the music of Pakistani singer Ustad Nusrat Fateh Ali Khan. Producer Shinichi Osawa of the Japanese electronica group Mondo Grosso brought her to New York to collaborate. Tokyo deejays Ken Yanai and Kei Kobayashi, who were playing her Polydor albums in dance clubs, flew her to Japan to record a live album and go with them on tour. Elsewhere in the universe, house music deejay Yukihiro Fukutomi remixed her cover of "Born under a Bad Sign," and Fatboy Slim sampled her version of "Higher Ground." She returned to Japan in 2011 to perform at the World Music and Dance Festival in Hakodate. She played and spoke their language. Ellen's album *Fear Itself* hangs on the wall of the Los Angeles County Museum of Art as part of artist Yoshitomo Nara's current show. His wall of sound memorializes the 352 albums that inspire him as he works.

One of her last collaborations was with tabla musician Cassius Khan. Trained in Indian classical music, he was also a lover of funk and rhythm and blues. They were family. *Mystic Bridge*, Ellen's last recording, is the music they made together.

At the time of her death, she was a few chapters into her autobiography, and filmmaker Alfonso Maiorana, co-director of *Rumble: The Indians Who Rocked the World*, had begun work on a documentary about her life. The UK's music magazine *MOJO* had just gone to press with a current interview and update on her career. In their next issue they followed with an obituary.

Ellen was remembered in the pages of the *New York Times*, the *Washington Post* and the *Globe and Mail* by Neil Genzlinger, Harrison Smith and Nicholas Jennings, respectively, whose reprints travelled the globe, including the *Times* of London. Their tributes hit hard as they knew what we had lost, sadly before a new generation even knew who she was. Despite the praise of true music aficionados, Ellen had yet to reap the rewards of her genius. ("No interest, no gigs and no money," she told Andy Morris in *MOJO*.) She was female, after all.

Some years ago, I wrote in her liner notes, "She travels in her van with equipment, clothes and the occasional bass player in the space in the back. Mementoes from her travels dangle from her rear-view mirror and pictures of friends adorn her dashboard. The deer whistles on the roof clear the road when she travels at night."

Ellen looked for the good in people and was a loyal friend, making each of us feel loved. She was proudly clean and sober (almost forty years) and she helped others to hang on. "So many people that I started out with, drugs and alcohol got them," she told me back in 1984. "And it almost got me. But I'm here and I'm real grateful for that." At the time of her death, she was living humbly, yet creatively, in Calgary, driving a school bus and making plans. She was seventy-five.

In my playlist, I've included (for selfish reasons) the Jimi Hendrix song "May This Be Love." She dedicated it to me one night in 1987 at an album release party in Toronto. For a moment, I felt like a big shot.

KONELINE: OUR LAND BEAUTIFUL

An Interview with Nettie Wild

Salt Spring Film Festival series, February 23, 2017

One night at a screening in Powell River, BC, a man left the theatre "steaming mad" at what he had just seen in Nettie Wild's latest film, *Koneline: Our Land Beautiful*. "Assumptions just keep piling up depending on who is watching and what they bring into the theatre," Wild tells me in an email. For a woman who has taken her camera behind the scenes of the Zapatista uprising in Chiapas, and filmed the radicalization of drug users on Vancouver streets as they fight to open a safe injection site, her exquisite tribute to the magnificent landscape of northwestern British Columbia and the people who live there may be her most contentious.

"The land was always, for me, the central character, which is what makes *Koneline: Our Land Beautiful* different than my other films. *Blockade*, for instance [a 1993 film about the land claims conflict between the Gitxsan and the descendants of the white settlers], takes place seven hundred miles to the south and pretty much deals with the same issue, but formally in a very different way. *Blockade* followed the central character [Gitxsan member] Art Loring, and while I was striving for different points of view, I was eliciting from the characters their political point of view.

"In *Koneline* I am striving to bring the viewer into a cinematic experience with the land through the eyes of different characters. Not so much talk. It is a search on my part to see if I can find the physical poetry in every character, and to see if I could be surprised, if I parked my assumptions about them, by that poetry. I was surprised. Many times over."

Koneline: Our Land Beautiful is filmed in a small corner of Canada most of us will never see. It is the traditional territory of the Tahltan First Nation and the location of the Red Chris Mine. It is the home of hunters, outfitters, linemen and miners; women and men (and children) who thrive in this beautiful harshness with physical and spiritual strength. Their attachment to the land is deep; they know change is coming.

Wild goes into the homes of language scholar Oscar Dennis (Hotseta Na-Dene), his parents, Mary and James, and other Tahltan families. She films their gambling games, house concerts and the inside of their smoke sheds. She accompanies them fishing and on a moose hunt.

With spectacular aerial shots, Wild travels with Heidi Gutfrucht, a local outfitter, on a harrowing thousand-mile trek north as she takes over a dozen horses and supplies across a rushing river and over the crests of mountains to where she will lead visiting hunters. "This is home," she says in the film. "People like me would die in the city."

Wild visits Teena and John Wright in their taxidermy-decorated Ta-togga Lake Resort, a lodge that caters to hunters and is a hangout for local children. The mine workers are represented, too. "I live up in the clouds," says one man. Another explains with a kind of awe that the samples he has removed from the ground are 192 million years old. An assistant driller, a Tahltan man, shares his knowledge as he assembles a heavy drill dropped by helicopter into his hands.

The mine is the easy target. It is the lifestyle of these northerners that some viewers find difficult to accept. There is rawness to life on the ground.

In response to my question about bias or lack of understanding expressed by the audience toward the people she filmed, Wild said, "There is far less criticism of the Tahltan than there is of non-natives working in the industry. And it drives northerners crazy when people are so quick to use what they mine out of the earth, and just as quick to criticize the workers who pull this stuff out of the earth. This is what Oscar Dennis means when he sighs and says, 'We need the mine.' He is not just speaking of Tahltan jobs at the mine site; he is speaking to the fact that he is a contemporary Tahltan who uses a cellphone, computer, truck and cannot see a modern world without them."

The viewer in Powell River walked out because of his opposition to big-game hunting and to the perceived ill-treatment of the outfitter's horses. "Up north in Smithers," Wild says, "we also had a big reaction to the killing of the female moose, which precipitated a debate about First Nations hunting."

In the beginning, Wild was "completely closed out of the mining industry" until Harvey Tremblay, the owner of Hy-Tech Drilling, "said yes, instead of no, to my camera. He said that he was not ashamed of what he did and if people had a bone to pick with him, then he was ready to talk to them. He thought that the mining industry as a whole should do the same, so he gave our camera to his diamond drilling crews and this encouraged Pretivm Resources to allow us to film Harvey's crew at their Brucejack mine site.

"On the Tahltan side, access was also initially problematic. The woman running the blockade asked me if I would contribute my truck to help block the road for a couple of nights. I explained to her that I couldn't do that because it would destroy my access to the mining side. I tried to argue that my camera might prove to be more useful to her than my truck. She was not convinced and denied me access to the blockade. So at one point I did not have any access to either the mine or the blockade." (Wild later films some difficult conversations between the elders and Chad Day, the young president of the Tahltan Central Government, and officials from the mine and the BC mining ministry.)

"Imperial Metals, the company who owns the Red Chris Mine, which was being blockaded by the Tahltan, never did give me any access. Rokstad Power, which was building the transmission line, however, allowed us to film, and that resulted in one of the most unlikely and poetic sequences that I have ever filmed. Every frame had its surprising poetry."

But a favourite scene for Wild was when the community came together to rescue the salmon that had been cut off from their spawning grounds by a rock slide. With bare hands, fishing rods and helicopters, the salmon were transported around the slide and back into the river. "I really like this scene because it uses the technology so often linked to industry to try to help save the salmon, and the effort could only work with the DFO [Department of Fisheries and Oceans] working with Tahltan Fisheries and community members, First Nations and white.

"My sense about the north is that those folks live the controversy. We talk about it. I doubt there is a Tahltan family for instance that does not have someone working in the mining industry at their dinner table. And every table also has someone who has blockaded a proposed mine or seized a drill rig. This is a complex world that they are living.

"I came to see my role in it all a bit clearer, which was a real liberation. I think there is a real role for art to play in these controversial times. I found that my job was to create a cinematic experience, not to articulate a polemic. It's not my job to offer up solutions. It is my job to park my assumptions and seek to find the poetry and beauty in complexity. To frame the familiar in an unfamiliar way to see if both myself, as the filmmaker, and my audience can be surprised."

In *Koneline: Our Land Beautiful*, Nettie Wild shares an emotional space with photographer Walker Evans. She takes an even-handed and loving approach to the people she meets, and an unflinching view of their lifestyles. Her approach is dignified and daring, and the land is truly beautiful.

CULTURE CLASH

THE 35TH ANNUAL VANCOUVER FOLK MUSIC FESTIVAL, JULY 2012

Words & Pictures, 2012

I started hanging out backstage at the Vancouver Folk Music Festival over thirty years ago. My first experiences behind the fence were as a music journalist and later as the emcee of my own stage on Sunday afternoons. Like many who return year after year, I walk on site with a well-developed sense of anticipation. I am a member of an old guard and I am devoted.

The thirty-fifth annual festival was held last July (2012) at its permanent location at Jericho Beach Park, a magnificent grassy space touched by the beaches of the Pacific Ocean and framed by British Columbia's Coast mountain range. For a performer, the view from almost any stage is breathtaking, especially at sunset. For a music lover, it is a beautiful dancing piece of paradise. My perfect time seems to be at the beginning of the evening concerts. The sun is moving toward the horizon, shooting a blinding beam across the grounds. Flickering shadows block the light as thousands of people are on the move. They are strolling, dancing and kicking up dust. I hear applause and the testing of microphones. Somewhere there are always drums.

The musical complexity of this year's festival received high praise. Gwen Kallio, the festival's publicist for the past four years, believes it is artistic director Linda Tanaka's respect for folk music and for this festival's history that makes it work. Sitting backstage, she describes Linda's programming as "a treasure trove of music. Gold coins on top that you know are valuable and then discovering the rare and brilliant stones underneath." In a previous incarnation, Gwen was the festival's hospitality coordinator. She also managed Rare Air, Moxy Früvous and Lillian Allen and the Revolutionary Tea Party, all of whom performed here. Her head and heart are in this business.

Valdine Ciwko, a newly elected board member and the festival's first full-time publicist back in the day, compares Linda's instincts to the contributions of Estelle Klein, the creative force behind the Mariposa Folk Festival and the originator of the workshop format now copied by almost every festival in the world. It is the "synergy" created by knowing how to mix and match. "It is the surprises that happen when Alejandra Robles, Los Gaiteros de San Jacinto and Cedric Watson meet for the first time on

Saturday afternoon on Stage 6 and break into a spontaneous collaboration. They didn't realize what they had in common until that moment." But Linda knew.

Likewise, Gary Cristall, a founding director who shaped this festival with the power of his political convictions and musical connections worldwide, has nothing but praise for Linda. "She single-handedly preserved what is best about this festival, artistically, financially and organizationally, *while no one noticed*. Her accomplishments are amazing." When I comment on how quietly she goes about the festival business, he refers to her "excessive modesty."

As the founder of the Salmon Arm Roots and Blues Festival and artistic director for at least twenty-five years, she is "the last one standing from that northern circuit," Gary says. When Linda headed to Vancouver to take over from Dugg Simpson, she left her old festival with a surplus well over $300,000—the mark of a woman who works until the work is done.

This year, Linda received an overwhelming vote of confidence as over sixty people attended the annual general meeting to elect a solid group of board members, including Valdine Ciwko, Anne Blaine and musicians Linda Hoffman and Amy Newman. As Anne Blaine, who worked as office administrator during the Cristall years, explains, "I was supposed to be teaching in some small northern town. The festival changed the whole direction of my entire life." Everyone has a stake.

For the audience last summer there were many opportunities to have that transformative moment. On the main stage Friday night, Shari Ulrich, Rick Scott and Joe Mock, in their beloved Pied Pumkin formation, ushered in the very first wave with their still-original West Coast sound. Later, with some help from festival staff, Dan Mangan acquired a ladder and climbed off the stage and into the audience, leading them swaying and singing as the festival lanterns appeared in the background. On Saturday night, K'naan, a long way from his childhood in Somalia, paid tribute to Neil Young when he sang "Heart of Gold." However, on Sunday I watched the screaming fans of the truly wild Johnny Clegg Band rush the stage, pushing aside those occupying the blankets at the front, even the sleeping children. These new occupiers were not content to dance in the designated aisles. This is where my culture clashes.

Backstage in the performers' lounge, a string of lights and the cast-off colours from main stage create the atmosphere. Musicians come and go in the semi-darkness, identified by their native language, cowboy hat or secret cigarette. (You mean you really *can't* smoke in here?) On this particular evening, Roy Forbes and his mate, Lydia Dixon, take their place at one of the long tables surrounded by friends, including Joe Mock and Rick Scott. At the other end of the table, Stephen Fearing and Andy White are hanging out with Joelle May from Folk Alliance in her vintage Sherpa jacket. Wazimbo from Mozambique has signed a CD for producer Steve Edge. Jack Schuller, who for years championed independent artists through his Festival Distribution business, is speaking highly of Dala and Good for Grapes.

Former staffer and volunteer Carol Herter calls it "the committee," anyone with institutional memory who shares their stories and "keeps the festival honest." This night the committee recalls the time a certain actor-turned-musician insisted that his limo be brought onto the festival grounds to pick him up from behind the stage, and the year an action star travelling with one of the performers insisted on introducing his friend from main stage and then having chairs brought up so that he and his entourage could sit off to the side. I guess he didn't read the part in the festival guide about chairs not being over four inches from the ground.

Anne Blaine remembers when all the performers were paid the same amount and everyone was required to participate in at least two workshops. If you wanted to play at the festival (and almost everybody did), "the performers bought into a belief system as well as the audience." She described the weekend as a big family reunion, a chautauqua, a political atmosphere but not adversarial. "It was a piece of what people wish the world could be."

For Shari Ulrich, sitting backstage with her two children, musician Julia Graff and reunited son Mike Magee, this moment is something she never could have imagined thirty-five years earlier. "The sense of history the musicians and audience have with the festival is unparalleled. To be able to share something that's been so special in my musical life with my family is wonderful."

Quite unexpectedly, I have my "festival moment" when I'm caught off guard by Ani DiFranco. I hadn't seen her since she first performed here as a teenager. Sunday night she walked out onstage, alone, all grown up, with only her words and her guitar and what Gary Cristall calls "the three chords and the truth." I actually started crying at one point as I listened and looked out over the site. What happens here still matters.

THE SONG REMAINS THE SAME

THE SHARED SPIRIT OF WOMEN'S MUSIC

34th annual Vancouver Folk Music Festival program guide, July 2011

It's been over thirty years since the Vancouver Folk Music Festival (VFMF) listed a workshop called A Good Woman's Love in the program guide. That same summer, "Feminist" appeared alongside "Gospel" and "Celtic" in festival publicity. Famed and former artistic director Gary Cristall had sent talent scouts to the Michigan Womyn's Music Festival. Tipped off by women in the ranks, he took note of a movement being labelled feminist music or women's music and called someone who called someone else. In the decades that followed, the VFMF would become the major supporter of women's music in Canada.

"Women's music" was the creative voice of women's liberation. It was at once a spontaneous outburst of euphoria and a reaction to that nameless emptiness so many of us felt turning on the radio. It was all about airplay. If you didn't hear it on the radio, you would probably never hear it at all. We were told women couldn't play music and if they did, no one would listen. For the mighty women who persevered (*and there were many*), the stories of their suffering or isolation are now legendary. These were very different times. Our history was hidden from us. It was discarded in used record bins, reinterpreted or left out completely. Women's music not only fought the power, it took the power.

Cris Williamson, appearing at this year's festival, was a reluctant catalyst. She had found her voice early and as a songwriter had shown her confidence and independence. Signed to a major label, it was her debut studio album (found in a used record store by singer and musician Meg Christian) that brought her to the attention of a group of relocated radicals considering their next move. While being interviewed on an early feminist radio program in 1973, Cris made an offhand remark that someone ("you") should start a women's music label. Within the year, the newly formed Olivia Records would record *I Know You Know*, Meg Christian's groundbreaking album of "women-identified" original songs, but it was Olivia's second release that would become the most influential women's music collection of its time, Cris Williamson's *The Changer and the Changed*.

The launching pad that was Olivia now became a landing strip as many musicians who were already in the business arrived at Olivia to offer their services. They produced and engineered albums, played backup, arranged music, raised money and packed boxes. Women taught each other. This was the big idea. By the mid-1970s, a renegade network of women's coffee houses, bookstores, women's centres and festivals supported by other women-run recording labels and production and distribution companies, publicized by a growing number of female music journalists and historians (the late Rosetta Reitz comes to mind), began to spread throughout Canada, the United States, parts of Europe, New Zealand and Australia. It was mail order and word of mouth. It was revolution.

Looking at this year's lineup of women, a generation later, we may take choice, opportunity and independence for granted. Corrine West chose the life of a nomad. Gillian Welch felt the creative freedom to play bass in a goth band and drums in a psychedelic surf band before discovering the Stanley Brothers. Wendy McNeill took herself from a childhood love of Dolly Parton and Porter Wagoner to the Velvet Underground. Kendel Carson began fiddling at age three. Emily Wells channelled Screamin' Jay Hawkins. Their musical influences reveal a strong, expansive knowledge of history. (Jenny Whiteley swam in the talent pool.) Most likely, they were encouraged.

Diana Jones was inexplicably drawn to music of Appalachia, imprinted on her soul from her birth family. Kathryn Calder found comfort and inspiration in her experience caring for her mother. Mary Gauthier braved her battles with substance abuse and rejection. Samantha Crain revealed her duality "singing from confidence and desperation." This is richness expressed in the integrated, appreciated and shared spirit of women's music. As Rosanne Cash learned by example as a member of one of music's most revered families, the best stories are always the truth.

Today music can be created almost anywhere and uploaded to the cloud. What once took a national movement, we can do mostly from our phones. But this weekend, as we listen to the young ones and walk among our pioneers, it will still be the human connection to the music that makes all the difference. As Cris Williamson wrote many years ago: "When you open up your life to the living, all things come spilling in over you. And you're flowing like a river, the changer and the changed." The messengers may be "changing," but in the best possible way, our song remains the same.

FERRON

THE BEST OF OUR TIMES

18th annual Vancouver Folk Music Festival program guide, July 1995

I sometimes think I know how musicologist Alan Lomax felt as he held his field recordings in his hands. In my collection I have Ferron's white albums; those first tentative homemade projects recorded on two tracks. The ones with the pencil drawings and cloudy photographs. The raw sounds from another time.

Like many people who were a part of the women's movement in Vancouver in the '70s, I recognize the names that are among the credits. I remember the night at the Full Circle Coffee House when Ferron asked us to all come down to the studio the next day to sing along on *Testimony*. I could have been there, but I stayed out too late.

In those days, Ferron was a point around which many of us could gather. Despite her shyness, her reluctance to talk or raise her head, she could command an audience. The early women's movement was not an easy place to be. It was where women came when they escaped. Some were hurting. They were angry and full of hate. Others were excited, inspired and deeply concerned about their sisters. Many were both. It was also a time of conformity. We could ask all the questions we wanted, but the answers had to be the same. Ferron had other ideas.

When some of the most popular women's music rallied women to action, Ferron's music required women to sit down. We had to listen. We had to think. Even in the beginning, she wouldn't let us off easy. She had no solutions, only different ways of looking at things. She excluded no one. Her emotional universe was somewhere out there, past prejudice, past fear and into those wide open spaces. When women were trying to pull themselves together, she was saying, Let it come apart. She knew that from the bottom, we could see the whole world.

Gayle Scott knew this, too, and her fifteen-year partnership with Ferron began the night after a concert when Gayle picked up some boxes of Ferron's albums and carried them out to the car. They met for the first time that evening. Together they travelled the continent.

In the beginning it was floors, sleeping bags, small towns, way too many people, and equipment crammed into sometimes barely functioning cars. Their early days were very much the picture of the struggling, independent musician, except they were part of a brand new movement. All across the country, feminists were coming together to organize, create and support the spontaneously named women's music phenomenon. Women were forming their own production companies, their own labels and their own music press. Ferron and Gayle Scott were a major part of the cultural uprising. They helped set the standard.

Gayle had the drive and the skill. She had already worked in advertising and promotion for film. She was a photographer. She was self-employed. She understood Ferron and had a strong desire to protect her. She also believed it was possible to be involved in the music business in an enlightened and ethical way. Ferron trusted her completely and they believed in each other. Together they recorded *Testimony*, *Shadows on a Dime* and *Phantom Center*. In time, they played every music festival, major folk club and significant music hall and auditorium in North America. I sat fourth row centre, in 1987, the night Ferron played Carnegie Hall.

It is true that political criticism, media praise, outpourings of love and fanatical fans did not alter Ferron from her course. And that was never more apparent to me than on that night at Carnegie Hall. As she looked out on a fractured movement, a great room full of women divided by race, sexual orientation, spiritual beliefs and other ideological barriers, she asked us, as she had in the '70s, to take a new step in an old direction. With her song "Harmless Love" she simply said, Make love, not war.

Ferron took a new step herself after the release of *Phantom Center* in 1990, when her partnership with Gayle Scott began to come to its natural conclusion. In the wake of this major change, she started her label Cherrywood Station. She released a collection of instrumental music, *Resting with the Question*, and a live recording from the Great American Music Hall, *Not a Still Life*. She experimented. Then, after years on the road, after living on Saturna Island, in Provincetown, Santa Fe and Mexico, she arrived at a new place. There was an acre of land, blackberry bushes, a recording studio, three dogs and Marianne. She found her way back to the garden. Eventually their daughter was born.

Ferron said to me many years ago, "You don't have to be totally gifted and struck by God in order to stand up in front of people and say your piece." But I think those who know her music would agree that she has been touched by the light. She speaks a language all her own. She writes the way a painter paints. She makes you come outside. Now, past her fortieth birthday, she has literally grown up. She is rooted like a tree.

In the world of music journalism, analogies flow when describing Ferron's music, especially her recent CD *Driver*. For me, it's another chapter in her book. It's like looking at her photographs or reading her journal. For Ferron, being intimate is more than her trademark. It is her way of life. It is also what makes her one of the greatest songwriters of our time. It is through her that we find ourselves at home with strangers, all of whom are thinking, Ferron and I are the only ones here.

THE REAL ELLEN MCILWAINE (1975) / EVERYBODY NEEDS IT (1982) LINER NOTES

Stony Plain Records reissue, 1995

I first got word of Ellen McIlwaine's talent in the 1970s. It travelled to the West Coast on the wheels of Volkswagen buses driven by people who had actually seen her, and they dropped her name along with Genya Ravan and Tina Turner when talking about women who were kicking out the jams. Only with Ellen, there was more. They talked about the power with which she played her slide guitar. It was almost unimaginable.

Ten years later I witnessed it for myself and I felt like Mama Cass watching Janis at Monterey. We were all stunned. It was a sunny day at the Vancouver Folk Music Festival. Ellen was onstage in a whirl of hair and sweat, her voice matching note for note the squeal of her fingers on the steel strings of her guitar.

In that July heat, she was a boiling contradiction. Pink skirt. High heels. Her rhinestone barrette was catching the sun. But she was the real McCoy and she was giving us the goods. When she was finished playing, I couldn't breathe. I've since learned that Ellen McIlwaine is not so much a contradiction as she is an amalgamation. The adopted daughter of American missionaries, Ellen grew up in Japan. She spoke Japanese and attended an international school run by Canadians. Her musical tastes were integrated as well. On Armed Forces Radio she listened to Fats Domino, Trio Los Panchos, Ray Charles, Professor Longhair and Peggy Lee.

She began playing piano at a very early age and was well on her way to developing her famous New Orleans style when her family returned to the US. For a young woman who referred to white people as "foreigners," moving to Georgia at the beginning of the civil rights era presented some problems. It was also an incredible opportunity.

Living in Atlanta, Ellen was exposed to almost every legendary R&B artist who was touring at the time, including Aretha Franklin, Bobby Bland and B.B. King. James Brown had his own TV show. Gospel music was on the radio. Ellen McIlwaine had the fever. What began in Japan was reborn in the southern tradition.

In 1966, Patrick Sky found her and convinced her to come to New York. Although younger than her contemporaries, Ellen played club dates with Muddy Waters, Howlin' Wolf, Elvin Bishop and John Hammond. She was particularly encouraged by a young Jimi Hendrix, who asked to sit in on her sets at the Café Au Go Go. She was with him when he wrote "The Wind Cries Mary" and it was from him that she learned how to use her voice like another guitar.

New York was also the place where Odetta crossed the floor of a Greenwich Village club to kiss the cheek of this shy, red-headed guitar player who had just finished her set. It was perhaps an acknowledgement of promise. It could have been a kiss for luck. Ahead of Ellen McIlwaine was one long highway.

Ellen returned to Georgia in 1968 and formed her first band, Fear Itself. They recorded an album, which was raw and wild. It's now a collector's item. Her next album, *Honky Tonk Angel*, was recorded live at the Bitter End in New York in 1972, and the title cut for the album *We the People* was recorded in concert at Carnegie Hall in 1973. This album featured eight original songs, with the background vocals on specific cuts by the Persuasions and the West 44th Street Noise Choir.

(The song "We the People" became a favourite of Johnny Winter's, and Ellen watched him in silence one night at the Electric Ballroom as he sat in his dressing room, with his failing eyesight, picking out the fingering.)

In 1974, Ellen was featured on Polydor's *The Guitar Album* with Eric Clapton, T-Bone Walker, Rory Gallagher and John McLaughlin. The following year she recorded *The Real Ellen McIlwaine* with members of Montreal's Ville Emard Blues Band. On this album, she sang and played songs by John Lee Hooker, Stevie Wonder, Tracy Nelson, Jack Bruce and Pete Brown. She also recorded six more original compositions and illustrated the inside cover with her own artwork, featuring a self-portrait and a drawing of Jimi Hendrix.

Ellen was back in New York in 1978 to record *Ellen McIlwaine* with the jazz fusion duo of John Lee and Gerry Brown. That same year the mayor of Atlanta, Maynard Jackson, declared the first day of spring Ellen McIlwaine Day. She was also made Lieutenant Colonel, Aide-de-Camp, to Governor Busbee of Georgia in recognition of her contribution to the arts. In 1979, her name was added to the honour roll of *Who's Who in America*.

Two more albums followed. *Everybody Needs It*, featuring Jack Bruce on bass, won the National Association of Independent Record Distributors (NAIRD) award for Best Rock Album of 1982, and her eighth album, *Looking for Trouble*, released on Stony Plain Records in 1987, was picked as one of National Public Radio's top twenty records for 1988.

These accomplishments are impressive and eight albums is certainly a decent body of work. But it is her life that is remarkable. She is devoted to her music. It makes her heart beat. Although she has set up housekeeping in Georgia, Connecticut, New York City, Montreal, Toronto and Calgary, her life has been spent on the road. She is at home on the stages of rock clubs, blues houses and festivals. She travels in her van with equipment, clothes and the occasional bass player in the space in the back. Mementoes from her travels dangle from her rear-view mirror and pictures of friends adorn her dashboard. The deer whistles on the roof clear the road when she travels at night.

She's cleared the road for other guitarists, too. As young female musicians rise to prominence, they benefit, sometimes unknowingly, from Ellen's thirty-year survival in the business. She has always been independent and she's called her own shots. She has suffered the consequences of being first but she has ultimately shown in the light. Guided by her southern ghosts and psychedelic past, her rebel yell has grown into a banshee's wail. To listen to Ellen McIlwaine today is to hear the evolution of the sound.

RITA MACNEIL

HONEST EMOTION OVERSHADOWED
BY UNFORTUNATE SOUND

Nightshift column, *The Georgia Straight*, December 16–23, 1988

(Review of December 10, 1988, concert at Queen Elizabeth Theatre, Vancouver)

She made a magnificent entrance. Without introduction, Rita MacNeil walked onstage and began to sing. But the magic ended there. The words to "Walk on Through," a testimony to surviving malicious gossip, were drowned out by her band, which sounded as if it was giving a rock concert all its own.

Rita MacNeil could stand alone in a field and move mountains with her voice. The images in her songs are as powerful as a Dorothea Lange photograph or a painting by the socially conscious Norman Rockwell. For many, Rita is the true sound of music, because she gives voice to a range of individuals generally left out of popular song. It is important that we hear her when she sings.

Rita's first set included "I Believe in You," "Everybody" and "She's Called Nova Scotia" from her first major-selling album, *Flying on Your Own*. She received her first burst of applause for the latter song—because she removed her shoes. But the volume of the band made every song sound alike and seemed to push Rita through her lyrics, instead of allowing her to linger over notes with the band rising up behind her to sustain an emotion. The wall of sound surrounding "Fast Train to Tokyo," her last song before intermission, was almost too much.

During the break, though, the sound techs were asked to pull back the band. They did, and in the second half of the concert, Rita MacNeil slowly emerged.

The first sign of change came with "Reason to Believe," the title track from Rita's latest album. Written for her mother, Renee, who encouraged her shy daughter to sing but "who couldn't wait around for [her] to make it to the stage," Rita silenced and moved the audience as she sang of a loving parent "who is only a memory."

Her original Christmas songs were well received, but her signature song, "Working Man" (inspired by stories told to her by retired miners), brought the audience to its feet.

"Flying on Your Own" and "When Love Surrounded You and I" were delivered in the first encore. After removing her hat and blowing a kiss, she was back for a second. This time Rita took the hall by surprise with her version of Sam Cooke's "Bring It on Home to Me." For the first time, I saw a true blues singer living inside her body.

TERILYN RYAN HOSTS HEN NIGHT

The Georgia Straight, February 6–13, 1987

Had Hen Night been a tradition in this city, perhaps we would have contributed a legend or two to country music by now. However, judging from the talent participating in the monthly female jamboree at the Railway Club, we still have a fighting chance.

The creator of Hen Night, country singer Terilyn Ryan, is a story all by herself. For almost fourteen years, she's played the country music circuit in BC and Alberta, raising her son at the same time. She worked as a waitress and cook when the need arose and wrote, recorded and distributed two singles.

Last year when throat problems forced her to slow down, Terilyn took a cooking job at the Patricia Hotel. A month after she moved in, she organized a regular Saturday afternoon jamboree, which attracted Danny Mack, Herald Nix and members of the Rockin' Fools. Three months

1984, Vancouver: Country singer Terilyn Ryan never stopped working. Until her son started kindergarten, she was on the road and could be found doing sound checks in the afternoons before her gig.

later, she hosted a female jam session (she's done this before in the Kispiox Valley and in Penticton) and it also became a feature at the hotel. In August she moved Hen Night to the Railway. After a fall hiatus, it recently resumed on the second Monday of every month.

The band members change, depending on who's working where, and they only meet for one rehearsal. One might hear songs by Rosanne Cash, Patsy Montana, the Judds and Janie Fricke, "Loco-Motion," "Mountain of Love" or Terilyn's cover of Loretta Lynn's "Don't Come Home a Drinkin' (with Lovin' on Your Mind)."

If there's any justice, Hen Night should become a firmly established tradition in Vancouver. Naturally it's encouraging to see so many female musicians in one place having such a good time. But it is worth remembering that it is at the beginning of a performer's career that raw enthusiasm is most evident. And this is exciting to watch.

JANIS JOPLIN

BURIED ALIVE IN THE BLUES

Radio Waves, Vancouver Co-operative Radio program guide and magazine,

October 1984

Historians say that adolescence was unkind to Janis Joplin. Her skin was a mass of pimples and her pretty blond hair turned mousy brown. She was overweight, oversensitive and overread. It is written that the pain of unattractiveness turned Janis into a tough, swearing, beer-drinking tomboy who rebelled against her destiny. If they mean Girl Scouts, the typing pool and the mating game, then historians are unkind as well.

It's true that Janis was different. She didn't want to go to prom. She wanted to paint. She didn't like girdles and she wouldn't wear makeup. She read books by Jack Kerouac and she listened to black music. In 1963, this was tantamount to mutiny. Janis had no friends.

Her California experience wasn't much different from her life in Texas. When she joined Big Brother in 1966, the band was distressed. They were under the impression they were getting a sexy girl singer. One they could have fun with. Instead, they got a fat and homely Texas girl in a ponytail and mannish tops. The dreams of Big Brother and the Holding Company were shattered. Big Brother fans weren't exactly knocked out either. And there were times when people shouted for her to get off the stage. It's a wonder she didn't quit.

Then came the summer of love and Monterey Pop. No one was more surprised than Janis when her rendition of Big Mama Thornton's "Ball and Chain" stopped the show. Three months later at the Monterey Jazz Festival she brought the audience to its knees. And her New York City debut in February 1968 was pandemonium. (After four encores, a stunned audience reared back and charged the stage.) That same year, she appeared on the cover of *Time* magazine, and Aretha Franklin called Janis the most powerful singer to emerge from the white rock movement. She was twenty-five years old. In two short years she would be dead of a heroin overdose. The girl in mannish tops had become a legend. But she had also become a target.

Her sexual exploits, both real and imagined, were heavily reported. Did she like men? Did she like women? Did she like younger lovers? Why wasn't she asked to her high school prom? Was it true she was voted the ugliest man on campus? Did she consider herself "liberated" or just one of the guys? Why was she so fat?

Janis was also a victim of concert scams and bad promoters. On one tour, she was greeted with half-empty halls and cancelled performances. Although the entire fiasco was the work of an inexperienced promoter, Janis was led to believe the tour failed because no one liked her. On another occasion, fifty thousand people sat in a field waiting for her to arrive. Unfortunately, no one told Janis. Eventually the promoter involved in this concert went to prison.

But what the media and poor management started, local officials finished. Janis was blamed for every rock crime of the period. After the murder at Altamont, which had absolutely nothing to do with her, Janis was banned from performing in several states.

In time, Janis grew disillusioned with her audiences. She wanted to slow down, but she said her fans weren't happy unless she incited them to riot. She told a reporter the year before her death that she didn't think people could enjoy her music unless they thought she was destroying herself. Southern Comfort must have concurred because they sent her a fur coat. But contrary to myth, Janis battled her addictions. She never missed a scheduled performance and she never used before a concert.*

The real tragedy is, of course, that her critics overpowered her supporters. Obviously Janis knew she was a target. She'd been one all her life. But to those who understood, intuitively or otherwise, Janis was a target because she was a symbol. In every small town and community across North America, there was at least *one* young woman who dared to be different. Janis Joplin sang to her.

Janis died on October 4, 1970. Since then, there have been some changes made.

This month on Rubymusic *Connie Kuhns will be presenting* Buried Alive in the Blues, *a four-part documentary on the life of Janis Joplin.*

*At the time of this essay, the life of Janis Joplin hadn't been fully explored, as she had not yet received, in death, the critical and historical acclaim that was her due. Howard Alk and Seaton Finlay wrote and directed the 1974 documentary *Janis*, but only a handful of books had been written, most notably Myra Friedman's 1973 biography of Janis, *Buried Alive*, which was part of the inspiration for my radio series.

In the following years, several important books, specifically *On the Road with Janis Joplin*, by her friend and road manager, the late filmmaker and author John Byrne Cooke, and the American Masters documentary *Janis: Little Girl Blue* have shone a much brighter light on her drug and alcohol addictions, which, in the end, she was unable to overcome.

RUBYMUSIC

A HALF-HOUR OF MUSIC BY WOMEN ARTISTS

Vancouver Co-operative Radio program guide, August 1981

Rubymusic went on the air on Vancouver Co-operative Radio, CFRO, on May 15. The following is an interview with Connie Smith (Kuhns), *Rubymusic*'s creator and host. Promoted as "one half-hour of music by women artists," we began the interview by asking Connie to define women's music.

CK: Women's music is anything and everything that a woman writes, plays or sings.

CFRO: Then what is feminist music?

Feminist music is usually written with an analysis in mind. The songwriter has reached certain conclusions about her life and adheres to political or personal guidelines; guidelines set by her own consciousness or by a group. Often this music is generated by women-owned and -operated recording companies—Olivia for example. Most popular lesbian music falls into this category. But for the purposes of *Rubymusic*, I don't usually differentiate between the two. It's all women's music as far as I'm concerned.

You did a show called "Blue Notes." Isn't blues rather humiliating music for women?

On the contrary. Blues and jazz contain some very aggressive, strong-willed lyrics. Just listen to Billie Holiday's "Baby Get Lost," "No More," "Ain't Nobody's Business If I Do," "Now or Never." These are all excellent examples of a woman asserting herself. It's true blues can hurt. But then so does asserting yourself sometimes. "Blue Notes" was a finely tuned show. I included Gwen Avery's "Sugar Mama," Holly Near's "Get Off Me Baby" and Joplin's "Little Girl Blue" with the Holiday material. It was a very strong program. One of my favourites.

What do you think of country and western music as it pertains to women?

Country and western music is also underrated. Its lyrics are unpretentious, honest and completely to the point. Aida Pavletich [*Los Angeles Free Press*] once said, "The themes may be trite, but they are the values that people kill for." I don't agree that the themes are trite, but it's true that country and western songs cover the most basic details of a woman's life. As with blues, the field is replete with women songwriters literally shouting out women's reality.

Who do you think are the outstanding country songwriters?

Dolly Parton has written some excellent material and in some circles she is recognized as an accomplished songwriter—not as a woman of large proportions. Loretta Lynn is another songwriter I respect. "Don't Come Home a Drinkin' (with Lovin' on Your Mind)" is the only song of its type that I know of—not a trite theme at all. And "One's on the Way" exemplifies perfectly a country woman's ambivalence towards a big-city women's movement she can't understand. Complementing this material is the feminist genre of country and western. Willie Tyson, Woody Simmons and Terri Garthwaite for example. Then there is the new breed: Carlene Carter with her new wave album cover, Juice Newton and Tanya Tucker. Tanya brings a sexuality to the stage not previously seen in country music.

Why do you think country and western wasn't acceptable at one time?

It wasn't sophisticated enough; too working class perhaps. There was prejudice towards the country accent as well as an unwillingness to listen to some basic truths. Country and western women inundated their music with songs of divorce, abortion, adultery, alcoholism, passion, revenge. They said what most people were embarrassed or afraid to say, which doesn't exactly make someone popular.

Has anything been overlooked as far as pop music is concerned?

Absolutely. Nineteen sixty-four produced one of the most feminist songs in popular music, Lesley Gore's "You Don't Own Me." The lyrics of that song contravened everything that young women were being told at that time. Ironically, it was written by a man. Helen Reddy's "I Am Woman" was another landmark song. She first wrote and recorded the song in 1970 over the objections of her producer, who thought the song "too butch." She also expressed sympathies with certain women's issues, which got her into lots of trouble. NBC required her to shave her armpits and wear a bra, the critics condemned her and ridiculed her every time she made a public appearance, and factions of the women's movement criticized her for being too successful. However, by 1972 "I Am Woman" was selling twenty-five thousand copies a week—seven out of ten to women. That song reached women everywhere. Laura Lee is another unsung heroine. Her one album *Women's Love Rights* is blunt and powerful. She made it briefly as a cult figure but disappeared into obscurity.

Is it difficult finding information about *Rubymusic*'s featured artists?

Sometimes. Generally, I can find some information once I figure out where to look and how to look for it. But occasionally I run into dead ends.

What are some of the stories you've discovered?

I didn't really discover anything. I just look at an established fact differently. For instance, it's no secret that Carole King took her baby to work with her every day when she was songwriting in the Brill Building during the late '50s. But it becomes a woman's story when placed in the context of a nineteen-year-old mother without a full-time babysitter and without a lot of money trying to make it as a songwriter.

Carole kept her baby, Louise, in a playpen near the songwriting cubicle and would check on her throughout the day. During this period, 1958–1968, Carole co-wrote over two hundred songs and her baby grew up to become a songwriter and singer herself. Another example are the girl groups such as the Crystals and the Ronettes. They cease to be the dumb '60s girl sound when the lives of these young women are taken into consideration. Firstly, *they were girls*. They were all in their teens when they began singing professionally. They were all from the poorer neighbourhoods of New York City, Philadelphia, Detroit, and they all wanted to sing more than anything else in the world. It just so happened their street sound was exploitable.

Who do you consider to be the most important contemporary songwriters?

That depends on the genre. For my own personal tastes, I'd say Carole Pope [Rough Trade], Marianne Faithfull and Nona Hendryx, although I haven't heard much from Nona in several years.

Why those women?

Because they are daring. They speak the unspeakable yet they are integrated.

What about women's recording companies?

With the help of Olivia artists, particularly Linda Tillery and Mary Watkins, feminist and lesbian music is slowly moving out into the world. Once the buying public stops being afraid, I think the broad-based appeal of this music will become apparent. It will also be good financially for the studios. Holly Near from Redwood Records has done much to further this cause.

Why is it important to have a show such as yours?

Because women have a vast musical history worthy of appreciation. I believe all of this music should be available and should be approached with an open mind. On *Rubymusic* I provide the music and the information. I let the listener go from there. Women don't need to be told what to think about music. They can figure it out for themselves. Besides, it's a lot of fun.

EPILOGUE

Meg Christian Concert Review

Kinesis, May 1976

And we will dance after all these years
Of crying, and self-denying ...
And begin ...

So it was, as two hundred women, in out of the rain, gathered under Ms. Christian's musical shelter to celebrate the theory and practice of sisterhood.

For an hour and a half, she commanded our emotional levels as we identified and relived our own experiences through her songs. Her music was her catharsis, as it was ours.

From her album *I Know You Know* she entertained us with "Hello Hooray," "Scars," "Ode to a Gym Teacher" and "Song to My Mama," the latter of which she called "the song my mama never heard." She spoke at length and almost lightly of conversations between herself and her mother regarding sexual preference and privilege. But as she sang, she beat the side of her guitar with the same force that she must have used on her kitchen table the night the song was conceived. Anger, pain and alienation pouring out through her fingers, her face, her soul.

New material included a song to her cat, Alix Dobkin's "Mary B" and the Four Seasons' oldie "Sherry." With a raised consciousness, the lyrics to "Sherry" held an entirely different interpretation. Her audience was very responsive.

Even though Ms. Christian considers herself "a guitarist who sings," her voice was rich and resonant. And her professional presence was very human and very woman.

She elaborated on the importance of involvement in the women's movement. There was too much energy, she said, being generated at the concert to let subside when we all dispersed. She strengthened her viewpoint with the tune "Where Do We Go from Here?"

We ended the evening with applause, solidarity and tears.

THANK YOU

DEBRA ROONEY

Mary Schendlinger
Liza Keogh

Geist
AnnMarie MacKinnon
Michal Kozlowski
Mary Schendlinger, Stephen Osborne

The Georgia Straight
Charles Campbell

Hot Wire
Toni Armstrong Jr.

Kinesis
The Radical Reviewer
Emma Kivisild, Claudia Macdonald, Cole Dudley
Nancy Pollack, Pat Feindel, Jan DeGrass, Nicky Hood, Janet Barry
Cy-Thea Sand, Barbara Herringer, Barb Isaac

Kurated
Kris Klaasen

Herizons
Penni Mitchell

Rogue Folk
Steve Edge

Vancouver Co-operative Radio, CFRO
Vinny Mohr, Peter Royce, Peter Grant, Bruce Girard, Corrine Douglas,
Allen Jensen
Elaine Arrowsmith, Lara Perry, Peter Thompson, Jill Mandrake
Brent Kane, Kandace Kerr, Tom Thompson
Janie Newton-Moss, Dorothy Kidd, Barbara Cameron, Ina Dennekamp
Jim Stewart
Brent Gibson, Bill Grant, Bill Hood, Michael Wilmore
Ron Simmonds, Paul Norton, Jim Burnett
John Orsick, Nou Dadoun, Karen Konstantynowicz
Jill Pollack, Aubrey Dayman

Vancouver Folk Music Festival
Gary Cristall
Dugg Simpson
Anne Blaine, Gwen Kallio, Carol Herter
Valdine Ciwko, Nadine Davenport, Jack Schuller
Si Garber

The Designers
Kris Klaasen, Elaine Littmann, David Lester
KAth Boake W., Britta Bacchus, Debra Rooney

Backstage
Jim Rundstrom, Rick Davenport, Tom Harrison, Michael Sasges,
Brian Antonson
Judy Segal, Arthur Black
Rob Joyce, Joan Miller, Jill Davey, Terrah Keener, Terry McNeney, Pat Hogan,
Shari Ulrich, Gayle Scott, Ellen McIlwaine
Brad Chernoff, Karen Kolenda, Kaycee Marchant
Marv Newland, Rodney Graham, Nigel Harrison
Helen Mears
Kalen Wilde, Linda Story

Belmont Shore Tour Support
Jan and Bob Young, George and Gail Shannon
Louise Raish Gentry, Linda Summerville
Donna Stiff, Mary Sterton, Barbara Gotzi Olsen
Jim Weidman, Nick Bliga, Billie Burnor
Sandie Hanna Fairman

Along the Way
Mary Watkins, Ronnie Gilbert, June Millington, Linda Tillery
James Haskins

My Road Crew
Anne Blaine, Judith Barnett, Lori Wotherspoon, Sheila Perret

The Hometown Band
David Wisdom
and our children
Georgia Kuhns and Nick Wisdom

And to the women.

ABOUT THE AUTHOR

Connie Kuhns has a forty-year history as an essayist, journalist, photographer and broadcaster. Her essays have been finalists for Canada's National Magazine Award, Western Magazine Award and *PRISM international*'s creative non-fiction prize. Other essays have been finalists in the *Los Angeles Review* Literary Awards, the *New York Times* Modern Love column thirteen-word love stories and the Frank McCourt Memoir Prize, and named "notable essay" in the *Best American Essays* series. Her photographs have been shown in various formats, including in the *Washington Post* and the *Globe and Mail*. She was a finalist for Canada's Salt Spring National Art Prize, receiving the award for Outstanding Salt Spring Artist. For fifteen years, Kuhns was the producer and host of the groundbreaking radio show *Rubymusic* on CFRO, Vancouver, specializing in the history of women in music. She lives on Salt Spring Island, BC.